YES!

Ordinary people

CAN

make a difference!

TRUE STORY

A PRE-COVID SOCIAL EXPERIMENT

THE DARK SIDE OF AUSTRALIA'S DEFENCE INTELLIGENCE

MONICA BENNETT-RYAN

IN HIS NAME
PUBLISHING

A PRE-COVID SOCIAL EXPERIMENT

THE DARK SIDE OF AUSTRALIA'S DEFENCE INTELLIGENCE

ISBN: 978-0-6453513-5-4

Printed in Australia

IN HIS NAME
PUBLISHING

PO Box 148
Waterford Qld 4133
www.inhisname.com.au

Cover Design & Graphic Art
DONIKA MISHINEVA
www.artofdonkia.com

Photography
BRONWEN RUSSELL
www.bronsdesign.com.au

FOR MY FATHER

Flight Sgt Martin J Ryan
A216217
Who dedicated his life
to the service of his country
and died in service.

CONTENTS

CONTENTS

FOREWORD

This is a true story. It's an eye-witness account of the determined and deliberate intention of government to break the law and override the rights and freedoms of ordinary Australians at will. This pre-COVID social experiment happened ten years ago, inside the Defence Intelligence and Security Authority (DSA) located in Brisbane, Queensland. When my friends and I set out to expose the abusive behaviour and the rampant corruption it covered, people in high places wanted to put us in jail for broadcasting their secrets. Did we break the law? No! Did they? Yes!

Jail time for us was a real threat. In Australia, people who blow the whistle on government corruption or threaten government commercial interests can be jailed for between five and twenty years. So my friends and I had a lot on the line when we uncovered their malfeasance, but we loved our country more than we feared its betrayers. At that time, I had no idea we had uncovered a clear pattern of coercive bullying and manipulation that would reappear ten years later in the COVID response. This book is about that pattern.

Today, the organisation that ran the pre-COVID social experiment no longer exists, and the building I describe is no longer used by Defence Intelligence. After our story broke, DSA Brisbane was given a new name and moved to a different location. So, despite the fact that this story is true, this book is referring to now unidentifiable people in places that no longer exist. How very cloak and dagger!

The corruption we exposed was the kind that couldn't be seen. There was nothing on paper! The only proof was in a highly secure Defence database, inaccessible to anyone without the proper clearance. There was only one way to bring this corruption into the open, and that was through testimony. Very risky! Despite the risk, two amazing co-workers, Janice Weightman and Owen Laikum decided to stand with me openly. We three became known in the media as 'The Three Defence Whistleblowers'.

From a whistleblowing point of view, our story is extraordinary and flies in the face of all reason. We risked our lives and freedoms by going public without any evidence at all. Was it bold and stupid? It could've been, but it wasn't! Despite all threats and against all odds, we successfully exposed the corruption and stayed out of jail! Yet, we couldn't have done it without the help of some exceptional people, notably:

- ABC *Lateline* reporter and producer, John Stewart, who's foresight, professionalism, integrity and sensitivity was evident in all his reporting. He never betrayed our trust.

- The Former Labor member for Forde, Brett Raguse, who assisted us as we took our first 'baby' steps in exposing the corruption.

- Our unofficial barrister, Dayle Smith B.A. L.L.B. L.L.M. PhD, who generously offered his extensive expertise free of charge at the very time we most needed legal advice.

- Liberal Senator David Johnston who asked the hard questions in the Senate and greatly assisted in exposing the enormity of the problem the Labor Government of the day kept trying to either flatly deny or play down.

- The invisible army of unsung DSA staff (many more than Defence knew about) who bravely risked their jobs and freedoms to confirm the truth of our story anonymously to the ABC.

- And Finally, all our praying friends and family members who supported and encouraged us during this long battle.

We three Defence whistleblowers are ordinary Australians, and Christians. This is important because we gained our courage, strength and strategies from following the principles set out in the Bible. Prime Minister, Scott Morrison, has said, *"The Bible is not a policy handbook, and I get very worried when people try to treat it like one."* But he is wrong! The Bible *is* a policy handbook! By following the moral policies laid out in Scripture, we three were able to discern right from wrong, act with integrity, and employ a process that would expose unchecked government corruption that went all the way to the top.

The first nine chapters of this book are written like a novel to detail the methodical way DSA lured honest people into their web of cruelty and lies, our disbelief that they could care so little about Australia's National Security, and the steps we took to beat them at their own game. The last chapter shows how the COVID response mirrors the DSA method.

Looking back, it's easy to correlate our Defence experience with today's COVID nightmare. The same methods of division, coercion, bullying, deception, and corruption of law used by government and civilian officials against a few back then are now being used on a massive scale against all Australians. Can ordinary people, once again, stand against lies and corruption in high places and win? Yes!

Monica Bennett-Ryan

INTRODUCTION

In March 2010, whistleblowers wrote to three government ministers through their local Labor member, the former member for Forde in Queensland. They set out a pattern of conduct in the granting and administration of security vetting that involved a number of things, including bullying and harassment. They also raised the issue of corrupted vetting practices.

Defence's response and the response of the members of parliament was to simply ignore them. But worse still the Defence report went on to treat them as if they were cranks in a most arrogant and offhand way. It was not until the *Lateline* program, in May 2011, raised these issues that the whistleblowers were taken seriously and the Defence administrators and, indeed those people higher up the chain, were brought to any form of account to set out what had been going on.

We now know that more than 20,000 security vettings have been compromised—that is, people who work in the Prime Minister's office, people who work with the Minister for Defence, people who guard bases. And let us not forget what happened with respect to the terrorism plot over Holsworthy. These compromised vettings include people who guard embassies, embassies that can be troubled in terms of their current and previous political histories.

The Secretary of Defence, when this was raised with him in estimates, slapped it down, flicked it away and said that he was totally oblivious to the significance of the issue. He said on the record that a flaw in the data input did not necessarily lead to a flaw in the security clearance.

We now know that the flaws in the clearances from Defence went all the way into the ASIO system. This department's maladministration not only corrupted its own processes but also, through the electronic transfer, corrupted the ASIO understanding and capacity to review who is who out there doing sensitive and important security based jobs.

There are 5,000 top-secret security clearances that have been compromised. The simple question that we all must ask is: who is accountable? Who is responsible? There is nobody that this government has pointed to as being responsible. It is always a review, adverse findings and 'we'll fix it now'. Nobody is accountable. This is an absolute disgrace.

These whistleblowers were treated with contempt. They have now received the Inspector-General's report. The first line of that report is that there should be an acknowledgement that what the whistleblowers said from day one was true and correct. **We owe them a debt of gratitude**. The parliament owes these three brave people a great debt of gratitude for coming forward in the circumstances. They were derided and treated as cranks.

The Prime Minister was asked to commission this report because these three might have been in breach of the law disclosing what they disclosed.

The Inspector-General has the power of a royal commissioner. The Prime Minister had to convene this review and, as I say, it is damning. The evidence has been overwhelming that there has been endemic, entrenched maladministration. This report makes fascinating reading as to a level of incompetence that is Olympic gold medal class.

I seriously cannot believe this is not front-page news in most newspapers. There are 5,000 top secret security vets that have been compromised. Several thousand of them have been worked through, but we are two or three or four years away from resolving what has gone on here.

It beggars belief, and the minister was on television last night saying, *'Look, people have made mistakes and we all bat on.'* It is just appalling, and it fits wholly and solely into the track record and the performance standards of this government. It is just a disgrace.

Senator David Johnston

Ministerial Statement given to the Senate in the Parliament of Australia on 9 February 2012 by Senator David Johnston, Shadow Minister for Defence.

Didn't they know
the law applied
to them?

CHAPTER ONE

Australian law? Irrelevant!

Over the space of two years, between 2009 and 2011, Australia's National Security was severely compromised. This was not an accident. It was not a misunderstanding of procedure. And it was not poor management. It was calculated and deliberate.

The Queensland branch of the Defence Intelligence and Security Authority (DSA) was responsible for doing background checks on people applying for security clearances at all levels; restricted, confidential, secret, top-secret and above. The people being checked were applying to work in secure areas like Military Bases, Airports, Embassies and Government.

Approved security checks were, of necessity, slow and methodical, so the only way to speed the processes was to introduce shortcuts. The shortcuts chosen by the management of DSA were not approved and therefore not legal, yet they were introduced and enforced anyway.

In order to introduce these illegal processes, an elaborate web of deception needed to be created. The plan was that half the staff would uphold correct procedure while the other half would be trained in the illegal shortcuts. For this deception to work, the two groups had to remain totally separate from one another. If their worlds ever collided, the deception would be discovered.

Highly trained Defence analysts continued to uphold correct procedure while temporary employees were brought in to do the illegal shortcuts. Neither group knew what the other was doing. The strict social barrier created between these two groups was so effective Defence analysts generally had no idea why the turnover of temporary agency staff was so high.

The new DSA temps had to be prevented from finding out what they were doing was illegal, so from the start of their employment, they were subjected to sudden and intense brutality, experiencing isolation, segregation, discrimination, harassment, bullying and persistent threats, as 'encouragement' to do as they were told without question. These threats were jointly enforced by DSA management and the employment agency that found the temps for DSA. Despite being Australian citizens, agency staff suddenly found themselves in a place where the protection of Australian law was completely irrelevant.

Have you ever noticed how much extra work goes into creating a cover-up? Children give us plenty of examples. When my eldest son was six years old, he decided not to eat his vegetables. Leaving them on the plate wasn't an option, so he developed a sneaky plan. He knew no one wanted to remain at the table waiting for him to finish his meal and that little bit of knowledge was all he needed to bring his plan to life.

He learned to dawdle, playing with his food until everyone had given up waiting and left the table. Then, when no one was looking, he would slip away from the table and quietly scrape all but one vegetable into the kitchen tidy bin and return quickly to his chair.

When he caught my eye, he would manufacture a perfect hang-dog expression and ask, "Can I leave the table, please?" When I saw my sweet little darling had eaten most of his veggies, I would excuse him and watch him skip away from the table like a wild thing set free from an enclosure.

His plan worked well for a few weeks, until one day when someone happened to be in the right place at the right time to see exactly what he was doing. After he was caught out, he was made to eat his vegetables for real.

There is not much difference between a child who wants to cover wrongdoing and an adult who wants to cover wrongdoing. The process is basically the same, no matter how old one becomes. First comes the distraction, which covers the sneaky deed, then comes the discovery of the deed, followed closely by feigned innocence. When that fails, it's replaced by fake submission to authority while the next plan is quietly formulated.

The trouble is, all sneaky deeds of deception are fleeting and only last for a time because there is always someone in the right place at the right time to see what is really going on.

We three whistleblowers just happened to be three experienced parents in the right place at the right time to see the deception being played out by people who, like children, thought their deception would never be discovered. The constant threats of job loss, along with intimidation, segregation, isolation, bullying, harassment and general harsh treatment, were the not-so-nice distraction. The inappropriate and thoroughly illegal vetting processes were the sneaky deed, and feigned innocence and fake submission to authority were the first reactions after they were found out.

IN THE RIGHT PLACE AT THE RIGHT TIME

I didn't plan to work for the Defence Intelligence and Security Authority (DSA). I didn't know it existed, and I didn't apply for it! Australia tripped, and I sort of fell sideways through an open door. I don't know how it affected you, but the 2009 Global Financial Crisis, the global disaster over which Australia tripped, affected me directly. I lost the best job I'd ever had.

I'd been working as a full-time temporary employee of the Queensland State Government for several years in their Home WaterWise Rebate Scheme. It was a great job, filled with friendly people. There were very few disgruntled customers but plenty of happy rebate receivers, and it was a pleasure doing business with happy people.

This atmosphere of contentment permeated the whole office, and the workers got along so well that for years after the Scheme was forced to close, many of us still met for 'catch-up' luncheons a couple of times a year.

The point, though, is the Rebate Scheme was shut down six months early due to that pesky Global Financial Crisis, and so sixty of my colleagues and I suddenly found ourselves out of a job.

At the same time the WaterWise Scheme closed, other State government departments were ordered to amalgamate, which consequently meant no new person could now be hired unless an existing employee was willing to vacate their position. Yes, well! Who in their right mind would give up a secure government position in the middle of a recession? Virtually no-one! So suddenly, at the end of June 2009, I found myself without a job at a time when jobs had become very hard to find.

Needless to say, things were looking grim. I was the sole breadwinner for my family. My two older children were married and starting families, but my youngest son was still in high school, and I needed to keep a roof over our heads. I didn't want to end up homeless, but without a reasonable wage coming in that was now, for the first time in my life, a nasty reality. There was no time to sit around. I had to find a job, and I had to find one fast.

So the day after leaving my supposedly secure State government employment, I hustled to a recruitment agency, one that specialised in finding government positions and was met by a short, round, congenial looking woman in her late forties. I later discovered this sweet looking recruitment agent also doubled as the one and only, not so nice, DSA staff liaison officer. I explained my predicament and asked if I could be placed on the agency register.

"Can you type?" she asked.

I handed her my resume and told her I had about 30 years of secretarial experience, to which she responded, "You'll need to take a test."

I went through the humiliation of registration and a school-leavers database efficiency test and waited for the results. About an hour later, I was told I passed the test and had been placed on their books. I breathed a sigh of relief.

Then the round, congenial looking woman told me the truth. "We don't have any jobs at the moment. The government is not hiring."

Surprised by her sudden candour, I looked at the smiling face in front of me dumbfounded. Why had I just spent all day going through this time-consuming rigmarole if there were no jobs to be had?

"No jobs at all?" I questioned, returning her professional smile.

"None!" she said and closed my file. Resting her relaxed hands on top of my file, she tilted her head in a way that let me know her word was final. She wasn't even going to try to find me a job.

Without thinking, words tumbled from my mouth, "I really need a job. I don't want to walk the streets, destitute."

She shrugged her shoulders.

I left her office thinking I had just wasted a whole day when I could have been looking for work in more efficient ways, though I didn't have a clue what those more efficient ways might be, and I started to realise getting work this time might be harder than I'd thought. I didn't want to start feeling defeated, so I did what I was accustomed to doing at times like this, I prayed. I handed the situation over to God, asked him to help me find a job, and left it with him.

The next morning I received a phone call from the congenial looking recruitment agent, let's call her Dora, asking me to come back into the office.

"I've a job for you, Monica," she said, sounding pleased with herself, "all you need to do is come in and sign some official paperwork."

When I arrived at the agency, Dora took me into her office and told me what had happened.

"I couldn't sleep last night...at all...because of you." She settled herself into the leather swivel chair behind her desk. She wasn't smiling. "You haunted me all night."

"Pardon?" I asked, taken aback.

"I kept tossing and turning, trying to avoid your face." She was using her hands as she spoke. "I saw images of you in rags, destitute on the street, begging for food, and I couldn't stand the look on your face." She paused. "All I could think of was that you needed a job...and if I was ever going to get any sleep again, I had to find you one."

I was astounded! I couldn't respond! What does one do with this kind of information? Was this God? Had God just answered my prayer?

"So when I got up this morning, I knew what I had to do," she said. "There were four people I was thinking of firing anyway, so first thing this morning, I fired the four of them. You can have one of their positions."

My mouth dropped open! Again, I was dumbfounded! To say I was shocked by her candour and stunned by her news would be an understatement. I was wide-eyed! But I quickly recovered and regained my composure. "You said four positions?"

"Yes!"

"Can I bring three friends?"

"Yes," there was a slight pause, but then Dora added, "as long as they're registered with this agency, there won't be a problem."

"I know one person already registered with you." I waited while Dora picked up her pen. "Janice Weightman," I said as Dora wrote, "she was a Senior Administration Officer in the State Goverment. There are several others. We all lost our jobs at the same time because of the amalgamations." I rattled off a few names, "I'm not sure if they are registered with you yet. I'll contact them."

The words 'stunned', 'ecstatic', 'incredulous', even when put together, were inadequate to describe how I felt at that moment. I was over the moon, and I couldn't help smiling at God's sense of humour. He'd turned my face into a nightmare to get Dora's attention. That was not quite the image I had of myself, but very funny and creatively effective. In doing that one little thing, God had not only provided a job for me but for three of my friends as well. Amazing! I felt like I was floating.

"Just fill this in," Dora said as she handed me an application form. "You'll be working for the Defence Department at Victoria Barracks, so you'll need a restricted clearance to gain access to the Base."

I filled in the form and handed it back.

After checking it, Dora continued. "Defence is a different culture. Its workplace rules are different from other places, and so from our point of view, there are certain actionable offences. They include office gossip, office politics, complaining, criticism of Defence management or not showing up for work. Any of these actions will bring instant dismissal."

She began searching through paperwork as she continued. "The four people I fired this morning had been gossiping and complaining about the management for a while. Their criticism was not acceptable under the terms of their employment."

Ouch! Sudden death! It sounded a bit harsh. Was this normal practice?

Dora, guessing my thoughts, looked up from the paperwork, and her tone became confidential. "This is a long-term position, Monica. One of the four has only worked eleven full weeks in the last eighteen months. He was only turning up for work four days a week instead of five, so he had to go."

I relaxed again. That sounded reasonable. Eighteen months was a long time. Maybe this position had real long-term potential.

I later learned Dora's confidential tone was a flashing amber light that screamed, 'warning, warning, you are about to be lied to.'

"The job is not high-pressure," Dora continued, "it's just processing information packs for soldiers. You simply enter their details into a database."

Convinced this simple little role could be exactly what I needed, I indicated I was willing to take the position. "Sounds perfect!" I said.

Dora nodded and continued. "When they first work for Defence, most people experience a kind of 'culture shock'." She suddenly smiled. "You will. It's normal. You'll get used to it."

My mind flicked back to my experience the last time I'd worked for Defence, decades ago, when I was young and employed as a secretary to the Air Commodore commanding RAAF Wagga. I had loved that job! Yes, it was strange and different, the rules of grammar didn't exist, and everyday conversations were filled with acronyms, but I got used to it. I felt confident that I understood what Dora meant by 'culture shock', so I responded almost immediately, "It won't be a problem, Dora. On my resume, you'll see that I've worked in Defence before. I know what it's like."

She smiled.

I smiled.

It was a done deal.

She saw me to the door. "As soon as your clearance comes through, you'll start immediately."

I had no idea that I'd just been lied to or how big the lie was! I found out a short time later that nothing I'd been told was true. Nothing! What Dora had outlined was the exact opposite of the truth.

The position was not long-term or low pressure, and neither was it military. I was, in fact, entering into a short-term, high-pressure situation that was not run by the military but by civilians. That, I found out the hard way, was a huge difference, of mammoth proportions!

The simple information packs for soldiers were not so simple. They had no room for error! At all! They were actually security clearances for the military as well as for embassy employees, government officials and civilians, and the data I was entering would not only be embedded in a highly secure Defence database but would also end up in the ASIO database, no less.

I wasn't told I would be working for the Defence Intelligence and Security Authority, that I would be sworn to secrecy or that I would be required to undergo an intense examination of the last ten years of my life just to gain the correct level of clearance I needed to do this 'simple' job. In fact, I had absolutely no idea what I was walking into. Dora, it seemed, was short for Pandora. The position she presented was nothing like the nightmare I was about to experience.

WHEN FIRST IMPRESSIONS PROVE ACCURATE

I first saw Victoria Barracks on a beautiful, warm, sunny winter's day. It was the first day of my new job, and these old barracks were a quaint surprise. Located on a slight rise in the middle of cosmopolitan Brisbane, hidden behind a high brick wall, was a snapshot relic of the convict era.

It was a delightful sight! Heritage-listed stone and red brick buildings with hand-painted rust-red corrugated iron roofs and white painted cedar window frames, some still displaying their original mouth-blown glass, sat amongst vivid green lawns, ancient trees and well-kept gardens. It gave the impression of order, pride, honour, safety, endurance and care; things which were, in my experience, typical of Australia's military.

My father had been in the military all his adult life, and he died in service. Reminiscent of every Military Base I had grown up on or visited every other day or week until I was in my twenties, this neatness was familiar territory. It was like coming home. I felt safe.

After being met by Dora at the tiny red brick guardhouse flanked by two white-painted boom-gates, I was escorted along a sealed road, past a neatly manicured grass assembly quadrant, to a building that, without any stretch of the imagination, was entirely out of place. Discordant would be one way to describe it. Out of harmony with its surrounds, definitely! There was no other way to say it really; it was just plain ugly! And neglected as well, which was a surprise given its well cared for surroundings.

The grim-looking two-storey facade was square and windowless, and its dirty, unpainted grey concrete walls dripped with rust marks from the many short and jagged antennas which adorned its flat top. Like a discarded, oversized building block, it sat alone and disconnected from all the magnificent heritage buildings that surrounded it. The whole demeanour said, 'stay away'. There was no warmth, no welcome, no pleasantness about it. This was DSA headquarters.

When I realised this ugly building was our destination, I took a little more notice. Off to the side, amongst unremarkable garden shrubbery, a short stand-alone sign read *'Defence Intelligence and Security Authority',* and beside the sign, half a dozen unadorned cement stairs led up to the entry; a single, double-glazed, glass security door.

I was more than a little taken aback. As we climbed the stairs, I questioned Dora, "Intelligence and Security?"

As she pressed the security buzzer, her only response was a non-committal smile.

I held my breath, not knowing what to expect. Intelligence!This was the stuff of television! Despite my best efforts to suppress them, multiple visions of neatly suited British secret agent types in modern buildings with 'state of the art' equipment began to race through my mind and invade my thinking.

The door opened, and a tall, red-haired man of military bearing greeted us.

"A new staff member for you, Doug," Dora said as we bustled through the door and into the small glass foyer. It was tiny. We three filled a third of the room.

Without responding, Doug punched a code into the second, more solid security door, opened it and stood back to allow us to enter.

As I began to pass through the doorway, Dora turned to me, "I have someone to see, so I'll be leaving you now." She smiled at Doug, "Chao!" and abruptly left the building. Her sudden departure dumbfounded me. I hadn't been introduced to this Doug person, nor he to me. And, I had no idea of his role or what I should expect next.

This turned out to be my first, nothing-subtle-about-it lesson in DSA staff relationships. Both Dora and Doug made it clear I was not important enough to be greeted, let alone introduced.

They say first impressions count. Well, this first impression will stay with me for the rest of my life. I had just come from the happiest workplace on earth, a place of light, order, diligence and humour. What I was entering now was the exact opposite. My life had just swung like a pendulum from one extreme to the other. I had become familiar with workplace harmony, but now I had a sinking feeling I was about to become familiar with workplace misery.

Looking around, all I could see was darkness and shadows. There were no windows. The only light came from the filtered neon bulbs in the high ceilings. The walls were covered with old grey paint, which was chipped, scraped and dirty looking. Small, dark, three-person cubicles, known as 'pods' and filled with messy clutter, adorned every inch of space on each side of a narrow central stairway. The people I could see working silently in those disorganised pods were dressed as untidily as their workspaces in what could only be described as scruffy BBQ casual. And there was not one smiling face to be seen.

The heavy, depressive, unwelcoming atmosphere ripped the 'pleased to meet you' smile off my face, but before I could begin to wonder why everyone was so unhappy, Doug spoke. "I'm going to take you to orientation," he said and closed the security door firmly behind us. He didn't ask my name, nor did he seem interested in what it may be. Walking past me, he said over his shoulder, "Follow me," and began descending the central stairway.

The 1940s style stairs were steep and narrow, so I gripped the railing as I followed him for fear of stumbling. As we neared the landing on the next floor, I was surprised to see an open bank vault door blocking part of the stair exit. It was the old-fashioned kind, the type you see in classic movies, around 30cm thick and made of solid grey steel with a circular turning handle on the front.

Squeezing through the gap between the open vault door and the stair rail, I immediately did what most people do in such circumstances; I looked around the vault door into the space beyond to see what treasures it was protecting.

Another dirty room! A large one, though! From the ripped vinyl flooring, worn down to the black backing in patches, to a row of small, grubby, unwashed windows set high on one wall, it was just plain sad, the type of place you would want to avoid. Wall to wall, it was filled with filing cabinets, the old kind, army surplus, ex-World War II. They were all scratched, dented, grey, of course, and adorned here and there with stuck-on bits of partly lifting scraps of paper.

I found it strange that the only windows I had seen so far were in a vault. I began to wonder why anyone would put such a heavy security door on a room with windows. Surely, I mused, if someone wanted to break in, they would not need to struggle with a heavy security door when they could simply smash a window. But hey, what did I know? This was intelligence! Smarter minds than mine had thought this one through!

Where was Doug? I looked around and saw him in a room on the other side of the landing, opposite the vault door. I headed towards him.

It only took a second for me to negotiate my way, without tripping, around the high pile of discarded boxes and bags of shredded paper spilling out willy-nilly from underneath the stairwell and enter the room where Doug was standing.

No windows here either, but at least the walls looked clean. This long rectangular room was dominated by a table that could comfortably seat twenty. It was obviously the conference room. I discovered later it also doubled as the DSA staff lunchroom. A wall at one end was covered from floor to ceiling with shelving untidily filled with open stationery boxes. So I guess this room could be more accurately described as a conference room/ lunchroom/stationery cupboard.

"Take a seat," Doug said to no one in particular.

I sat down next to the only other seated person in the room, a very pretty young Islander lady with long, straight, black hair and greeting in her eyes. She was well dressed in smart office attire. I could tell she was new and that this was her first day because she was as overdressed as I was. We both attempted a polite half-smile, but neither of us said a word. Speaking didn't seem like the thing to do.

"Welcome to DSA," Doug said without a smile.

He was still standing as he handed each of us a well worn blue vinyl ring-binder containing about 60 pages. "Just familiarise yourselves with the contents of these folders. When you've finished reading, I'll get you to sign some paperwork." Then he looked directly into our faces and smiled. Well, he sort of smiled. He tried, I suppose. I gathered he wasn't used to smiling because his attempt didn't last long.

"I'm Doug," he said, holding out his hand.

I took his hand and shook it. "Hello Doug, I'm Monica." I still didn't know who this man was or what I should say to him. Was he from personnel? Was he a security guard? I had no idea.

"I'm Sara," said the pretty Islander lady, reaching past me to shake his hand.

"I'm going to leave you to it," Doug said. The faint hint of a smile was gone entirely, and he was already starting to move towards the doorway.

My eyebrows shot up, but I tried not to appear shocked that he was leaving.

Doug continued, "I'll be back in about an hour to take you to your work area." Then he turned and walked out the door.

Scratch personnel! Scratch security guard!

More stunned than surprised at this new turn of events, Sara and I looked at each other a bit nonplussed. Alone for an hour? What kind of orientation was this? We didn't speak. I had the strangest feeling we would be 'caught' if we said anything. I could only guess Sara had the same feeling because neither of us said a word.

We'd only been in the building five minutes, and we were already being squeezed into the DSA mould.

When Doug returned, he wasn't alone. A slender, pink-shirted, dark-haired man of Greek extraction came buzzing through the door behind him with a fixed smile and face agog with artificial excitement. "Hello ladies," he said in a sing-song voice, letting the s's hang in the air. "I'm Con, your agency team leader."

"Just fill in and sign this paperwork," said Doug, handing us each an Official Secrecy Acknowledgement form, "then Con will take you to your work area."

I took a moment to read the single-page form, "secure information... not to be disclosed... not to be published... during or after service... any breach... liable to prosecution." Hmm, not a problem! I'd signed one of these in a previous position when I worked as secretary to a Member of Parliament. No issues here! I completed the form and handed it back to Doug.

"Follow me, ladies," said Con, who proceeded to lead us, mincing walk and all, out through the door, past the over-flowing rubbish and back up the stairs. We passed the depressive main entrance landing and continued to ascend to the top floor.

Light! Windows! Now, this was more like it! The whole floor was flooded with natural light. And it was clean! I breathed a sigh of relief. At least I didn't have to work in the dark, depressive atmosphere downstairs.

Wall to wall windows ran along each side of the massive room centred around the top of the central staircase. The walls on this level were a clean shade of cream, and the floor was covered with freshly vacuumed grey-blue carpet. Beyond the windows, the tops of gently moving trees provided the welcome appearance of green shrubbery. It all looked very civilised, and I guessed correctly that this was where the executives worked.

Sara and I were led to the third two-person cubical in a line of five. It was only partly cluttered. "Make yourselves at home, ladies," said Con as he stood back to allow us to enter our new workspace.

The far side of the pod was all windows from desktop to ceiling, giving a feeling of openness and order. Outside the window, a sunlit treetop brushed the window ledge at desk height as it swayed in the breeze, and beyond the treetop, red-painted rooftops gave way to a panoramic sky view. Maybe working here wouldn't be so bad after all.

Sara took the desk by the aisle, and I was left with the undraped window seat. Bliss! I settled in and stood for a moment, enjoying the view.

"Are you sure you don't want this window, Sara?" I asked. I felt like I was getting the better position in the pod.

Sara smiled, and her smile was genuine. "No, you take it. I can see the tree from here."

We began to chat - girl chat - the usual 'get to know you' things like where we lived, how many children we had, and how we ended up in this job. We didn't notice no one else around us was talking.

Con bustled into the pod. "Ladies, ladies, pel-ease!" He was smiling his excited smile, but he had both hands in the air waving them like he was trying to stop an accident. He lowered his voice to an almost confidential whisper. "Talking is not allowed. You're here to work. Not to talk."

Oops! I looked at Sara. Her face was showing that 'getting to know you' glow. I decided to say something. "We're just getting to know each other, Con," I said gently.

"I know, sweetie," he said, and his voice seemed full of understanding, but then suddenly his tone changed, and his smile completely disappeared, "But it's my job to make sure you understand all the rules."

He proceeded to publicly rattle off to us a list of rules which were, I found out as time went by, ruthlessly enforced.

"Number one," he was still not smiling. "Agency staff do not talk to other agency staff about work or any other subjects during the course of a workday. If you wish to talk, you can talk to either myself or any of the Defence team leaders."

I wasn't sure I'd heard him correctly. "Do you mean, Con, that I can't speak to the person I sit beside all day, even about work?"

"Number two," he continued as if I had not said anything. "Agency staff will not talk to Defence Staff about work or any other subjects unless the Defence staff member opens the conversation. These two rules are not negotiable. Any breach of these rules will bring instant dismissal."

My mouth dropped open. Surely this wasn't right. I closed my mouth and tried to make sense of what I was hearing. Okay, this is intelligence. Maybe they have to operate like this. "Is this for security reasons?" I asked, hoping my question would also show my compliance.

No response. Ignored again!

"Number three: Agency staff will not ask questions." Con was glaring at me as he spoke.

Ouch! Talk about Jekyll and Hide.

"Everything here is on a 'need to know' basis. Everything you need to know will be told to you. If you need to refresh your memory about anything you've been told, you can go to a team leader. Any breach of this rule will bring instant dismissal."

Later I discovered Con had been nick-named 'the smiling assassin', obviously not without reason.

I wondered why he was doing this publically. Surely this should have been covered in orientation. But then, in a private orientation, questions would have been asked, and questions were not allowed.

"Number Four: Agency staff will not complain about the way DSA management conducts its business or any decisions the management makes. To do so will bring instant dismissal."

My head began to spin. Did this mean no one was allowed to complain about the rubbish flowing out from under the stairs? Was that why everything around us was so dirty and messy?

"Number five." Con sounded disconnected like he had said all of this many times before. "Agency staff will arrive five minutes before start time and be seated at your desk with your computer up and running before 800 hours. Three minutes late and your pay will be docked 15 minutes." He paused, but he wasn't finished; there was still more. "Agency staff will leave the premises at exactly 1600 hours. If you are found on the premises after that time, you will be considered a trespasser and instantly dismissed."

For goodness sake! Trespassing? What about Base Passes? Did they have no value?

"Number six: Unscheduled breaks will bring instant dismissal." Con handed us both a mini questionnaire. "You'll have a choice of one of two time-slots for morning tea and one of two time-slots for lunch. Once you choose your break time, it's fixed. If you are found on breaks outside the times you have nominated, you'll be instantly dismissed."

"Number seven: Agency staff positions at DSA are temporary and highly sort after. There are plenty more people waiting to take your place."

I glanced at Sara. She was no longer smiling. Her eyes were lowered, and she was studying the floor. I guessed we wouldn't be friends after all. As it turned out, I was right. From that time on, though we shared a pod for eight hours a day, we were never more than nodding acquaintances.

Con continued, "Any un-requested day off will be regarded as a resignation. And any requested leave will be given on the understanding this position may not be here for you when you wish to return. A medical certificate must prove any sickness, but even so, return to employment within DSA will not be guaranteed.

Con paused, but he was not finished. "Further, as agency staff, Defence is only required to give you one hours notice before dismissal."

Suddenly Con smiled at us, and his face was agog with excitement like it was at our first meeting. "But the good news is," he looked at each of us and took a long deep breath as if he was going to say something wonderful, "you, also, only have to give one hours notice if you don't like working here."

That was the good news? How horrible! There was something very wrong with this whole picture. Scary wrong! I just didn't know what it was. I felt like running, but I knew I couldn't; there were no jobs out there. Besides, this was an answer to prayer for me. Deep down inside, in that place where faith lives, I believed there was a reason God had gone to such great lengths to place myself and three of my friends in these strange surroundings, so, despite my growing misgivings, I decided to stay.

THE OPTIONAL NATURE OF PROCEDURES

The following day, 'formal training' began, and it was as disjointed and surreal as orientation. The first thing that struck me as strange was that Sara and I were taught separately even though we were trained at our desks and the same person was training us. I assumed we were learning the same thing, but as Sara and I were taught individually, I began to wonder if that was actually the case.

The second strange thing was the lack of procedure notes. Nothing was written down. We had to rely entirely on memory, which was ridiculous considering the importance and volume of the workload. But I reminded myself this was an intelligence agency; I had to expect things to be different. Nevertheless, I found it difficult to adjust.

How does a person learn without asking questions, reading notes, or following someone else's example? In every other training situation I'd experienced, I could ask a fellow worker, "what are we supposed to put in this field?" They would reply, "Oh, you just put this..." The light of understanding would come on, and I would continue my work with a hearty, "Thanks."

That was not the case in this role. We were not allowed to communicate. At all! So with no discussion, no written procedures, our trainer on a different floor, and instant dismissal for unscheduled breaks (like going downstairs to talk to a team leader), learning was exceedingly difficult. In fact, it didn't make sense to me. I had to keep telling myself this was intelligence. There had to be a reason they wanted things run like this. And anyway, who was I to question the way things were being done?

After learning how to enter restricted, confidential, secret and top-secret data into the specialised security database, I was told I would be sent for further training on entering data into the general military database. This new training would be done by military personnel.

Early that afternoon, Sara and I joined with a larger group of around six people. We weren't introduced because we weren't allowed to talk to each other. So, without a word, we were led out of the cement building block, along a pretty flower-filled garden path, to one of the iconic red brick buildings which so beautifully complimented the green lawns of Victoria Barracks.

We were met at the entrance to the building by a female army officer who asked us to follow her down a long, long hall to her office. I had expected computer training to be conducted in a training room with desks and computers, but no, it wasn't. And again, there were no notes. Instead, we all crowded around the officer's desk and watched over her shoulder as she explained the ins and outs of the system via her personal computer.

There was so much to take in; I thought my brain would explode. Then towards the end of our session, the officer made the most amazing statement. "I can't show you how to connect this data to the programs you use because I don't have the clearance," she said, not realising she had just dropped an almighty bombshell.

What? Did I hear right? This highly skilled military officer, who specialised in IT training, thought my clearance was higher than hers? My mind went into overdrive. The questions came thick and fast, and none of them had any answers.

Who did she think she was training? My clearance level was only 'restricted', the bottom level, no higher than a cleaner. Didn't she know that? Would she have shown me the things she did if she had known my actual clearance status? How could I, with a lower clearance than a military officer, access data she was not allowed to access?

I couldn't grasp the enormity of what I had just heard. It just wouldn't compute. I had inadvertently discovered that the work I was doing on a lowly restricted clearance, I should not have been doing at all. Yet, despite my lack of clearance, my job was to use classified systems to enter classified information up to and including top-secret level.

This was too deep for me. Surely smarter minds than mine had thought this through. I certainly hoped they had. Or was it planned by the same minds who'd put a vault door on a room with windows? Scary thoughts!

In the end, I put it down to my own ignorance and moved on. After all, how was I supposed to know how 'intelligence' worked? I had only been on the job for two days. The trouble was, like everything else I'd encountered at DSA so far, this just didn't feel right. It nagged at me, but I didn't know what to do about it.

A TRANQUIL OASIS IN THE MIDST OF CHAOS

The cavalry arrived in the form of three of my ex-State government employment friends. I so needed friends I could talk to about all this, yet I couldn't talk to anyone without the proper clearance. Janice arrived first, starting the week after I did. Cassandra and Jennifer arrived in my third and fourth weeks, respectively. We didn't waste any time finding a quiet place to have lunch away from everyone else and away from prying ears.

The place we found was gorgeous. It was as secluded as a 'secret garden' but huge, like a park. A long rolling green lawn dotted with mature trees of different kinds was fully edged with meandering garden beds held in place by chunks of sandstone and backed on one side by a ten-foot-high sandstone wall that ran down half its length.

The entry to this delight, hidden by parked cars, was behind the flagpole on the far side of the trim green quadrant. Two short flights of broad sandstone steps led down to a wide garden path which, after five meters, took a 90° turn around a massive shady tree and suddenly revealed a paved picnic area. This rather large area was home to five weather-worn, cedar picnic tables and a double brick bar-b-que which was next to, surprisingly, an extremely tall and elegant antique lamp post.

The view from the picnic area down the sweeping expanse of lawn gave a sense of peace, tranquillity and order. Just what we needed! Since no one else used this spot, not even the military in the adjoining buildings, we had our pick of the tables, and I decided to add a little humour and civilisation to our lunchtimes by adding a round, butter-yellow tablecloth. Lunchtimes were wonderful. It was like we had entered a different world.

I discovered DSA staff avoided this particular place because of 'the lizards'. What lizards, I wondered? In all the time I was at Victoria Barracks, I only ever saw one rock lizard. And who is afraid of lizards anyway? I couldn't understand why anyone would prefer to eat in a windowless conference room/lunchroom/stationery cupboard instead of out here, in paradise.

"This is so beautiful," said Cassie.

"It's nice to be normal for a few minutes," said Jennifer. She didn't have to expand her thinking. We knew what she meant. This was a place where we could relax and be ourselves. We could talk to each other about anything, whether work, home or family. We could laugh and joke and discuss forbidden topics, like our horrific work conditions and the management practices of DSA.

"So you didn't get fired?" asked Jennifer.

I shook my head, "No, not this time."

"What happened?" asked Cassie.

"I couldn't stand working under that freezing air conditioning any longer. I had to choose between my health and my job. So I bit the bullet and made a complaint." I took a sip of my drink. "I fully expected to be fired."

"Monica's been rugged up at her desk with a coat, scarf and gloves for weeks," said Janice, filling in the details.

"It's like an arctic blast over my chair. Way too cold for me. And it's only in that one spot," I said. "It got so bad I couldn't use my fingers to type. They were too stiff."

"The air-con technicians have been in, but they can't fix it," said Janice.

"I was expecting 'instant dismissal' but, to my surprise, Con told me I would be moved to the middle floor instead. I'm now down in the dingy area with the analysts."

"So, they don't mean all those threats they made at the beginning," said Cassie.

"I think they do," said Janice without emotion. "Donna was fired yesterday."

Slightly built, with long fading red hair and a polished English accent, Janice reminded me a little of Agatha Christie's Miss Marple character, who also had a habit of coming straight to the point.

"That pretty woman with the long curly blond hair," I questioned, "the one who's always smiling?"

"Yes, she's the one," Janice said simply.

"Oh, she was such a ray of sunshine!" I remembered seeing Donna on every trip down to the vault-window filing room. Amid drab, dirty disorganisation, this slim, always busy young woman wore crisp, bright colours and red lipstick, making her cheery smile seem even brighter. "What excuse did they use this time?" I asked.

"She worked past 4.00pm. She was on the premises after hours," said Janice. "It didn't seem to matter that she had permission from her team leader who was working back with her. Erik and Dora decided to fire her."

Erik was the top boss. He was a middle-aged Scandinavian man of medium build and balding grey-red hair. He totally ignored agency staff. When we passed him on the stairs, he would not even shift his path to acknowledge there was someone on the stairs with him. He didn't speak to us, nor did he make eye contact. Even so, he was a micro-manager who controlled everything in the cement building block by emailing orders from behind closed doors. We called him the puppet-master because he pulled all the strings.

"How can you be fired for working after hours with permission?" asked Jennifer.

"You can't!" said Cassie.

"She was!" said Janice.

"So much for being conscientious," said Jennifer. "Why did she work back when it was against policy?"

"She was given a job which needed to be completed that day, but completing it meant going over time," Janice said.

"Ah! Catch 22!" said Jennifer.

"Dora and Erik didn't even speak to the team leader who gave her the task and stayed back with her," Janice continued, filling in all the details.

"Sounds like a set-up," said Jennifer.

"It does!" agreed Cassie.

I was puzzled. "She was a good worker. Why do they throw away so many good people?"

Jennifer frowned as she looked at me. "How many have been let go since you started?"

"Well, let's see," I said. "There are the four of us, plus Sara, who started with me and Zelda, who started with Janice.

"If six were hired, six were fired," said Jennifer.

"Six in four weeks," said Janice.

"With those figures, they would be going through around seventy agency staff per year," I said. "Could that be right?"

"One thing we can be sure of," Jennifer predicted, "we won't last long. Our turn is coming."

We all nodded in agreement. In a few weeks, we had all seen enough to know that what Jennifer was saying was true. We were doomed. Donna was living proof that good workers were not immune.

"Maybe we should just talk to Dora, you know, reason with her," Cassie suggested.

The rest of us slowly shook our heads. We knew by now Dora was the enemy. No mistake. DSA said, 'hit them', and Dora said, 'how hard?'

Jennifer frowned, "Seriously though, is there anywhere we can go to make an official complaint?"

"We can't go to Dora, and we can't go to Defence, so where do we go?" I asked, "there must be somewhere."

We sat in silence for a moment munching on our lunches and considering the possibilities. Yes, where could we go to complain? Agency staff were the 'meat in the sandwich', so to speak. We didn't work for Defence directly. They didn't pay us, so we couldn't go through any of their channels to make a complaint. Though the agency paid us, we didn't work for the agency directly. Our work was classified, and we couldn't tell them about it, so we couldn't go through any of their channels to make a complaint. Neither could we go to any outside agency, like the Ombudsman, because it would breach the Secrecy Act.

"I think we're in a bit of a pickle," said Janice.

We all chuckled, a sad, involuntary, hopeless kind of chuckle. She was right. We *were* in a pickle!

The threat of 'instant dismissal' was constant. Plus, Dora had made sure we all understood that those dismissed would not be considered eligible for any future position. Complaining was a dismissable offence. In other words, we were doomed if we complained, and we were doomed if we didn't.

Cassie shook her head. There were no words.

I often felt a pang of guilt that I'd involved my friends in this horror story. We had all stumbled into a living nightmare. If any of us had known in advance about the horrors which lurked behind DSA's coded doors, we would've turned away and looked for work elsewhere.

Nevertheless, being together was a God-send. Our lunchtime chats helped clarify what our eyes were seeing and provided a forum for questions that may not have otherwise been asked.

Through our candid lunchtime conversations, we all came to realise there was no easy way out of this situation. The simplest solution was to find another job, which was complicated because new employers wanted a referee from the most current former employer, and we were not likely to get a referral from either Defence or Dora. On top of that, the global recession had made jobs almost impossible to find. So, we quickly realised that all we could do was put our heads down, do our work, obey the rules, and wait for the hammer to fall.

THE GULF BETWEEN MILITARY AND DEFENCE

Those first few weeks at DSA were like an emotional roller-coaster. Working there was exhausting! Like every other agency worker, I didn't know, from one day to the next, if I would keep my job or if my friends would keep their jobs. In a few short weeks, I'd become used to being isolated, constantly threatened, and made to feel as disposable as a used tissue. All I knew for sure was that something was very wrong, and everything seemed upside down. Worse, trust was in very short supply.

I realised I no longer had the protection of Australian law; it didn't seem to apply within DSA.

I couldn't trust Con, my agency team leader. I'd learned that he reported everything any of us did and said to Dora. If a look could be construed as criticism, Con made sure it was, or if a light-hearted comment could be mistaken as dissent, Con, the smiling assassin, made sure it was.

I couldn't trust Dora. She was just a puppet on one of Erik's strings; her whole motivation was to please Defence.

I couldn't trust Defence personnel because I'd discovered their smiles were just masks that hid daggers. I was safe as long as one of them didn't smile at me. If they smiled, I knew I was about to be deceived, used, or fired. A smile meant I was in big trouble. Now I understood why no one smiled - why Doug didn't smile during orientation. In DSA, smiles were deadly, and misery and mayhem were the order of the day. How twisted! How insane!

There was nothing normal about any of this behaviour. But what I couldn't understand was why. Why were they like this? This was not the Defence I'd grown up with. My father would have been horrified by this behaviour. But he was military - this was not!

Suddenly the light came on. That was it! That was the difference! I suddenly understood. The military was not Defence, and Defence was not military. The difference was huge!

I'd always held Defence in high esteem. Like most Australians, I believed Defence was our protector; there to keep us safe and protect our rights as Australians. That long-held belief had just been shattered into a million pieces. Like a pin bursting a bubble, my fantasy world had been blown apart before my eyes.

This Defence was not my protector. It was not keeping me safe. It was not keeping anyone safe! And it was definitely not protecting my rights as an Australian.

This Defence was the opposite of everything I'd always loved about our military. Until that moment, I didn't realise Defence and our military were worlds apart. But the glaring reality was - these people were *not* military!

Before my experience with DSA, I tended to lump Defence and the military together. I had put them both way up there on a pedestal. This was mainly because of my father and the respect for the military he'd instilled in his children. I grew up proud in the knowledge that our military were never aggressors, only defenders; clothed in honour, hard-earned and well-deserved.

The trouble with my pedestal fantasy was that, in reality, the military only made up a small part of Defence.

The majority of those working under the Defence banner seemed to know how to manipulate military protocols and illegally use them to coerce civilian workers in order to further their own agenda's. They'd learned to use the light of military glory to cover their inglorious actions.

When the bubble burst, it swept the non-military off my pedestal. Our military is still up there and always will be, but the non-serving civilians working under the Defence banner do not deserve the same honour as those in the military itself. Our military is our protector and always will be, but these people, these bureaucrats, were a disgrace.

There was no honour in DSA. It was easy to see, really, like black against white.

The stark contrast was evident from the moment I arrived at Victoria Barracks. Everything in the hands of the military was neat and ordered, while everything in the hands of the DSA civilians was disorganised to the point of chaos.

I'd never been treated cruelly by any member of the military at any time in my life. In my experience, they'd only ever been helpful to civilians in times of trouble, lending a helping hand and going the extra mile whenever possible.

The news coverage of the soldier holding a toddler during the 2010 Queensland floods is a perfect example. He was taking the child to a helicopter but wasn't just transporting the child; he had his hands over the child's ears, protecting the little one from the noise and wind of the rotors. Beautiful! That's our military!

In predictable polarity, cruelty was the order of the day within DSA. Human dignity was a foreign concept. Coercion, threats, bullying and injustice were like mother's milk to them. I'd discovered the hard way that many of the civilian bureaucrats within DSA who ride on the back of military honour have no honour at all.

But I hadn't seen the worst. I'd only dipped my toe into this foul swamp. There was more to come – much more.

> *Defence Minister Stephen Smith says an internal Defence Department review has found serious maladministration flaws.* (ABC News 21 Sept. 2011)

Didn't they care
about
the consequences?

CHAPTER TWO

No facts? Use fiction!

From 2009 to 2011, the management of DSA Brisbane forced its agency staff to falsify official data and pass that data on to ASIO as checked and accurate. If there were no facts, information was made-up!

> *A Defence review found that procedural errors led to false information being passed to ASIO.*
> (ABC News 21 Sept. 2011)

When news of this corruption finally emerged in the media in 2011, people were incredulous. They were not only shocked by the allegations against Australia's trusted Defence Intelligence and Security Authority but they also found it hard to believe their Defence Department would order their workers to do such a thing. Further, they couldn't understand how so many people could claim they didn't know that what they were doing was wrong.

The implications for Australia's National Security were enormous. It was alleged that tens of thousands of security clearances had been granted, from restricted right through to top-secret, despite being based on false information.

Considering these clearances covered people who worked in highly secure places like military bases, embassies, government offices and airfields, the real potential for disaster, particularly during visits by overseas dignitaries, like British Royals or the American President, was disturbing.

Once it was exposed to the media, this appalling security breach was finally acknowledged and addressed. As a result, the slow and cumbersome wheels of resolution began to turn.

Clearances done during those two years were counted and put aside to be rechecked with the promise that, as they were rechecked, the potential threat would grow smaller each day. Yet, despite the action being taken to reverse the damage, the original question remained. How could so many people falsify data, for so long, without knowing that was what they were doing? How could so many be so deceived? I believe the answer to that question can only be found by looking at the deliberate and calculated nature of the callous deception of staff.

At first, I didn't know that what I was doing was wrong. I was doing what I was ordered to do. It took a long time, nearly seven months, for me to uncover the corruption. I could only do so then because of the multiple exceptional circumstances in which I found myself. If events had not unfolded in the particular way they did, none of the whistleblowers would have seen through the deception.

HOW AND WHEN THE DECEPTION BEGAN

I arrived at DSA just in time to see the beginning of the deception and how it was both subtly and forcefully introduced. The corruption was not an accident. It was not an administration flaw. It was, as I mentioned earlier, deliberate and calculated.

As I write this, I am painfully aware that the same deception played out on a small scale back in 2009 is now being played out on a large scale throughout Australia under the guise of the COVID health crisis. But we'll get to that later. There are just too many similarities between the two for my experience at DSA to have been anything but a test run.

The deceptive plan was in place and ready to go before my friends and I knew about DSA, were lured into their trap, and coerced with force into implementing their illegal plans. This deception was jointly embraced and propagated by both government and civilian bodies working in unison.

There was a space of three weeks from the time I was hired until the time the planned corruption began. During this period, the government and civilian officials worked together to form us into the mute robotic slaves they needed us to be for the plan to work.

They isolated us, shut down communication, made threats and bullying part of the normal daily routine and held the threat of termination of our jobs over our heads. The threat of joblessness was made even more effective as we were in a global recession and jobs were scarce. These power mongers were not going to let this global crisis go to waste. We were merely guinea pigs in their social experiment. Does any of this sound familiar?

Then, the real deception started!

Highly skilled DSA analysts were trained to check the accuracy of the information provided by military and civilians who were applying for security clearances before sending a report about the new clearance rating to ASIO. That report to ASIO signalled the completion of the DSA process and was only done once all the data being sent to them had been verified as accurate. This was the only correct and approved vetting procedure - and that was the problem! This efficient procedure was in the way and had to be disposed of for the corruption to work.

That's where we came in. This is why agency staff were all trained separately and why we were forbidden to speak with the DSA analysts.

For the first three weeks, while we were being squeezed into the DSA mould, agency staff were actually being taught to do what analysts do; check the applications for accuracy, send those with problems to the analysts and finalise the rest ourselves by sending their reports through to ASIO. We didn't know that what we were doing was illegal. We didn't know that reports to ASIO could only be sent by DSA analysts.

But that wasn't the deception. That was just the training for the deception.

Three weeks after I arrived at DSA, agency staff were suddenly ordered not to reject any applications. Nothing was to be sent back to the applicant or through to the analysts. Whether they had complete data or not, the information provided on all applications for 'Restricted', 'Confidential', 'Secret' or 'Top-Secret' level clearances were to be entered into the database and finalised by us; that included sending the completion report to ASIO.

I had no idea this new process had been set up to bypass the analyst check. None of us knew that we were illegally sending reports to ASIO as complete before information had been checked or even received by analysts. DSA management cleverly hid that little bit of very important information from both the agency staff and the analysts, though it didn't remain hidden for long.

ASIO database security went berserk! The ASIO database would not accept reports with information gaps. This meant that if there was even one 'field' left unfilled in the electronic report, it would reject the whole report as an 'error'. Since most of the reports being sent by agency staff had a lot of missing information, the number of ASIO bounce-back 'errors' suddenly skyrocketed.

I was amazed DSA management didn't know this would happen! What amazed me more was that even after they saw the new procedures were causing problems with the ASIO database, they defied logic and all reason and insisted we continue to use their new procedures anyway! Unbelievable!

This was the direct 'cause' that produced the 'effect' of the greatest security scandal in Australia's history; the DSA security clearance scandal. There was nothing accidental about it! It was not only deliberate, it was enforced with threats!

"Ya makin' too many errors, Monica," I jumped! I didn't know Jack had walked into the pod and was standing behind me.

Jack, a short pompous bulldog of a man in his late forties, had the job of training agency staff in the new procedures; and he did this loudly with humiliation as his preferred training method.

"What ar'ya gunna do about it?" he bellowed at the back of my head loud enough for the whole floor to hear.

"I'm sorry," I said, turning my chair around to face him, "I'll correct them now." At this stage, I didn't know rejected ASIO reports were called 'errors'. So, thinking he meant typing errors, or data entry mistakes, I held out my hand, expecting him to give me the files which needed correcting.

"Errors never come back to the person who makes them," he blustered. It was obvious he wanted everyone to hear what he was saying. "But we keep a record of how many are made, and if y'make too many, you'll be replaced."

Oh, no! As I withdrew my hand, my heart sank. I was getting the sack.

"You've got till the end of the week. If y'can't get y'errors down by then, you'll be replaced." With no further explanation, Jack left the pod.

I was devastated. Replaced was the DSA word for fired. I'd seen this happen to others so many times. I guessed I would be the next one given one-hour's notice and escorted off the Base like a criminal. Oh, well! I suppose it had to happen sometime! I spent the rest of the day being super careful, double-checking all my entries. It slowed me down, but what else could I do?

The next day was the same. "Ya still makin' too many errors, Monica," Jack announced loud enough for everyone on the floor to hear him berating me. "And ya'need to get y'speed up. Yesterday y'didn't process enough applications."

I scanned my memory, searching for something I may have missed. There wasn't anything. I knew my work was accurate. I had double-checked all my data entries. I couldn't let this accusation pass. I had to speak up. I was losing my job anyway.

"Jack, I made sure my data entry was accurate. I double-checked everything." My voice had an edge to it. I was starting to feel angry. "That's why the number of applications dropped a little. I was just trying to be accurate. I don't understand how I could still be making errors."

I wanted to ask, 'what errors am I making?' but that was not allowed. Not being allowed to ask questions was just plain stupid, right up there with vault-window mentality. I glared my frustration.

Suddenly Jack backed down and stopped yelling. "The errors aren't in y'typing or accuracy; they're in y'data entry. Y'not fillin in all the fields."

Oh! This was different. I hadn't heard this before. I sat back in my chair as he continued.

"If all the fields arn't filled in – when y'send the ASIO report – it'll bounce back – those bounce backs are called 'errors'. He seemed pleased with his explanation. "Y'makin' too many errors of this kind. Y've got one more day. If y'don't get it right tomorrow, y're out the door."

As he turned to walk away, I stopped him. "Jack," I said, "I need a list of the fields the ASIO database is sensitive to so I can keep it beside the computer to check my data entry."

He stepped back and laughed, a kind of shocked half-laugh, then shook his head like he couldn't believe what he was hearing and, without saying another word, walked out of the pod.

A few seconds later, I heard him talking loudly with Betty, another DSA team leader at the far end of the room, about forty metres away. They were laughing, and I heard my name mentioned. "Oh, what?" boomed Betty for the whole floor to hear, and they both laughed again.

I stood up and looked over the top of the pod dividers in the direction of the voices. Jack was walking away from Betty towards his pod, his face red from laughing, but his final parting comment to Betty was loud enough for me to hear clearly. "As if we'd write anything down!" he bellowed, and they both laughed again. Suddenly, Jack looked across the tops of the pods and fixed his eyes on mine. There was no laughter in his eyes.

I sat back down. I was not going to get my list. Why would I? He was right. They didn't write anything down. Not orientation instructions. Not procedure notes. Certainly not lists!

My job was on the line. I had to work this out. I sorted my files into those which had all their information and those which didn't, entering each of them into the database. I didn't have a clue which fields were safe to leave blank and which fields would cause an error. But this was life and death for me now, job-wise, so I changed the rules.

If an application had complete information, I sent the report to ASIO. If it didn't, and around 30 to 40 per cent didn't, I held back the ASIO report, wrote out the missing information onto a yellow sticky note, stuck it on the front of the file, and took the file to an analyst so that the applicant could be contacted for information.

Then I waited to see what would happen - if I would still have a job the next day.

The next day was a Friday, and it was not until just before knock-off time that Jack came to my pod. I'd spent the whole day not knowing what management had decided, and wondering if I'd have a job to come back to on Monday.

"Look what y'can do when y'try," Jack said. "Y'didn't make any errors yesterday." He was smiling at me. Oh-no! This was not good!

"Do I still have a job?" I asked, forgetting that I wasn't supposed to ask questions.

"The jury is still out on that one," he said. "Erik hasn't made up his mind, so y'll find out on Mond'y." He was smiling as he walked away.

Great! I had the whole weekend to continue not knowing, wondering, worrying. Fantastic!

This, I'd discovered, was another one of their nasty little habits - something they did simply because they could.

They would save their worst news for Friday afternoon, knowing it would ruin our weekend. It gave them a lot of pleasure. It gave us a lot of pain. Like children torturing insects, they were just plain mean. No wonder Jack was smiling.

This nasty, childish torture-loving attitude has permeated the COVID response. The power-mad orders given by Premiers were always predictable. The public caught on early that Premiers would align their most severe restrictions to a major holiday like Christmas or Easter, School Holidays or Anzac Day. And we were always right!

ORDERED TO FILL IN THE BLANKS

Janice and I travelled to and from work together on the same bus. The walk to the bus that afternoon gave us the opportunity to chat.

"What did they say?" She looked at me with concern in her eyes.

"They did the Friday afternoon torture trick," I said, trying to make light of their nastiness.

"Oh, no!" She shook her head. "So you have to go through the whole weekend not knowing?"

"Yep!" I nodded.

"What's wrong with these people?" She asked, not expecting an answer. "This is not normal."

"Tell me about it," I said and grinned. "They're not going to ruin my weekend. I've got other things to think about, nice things."

"I hesitate to tell you what's going on in my world," Janice ventured almost apologetically, "you've enough on your plate."

"Spit it out..."

"All right, well, umm...I'm a little concerned about what happened today," she stopped walking and turned to me. "Would you like to have a coffee? We can't talk about this on the bus."

Once we were settled in a nearby cafe, Janice opened up. "I was told to delete data today."

"What?" I was shocked. "What do you mean?"

"Well, you know they've given me the job of clearing the backlog of top-secret files."

I nodded.

"I'm supposed to enter them and then send the ASIO report, but they keep bouncing back because of the information gaps."

"Yes, that's normal," I said.

"I usually attach a yellow slip to those with blanks and give them to an analyst."

"Yes, I started doing that today, too."

"Well," she paused and sighed, "they don't want us to do that. I was told to fill in the blanks."

"What?" I said, "You can't!"

"Apparently, analysts do it all the time."

"Well, yes!" I responded, wondering why this was an issue. "It's their job to contact the applicants, get the details and fill in the blanks."

"I know that, but that's not what I mean." Janice took a sip of coffee. "She said they fill in the blanks without referring to the applicants." Her eyes were searching my face waiting for my reaction. "Monica, I'm worried the applicants could get into trouble later for giving false information - information they never actually gave!"

"No!" I shook my head in disagreement. I couldn't believe what I was hearing.

"She told me that if I didn't have the birthdates for siblings, I should delete all reference to siblings, then the report would go through without an error."

My mouth dropped open. "No way!" I was stunned. "How can they delete data?"

"I told her I wasn't comfortable doing that and would continue handing the incomplete files to an analyst." Janice paused, waiting for my response.

"That can't be right, Janice. Surely not!"

While we sipped our coffee in silence, I was searching for reasons.

"Maybe she's just fobbing you off." I said.

"Well, I was giving her a lot of files with yellow slips," Janice conceded, "but that's not the worst of it. This afternoon, I came across an application which had children's names but no birthdates."

"You didn't delete the kids..." I said.

Janice shook her head. "No! I wouldn't!

I nodded. This was bad. Really bad!

Janice continued. "Anyway, Helga was there, you know, one of the team leaders from the top floor. So I tried to ask her what I should do. She didn't want to talk about it, so when Jack walked through the door, she called him over and told me I should speak to him."

A stranger walked past our table, and not wanting to be overheard, Janice lowered her voice and continued. "He sat down at my computer and began entering false birthdates for the children."

My eyes widened. "False birth dates?"

"I swear!" She put her hand over her heart, "yes, false birth dates. And he explained how he was calculating the dates so I could do the same."

"What do you mean?" I couldn't believe my ears. This was way past bad.

"He said I should check the birth dates of the parents and calculate a reasonable date for the birth of each of the children from their parent's birth dates." She could see the astonishment on my face. "They were completely made up, Monica. Totally fabricated!"

"What did you do?" I whispered, shocked.

"I told him this was false information, and I didn't feel right giving false information to ASIO."

"And?" I whispered. My brain was numb. I was holding my breath.

"He said ASIO had no problem with it. They knew the database was too sensitive, and they would be able to pick up any discrepancies at their end. He said it was just up to DSA processors to get them through the database."

I sighed with relief. "Oh! Okay, so it's not so terrible, Janice. If ASIO has approved this, who are we to buck the system?" I thought about it for a minute. "This is intelligence, Janice. We're at the bottom of the pile. How can we possibly know what decisions have been made at high levels?"

"We can't," she agreed.

"Smarter minds than ours, Janice," An image of the vault-window room flashed through my mind. This time I pushed it aside, "What do we know?"

At that point in time, I didn't see the corruption. I couldn't imagine DSA would lie to us about something as important as intelligence. I couldn't believe DSA would encourage its staff to deceive ASIO. I couldn't believe our Defence Department would order staff to compromise our National Security. And in my wildest dreams, I would never have thought anyone working for Australia's Defence would deliberately place so many Australian lives in jeopardy. I couldn't believe any of that, and so years later, after the story broke, I could easily understand how hard it was for the Australian public to believe the story was true.

I knew that DSA staff were sloppy, dirty, messy and just plain nasty, but I didn't believe for a minute they would betray Australia or Australians. Not for a minute!

I thought we were being told the truth. So did Janice. So did all the other agency staff. But the cold, hard reality was we were all being deceived and being trained to deceive.

Every one of us was kept isolated from the other. We were all taught separately and were not allowed to talk to each other so that we couldn't compare notes. We were always under constant threat of job loss, which served to deter us from questioning what we were being ordered to do. And the disposable nature of our employment kept us bowing to the assumed wisdom of the established long-term, supposedly know-what-they-are-doing Defence staff. Added to that, anyone who came close to finding out the truth was fired.

When I look through the COVID haze today, I see the same disbelief at work in ordinary Australians. Surely our leaders would not betray Australia?

At the beginning of my time with DSA, I thought the sloppiness, mess, filth, disorganisation and chaos was just poor management or lack of discipline. But when I discovered the truth, I realised there was nothing accidental or undisciplined about it.

This was indeed a well-planned operation, executed with military precision. Isolation, segregation, intimidation, threats, bullying, lies, malice, deceit, and treachery were all openly mixed into a cocktail of organised chaos, which served as an elaborate distraction to take our minds off what was actually going on.

As hard as it may be to believe, all the erratic border closures, disorganisation, isolation, segregation, separation, intimidation, job insecurity, threats, lies, deceit, chaos, confusion and wholesale treachery performed by our leaders against the Australian population during COVID is also part of a well-planned operation, designed as a distraction to keep us from seeing what our government is really doing.

The fly in the ointment for DSA, and one of the major reasons for their eventual exposure was our little group. Their plans failed because they couldn't keep us apart. When we got together, we compared notes. We discussed the inconsistencies, we recognised the outright lies and we began to realise that the chaos was just a coverup. At that point, we began to plan what we could do about it. The first big mistake DSA made was thinking that they could stop all discussion just by introducing isolation and forbidding communication inside their walls. They had no control over us outside their walls.

Despite what it looked like, small and insignificant, our little group was the beginning of the end for their sneaky deception. They just didn't know it at the time. Neither did we.

EXPANDING OUR CIRCLE OF INFLUENCE

After the shocking discussion I'd had with Janice that Friday afternoon, I was not able to stop thinking about DSA. The more I tried to forget, the more I remembered, and so despite my best efforts, I couldn't concentrate on anything else. My whole weekend was ruined. By Monday, I was drained and exhausted.

When I dragged myself to work on Monday, I was fully expecting to be told to turn around and go straight back home - jobless. But, to my great surprise, that didn't happen. Shortly after I arrived and began my work, Jack came to the pod.

"Erik has decided to keep ya'on for a while longer." His face was expressionless - a good sign. "Y'didn't make any errors on Friday."

I breathed a sigh of relief and quietly thanked God for my second reprieve in as many weeks.

"By the way," he continued. "Con has been relocated from the top floor to the basement. He'll be commencin' in a new role and won't have the time he used to have to deal with agency matters."

I wondered what new job Con was doing. But I knew better than to ask, so I kept my mouth firmly closed, even though I was bursting with curiosity.

Jack read my face - interesting that he did - I would have to watch that. "Con's been placed in charge of correctin' all the ASIO errors. When y'make a mistake, he's the one who fixes it," he explained. "He's flat out at the moment, so don't contact him unless y'need to."

He turned to leave but then paused like he had something else to say. "If everyone adjusts as well as you, he won't be flat out for long."

Was that a compliment? Shock of shocks!

As Jack walked away, he bellowed in a commanding, almost threatening tone, "Keep it up!"

Hmm, yes, well, that was more like it!

So, I was doing something right, but what was Con doing? Was he 'correcting errors' by filling all the blanks with false information? Surely not!

I couldn't wait to tell the girls I'd had a reprieve. They were as anxious to know as I was. When lunchtime came around, I bolted out the door, set up the yellow cloth in our usual spot and was soon surrounded by friendly faces.

"You look happy," Cassie said.

"It must be good news," echoed Janice.

"Yes, yes, yes," I said, grinning from ear to ear as we started unwrapping our lunches.

At that moment, two of our fellow agency workers, Owen and Jim, came down the path and around the shady tree, lunches in hand and great big smiles on their faces.

"Well, doesn't this look civilised," said Jim, pulling up a bench seat and plonking his lunch on the table.

"A bit too posh for me," laughed Owen. "Do you mind if we join you ladies?"

"Oh, I'm so glad you could make it," said Janice smiling her most welcoming smile. Turning back to us, she said, "Jim and Owen work in the dungeon with me. That's what we dungeon-dwellers call the basement. I invited them ages ago." She turned back to the men. "But this is the first time you've deigned to show."

I was already on smiling terms with Owen and nodding terms with Jim. Cassie had worked with both of them when she worked in the dungeon before being relocated to the top floor. Only Jennifer needed to be introduced. Jennifer shook hands across the table, and we began to eat our lunches. The dynamic had just shifted. We were glad to have them, they were glad to be with us, but no one was sure what to say.

"You were right, Janice. This garden is beautiful," Owen began. He was eating his lunch, and his gaze was taking in the broad expanse of lawn with its long-established trees and well-kept gardens. "This has got to be the nicest place in these barracks. How come there's no one else here?"

"Apparently, the lizards frighten them away," Cassie drawled, and we all laughed. The ice was broken. We chatted for a while, getting to know the guys, letting them get to know us.

Owen was a Samoan Australian, a family man, father to two young children and husband to a very pretty young wife. He pulled out his wallet and showed us a picture. So proud! He was a devout Christian, a joker and constantly walked around with a genuine smile on his face.

Jim was a tall, slender, quietly spoken, young, good-natured university student who had taken a break from uni and planned to go back to full-time study in 2010.

After a bit of testing, we discovered that these two men thought the same way we did. They saw what we saw, and they didn't like it either.

"We won't be in the dungeon for much longer," said Jim, opening up, "Owen's, going to the middle floor, where Monica is, and I'm going upstairs."

"It'll be your turn soon, Janice," said Owen.

"Oh, I don't think I'll be going upstairs," said Janice. "It seems they don't think I can do the job."

"Of course you can do the job," said Owen with a chuckle. "It's not rocket surgery..."

"You're breathing, aren't you? You're qualified!" said Jennifer, munching on her sandwich.

"Leave your intelligence at the door!" Jim concluded, summing up the way we all felt.

"It's not about what you can do, Janice," said Owen trying to be both blunt and gentle at the same time. "It's whether they like you or not."

"What do you mean?" asked Janice.

Owen turned to Jim, "Do you remember what happened to Kylie?"

Jim nodded to Owen and explained to us, "it was just before you all started."

"Kylie was fired because she didn't say 'hello' properly," Owen said with a hint of disgust.

"No way!" We chorused, all shaking our heads.

"Uh, huh," Jim nodded. "She came in one morning, said hello, but didn't smile submissively as she said it."

"The smiling assassin reported her for bad workplace attitude," Owen continued.

"Dora came in and fired her that day," Jim concluded, taking another sip of his drink.

"That's not anywhere near legal!" said Jennifer.

"Who's going to know?" asked Jim

"Secret organisation and all that," said Owen.

"Con didn't like her," said Jim, shrugging his shoulders, "so she lost her job."

"It had nothing to do with her skills or work performance," Owen concluded.

"So they don't like me," said Janice. "Is that what you're saying?"

The men said nothing but their gentle eyes said it all. None of us knew how long our employment would last or how we would be sacked.

"Who is 'they'?" asked Cassie.

"'They' is Con," said Jim. "He's the one who decides who stays or goes."

"Is that why you call him 'the smiling assassin'?" drawled Cassie.

Jim nodded. "He's vicious!"

"Todd got the bullet today," said Owen, "another one bites the dust."

"Yeah," confirmed Jim. "He was talking to me, telling me a joke. I saw Con coming, and I signalled him to stop, but he just kept going. Anyway, the punch line had a swear word in it, and Con heard."

"Oh, no!" We all groaned.

"Con must've disliked him. He went straight upstairs to Erik and dobbed him in," Jim continued.

"Dora came in and fired him," Janice said. "The official reason was 'negative workplace attitude'."

"Poor guy," said Owen. "He was only here three weeks. He probably didn't know what hit him."

"They're all such hypocrites," said Jennifer. "We're surrounded by Defence personnel who swear all day."

"That's true," I nodded, "I'm amazed they're allowed to talk, let alone swear."

Owen laughed, "They don't seem to know how to talk without swearing."

"No fear of being sacked!" said Janice.

"One law for them, and another for us," said Jennifer. "We are second-class citizens here."

We all nodded. And sighed.

As strong as we tried to be, the pressure was getting to all of us. It was so hard to maintain a positive attitude when all we could think about was how agency staff were being treated, when we would be sacked, what excuse they would use when they sacked us, and who would disappear next.

Owen and Jim had brought just the boost we needed. That first day, as we were about to go back to work, Owen suddenly pulled up the tablecloth, reached under the table and began patting around as if he was looking for something. "Did you check for bugs?" he asked with a cheeky smile.

We all chuckled and warned him the eight-legged bugs under the table might bite! But we understood where he was coming from. He had verbalised something each of us had secretly wondered about but never put into words. Were our private conversations being monitored? We didn't know. He was joking, of course, we all knew that, but there was an uncomfortable reality in what he was implying. DSA personnel were sneaky and devious. Yep, here was a man we could trust.

THE FIRST OF FOUR SIGNIFICANT EVENTS

During the next week, the first of four significant events happened. The other three events would happen later, and they each played a major part in opening my eyes to the corruption the DSA managers were trying so hard to hide.

I was suddenly moved into a cubicle with three analysts. This was a silly move by DSA, for it meant I would be sitting next to people who followed the correct vetting procedure approved by Parliament. It would only be a matter of time before I discovered the double standard.

I had three pod-fellows; Crystal, who, despite the inhuman rules attached to agency staff was to become a firm friend, Linda, who turned out to be a trusted ally and Cleo, who seemed to be related to Attila-the-Hun.

After being introduced to my three new pod-fellows, I was basically left alone. So I sat quietly in my corner, doing my work, minding my own business and pretending I didn't exist. I must admit, I felt a little jealous that these three people around me had the freedom to chat with each other about whatever came into their heads; office gossip, jokes, hobbies, their families, what they did on the weekend and all the other usual things people talk about at work, while I had to force myself not to listen, not to enter in and not to offer up my thoughts as well.

This was particularly hard for me when a question was being asked about something work-related, like how to spell a particular word or the location of some building in the city. If I knew the answer, I still, with great difficulty, had to keep my mouth shut. It was like having an annoying itch and not being allowed to scratch. Argh! So frustrating!

Since I had trained myself not to listen to their conversations, my first real insight into the personalities of these three analysts presented itself a few days after my move. Another new agency person had begun, and as he would be carting files for the analysts on a daily basis, he was brought to the pod by Con and introduced.

"Hello ladies," beamed Con, exuding his usual fake excitement and enthusiasm.

Linda and I were seated with our backs to the aisle, so we turned around. I noticed, and was surprised, that Crystal was smiling a genuinely welcoming smile.

"This is Brian!" Con gushed as if he was Brian's best friend. "He has just started today and will be bringing you your allocations, so you'll be seeing quite a bit of him."

"Nice to meet you, Brian," Crystal was gracious in her welcome, "I'm Crystal."

"I'm Linda. Welcome to DSA," Linda offered.

"Hi! Bye!" Cleo said in a brash, off-hand way. She had not moved and was still facing her computer screen. Then suddenly, she turned, looked up directly into Brian's face and laughed a mean, challenging laugh.

Everyone was stunned. Brian didn't know what to do. Con stopped smiling and whisked Brian away. Crystal's jaw dropped almost to the floor.

"Cleo!" said Linda, and her eyes flashed her anger. "What a nasty thing to say!"

Cleo was still laughing.

"How could you be so mean?" Crystal was going pink in the face, "why did you say that?"

Cleo looked over at me and was still laughing as she spoke. "They never stay long." She was looking directly into my eyes and pointedly referring to me but speaking as if I wasn't there.

Crystal and Linda looked over to me to see if I was upset. I wasn't. I had come to expect this attitude from DSA personnel. Though I could see Crystal and Linda looking at me, my eyes were on Cleo. She was laughing into my face, but her eyes were as hard as nails. I held her gaze until she stopped laughing, turned her chair around and went back to her work.

Linda and Crystal watched me. It was like time was standing still. Then, when Cleo stopped laughing, Linda gave Crystal a knowing look, turned her back to Cleo and went on with her work.

Crystal was mortified. "I'm so sorry, Monica," she said softly. "We're not all like that." She was searching my face for a response.

"I can see that, Crystal," I said and smiled into her eyes. Here was someone with a heart. I liked her from that moment. That was the beginning of our friendship.

Cleo probably didn't understand what had just happened. Bullies usually aren't too bright. But we three understood that the dynamic in the pod had just changed. Now it was Crystal, Linda and me. Cleo had just become the odd-one-out.

That same day, Owen arrived on my floor. He was moved up from the dungeon to the desk I had vacated and was beginning to process applications. I finally had a truly friendly face on my floor.

The timing of his move was perfect, for chaos was about to erupt, big time!

Suddenly, the procedures changed again, and both Owen and I were now in the position to hear what the DSA analysts thought about the changes. Unlike agency staff, the analysts were allowed to complain about management decisions.

The implementation of the previous new procedures had caused an uproar amongst the analysts who, to my surprise, had not been told about them. They were insulted that their professional responsibility had been passed to untrained agency staff. And they complained long and loud that agency staff had now been placed in the position of telling them what to do.

The same kind of thing happened to doctors in the COVID crisis. Suddenly, bureaucrats untrained in medicine were overriding the professional expertise of doctors so that Australians were being given prescribed medication without the need to see a doctor. In fact, the medical opinion of doctors and their Hippocratic oath to ensure they 'do no harm' to their patients was made completely redundant.

The Minister for Health, Greg Hunt, a lawyer, not a doctor, took on the role of persuading all Australians to be vaccinated, no matter what their medical history, and without anyone checking if the vaccination would clash with the other drugs they were already taking. And through the coercion of fear, hapless Australians lined up to be vaccinated in make-shift tents, paddocks, and pharmacies. Were any warnings given about the side effects of taking this experimental drug? No! Unconscionable! But the precedent was set in DSA ten years earlier.

Within DSA, the calculated exclusion of analysts from the vetting process was a time-saving approach designed to allow more applications to be processed in a shorter time, making DSA more money. Yes, money! The bottom line, as usual, was money!

Clearances cost money. The people who wanted them had to pay for them. The higher the clearance, the more they cost. So, logically, the more clearances DSA could process in a year, the more money Defence could make in a year. Not just pennies, either! Clearances were and still are a multi-million dollar business. We were in a Global Economic Crisis, and this was DSAs solution.

The problem was, Janice, myself and other conscientious agency staff thought our roles in DSA involved keeping Australia safe, silly us! So, despite not knowing that DSAs 'streamlining processes' were illegal, we started doing the right thing anyway and sent applications with missing information to the analysts to complete instead of completing the corrupt DSA process from start to finish ourselves as ordered. Oops!

Our yellow stickers were the catalyst for everything that followed. A little bit of integrity destroyed a mountain of carefully arranged lies! The yellow stickers set up a domino effect which caused havoc! By means of those pesky yellow stickers, the Defence analysts found out what was being done and hit the roof because the responsibility which had long belonged to them and legally belonged to them had just been given to agency staff who didn't have any vetting qualifications.

They pointed out, and rightly so, that analysts had been properly trained to identify fake documents, recognise when extra data would be required, know when they could legally forgo an official document, and when the information provided was 'of concern' and would need further follow up. Now, suddenly, they only needed to make phone calls if untrained agency staff told them to? I didn't blame them for being angry! And two of us, Owen and I, were witnesses to their anger.

After just two weeks, those new 'you beaut' procedures were thrown out and replaced with another set. This time though, the analysts were aware of what was happening. So they went over the changes with a fine-tooth comb and continued to complain. With every complaint, the procedures changed again, with major changes being made every few weeks. This went on for months, causing great upheaval, discontent and confusion.

DSA management couldn't seem to get it right, and I began to wonder if they actually wanted to get it right. It seemed not! The rules kept changing even though the original procedures were still the only approved standard ratified by Parliament and should not have been changed, or new procedures implemented, without Parliamentary approval.

The physical reality for staff was that the procedures were constantly changing, yet nothing was written down, so every change needed to be committed to memory. For me, that meant my memory was sorely tested, and my flexibility was stretched to the limit. Nevertheless, I tried to keep up, we all did, but the place was in chaos, and it seemed nobody knew what was going on. There was nothing but confusion, anger and misery.

HOW THE HAMMER FELL ON JANICE

Two weeks after Owen and I changed pods, Janice's worst suspicions were confirmed. She was still working on the considerable backlog of top-secret applications, entering the data, sending the complete reports to ASIO and handing those with missing data back to the team leader or an analyst. The trouble was she couldn't keep up. Applications for top-secret clearances were coming in faster than they were going out, so the backlog kept growing. And Janice was the only one entering them.

"What are all these files?" Helga demanded to know, pointing to the overflowing tubs of files in the passageway outside the pod where Janice was working. Helga was a short, dark-haired, officious woman in her early fifties who was always abrupt and often nasty. She knew the files she was pointing to were top-secret files. Everyone did! It was written all over them in thick red marker ink! This was not about the files. This was about Janice. This was the beginning of the torturous DSA 'firing process'.

Helga was holding a large pile of top-secret files with yellow stickers on them (Janice recognised them as the files she had given back to Francine and Betty) and was staring down at the three large plastic tubs of files on the floor in the aisle outside Janice's pod. "They need to be processed," she barked, stating the obvious.

Without waiting for an answer from Janice, Helga dumped the files she was carrying into one of the already overflowing tubs and hurried out the door. A few minutes later, she was back with Paula, the second in command.

Paula was young, tall, slim, blonde, beautiful in a pale sort of way, and cold as ice! We called her the 'Ice Queen'! Like Erik, she refused to look at agency staff and avoided speaking directly to us whenever possible. When she couldn't avoid speaking to us, she would still avoid our faces. Her eyes would always look past us, to something or someone else as she spoke.

I'll never forget the time she held a meeting of all the Defence personnel in the pod next to mine, and so it was impossible for me not to overhear what was said. The analysts were being told about changes to their seating arrangements, and they were not happy.

Normally, Defence staff didn't get shuffled around every few days or weeks as we did, but now they were being ordered to move, yet were nevertheless being asked what they thought of the new arrangements. None of them held back. They told Paula they wished to stay where they were, pointing out that they were not agency staff and expecting her to listen to their group consensus. When they'd finished, she gave her response.

"I've told you how it's going to be," she said, emphasising this as her final word by turning to leave the pod, "get used to it."

As she left, the analysts began to grumble.

"Why'd she bother asking us?"

"So she could report she 'consulted' with us."

"A waste of time..."

"They never listen..."

Paula couldn't be pleasant, even to the Defence personnel. The analysts knew there was no point arguing with her or even trying to express an opinion. She would never act on their concerns. We knew that since Defence personnel were treated so badly, agency staff didn't stand a chance. We were simply sacked on the spot if we disagreed with her. And now poor Janice was about to get one of her vicious tongue-lashings.

"Why are there so many applications?" She was standing outside the pod and looking down at the tubs. "How many are there?"

"Around fifty," replied Janice, thinking it was easy to see how many there were.

"Why aren't they done?"

"Because I'm the only one doing them," Janice's tone was docile, "and I have other work."

Paula had picked up one of the 'yellow stickered' files. "Why is this a problem?"

"I don't have the correct dates to enter..." Janice began.

"Work it out!"

"But if the dates aren't there..."

"Put it through!" Paula threw the file back into the tub. "I want all of these processed today."

"Many of them will not get through the ASIO database," said Janice. Oh-oh, she was arguing. No one could argue with the Ice Queen and get away with it! Nevertheless, though Janice knew she was not allowed to have an opinion, integrity was knocking, and she had to answer the door, so she continued, "They'll just bounce back as 'errors'."

Paula froze. "How could you possibly know that?" The words shot out of her mouth like frozen darts, and her tone was scathing as if Janice had stumbled onto some hidden mystery she had no right to discover.

"That's what I've experienced..."

"Don't you worry about the 'errors'," Paula warned. Then, pausing to compose herself, she said calmly and far too sweetly, "you won't receive any blame for them." And without another word, she turned and left the room.

"Oh no," Janice thought, "I've done it now."

"Push them through," Helga barked at Janice as she hurried past her and scurried after Paula, out the door and back up the stairs.

That day, against her better judgement and knowing there would be a huge jump in ASIO errors, Janice obeyed her orders and put through fifty gap-laden top-secret applications, complete with reports to ASIO. Those fifty applications would later play a huge role in bringing undone the DSA coverup.

That day, Janice knew, as you know, when you know, when you know, that no matter how hard she worked, or how good her work, the repercussions for her brazen attempt at confrontation with Paula were coming, and coming fast! No-one could argue with the Ice Queen and get away with it. The dye had been cast. Janice's fate had been sealed.

She was right, of course. When the errors were counted the next day, Janice was blamed for them as expected. DSA management was becoming so predictable! She was relieved of her data entry duties because, they said, she was making too many errors. Of course! But, though she knew the Ice Queen would punish her somehow, she couldn't have guessed how degrading her punishment would be.

Her punishment consisted of collecting large, heavy tubs of mail from the buildings on the other side of the quadrant, carrying them down the long road and into the cement building block. Then, up and down the narrow stairs to deliver the mail to each person on each floor. It took several trips each day - and there were no trollies.

Brian, a solid man in his mid-thirties, had been doing this lifting and carting since his humiliating first day and was often seen huffing, puffing and sweating as he transported the heavy tubs around the building. Now Janice had been given this job. Unbelievable! This was a disgusting job to give to a slightly built woman just shy of sixty. It was way past bullying, way past harassment – this was abuse! But it didn't stop there!

She was also required to do the 'filing spreadsheet' and needed a computer to do the entries. The trouble with this was she was not allocated a desk and therefore had no computer. Talk about stress! Were they trying to give her a heart attack? It certainly seemed so!

From that time on until her final day with DSA, Janice wandered around looking for a spare desk and computer so she could complete her given tasks. I would often see her walking past my pod, holding a cardboard box filled with the office supplies she needed to do her job, looking for a place to sit, even for a few hours. Disgraceful!

Finally, she'd been forced into the dreadful self-defeating position of having to make a complaint, knowing that making a complaint would bring instant dismissal. But she bit the bullet and contacted Dora nonetheless.

"I thought I'd be hearing from you," said Dora. "Con told me you complained about management in front of the two new agency staff members."

Janice went cold. What a snake! Those two new staff were in the same small pod as Con. They couldn't help but overhear every conversation. Way to twist the truth, Con!

"I was merely asking for a desk," said Janice.

Dora wasn't listening. "You've also been complaining about the tasks you've been given to do."

"I don't think it's appropriate or safe for someone of my age to carry heavy tubs of mail..."

Dora cut her off. "If Defence wants you to shred paper all day or stand on your head, what is that to you? After all, you are still being paid the same as all the other contractors."

What did money have to do with it? Janice couldn't believe her ears. Where was the support?

"I'd like you to find me another position outside Defence, please, Dora," said Janice. "I took this job on the understanding that I would use my data entry skills. If I'd known I would be carting heavy boxes, I'd have turned this position down."

"There's nothing available," Dora said sharply, "you would do well to do the job you're paid to do."

"That's my point, Dora," said Janice, "I can't do my job without a desk and without a computer."

The phone clicked. Dora had hung up.

It was obvious Dora would not be of any assistance. She was sold out to Defence and would do anything Erik wanted. But why was Janice being forced to stay when so many others were sacked over nothing? Did they just enjoy torturing her? It seemed so! She had now tried to quit, but her resignation had been refused. Why? Was this Paula's revenge? Did she need to *see* Janice suffer?

It was also obvious that Con, the smiling assassin, was also behind what was happening to Janice. In hindsight, it was easy for all of us to see that if Con hadn't been so nasty, more people would have kept their jobs. He was one of 'them'. So was Dora. We - all the other agency staff - had been thrown to the dogs.

UNBELIEVABLE BRAIN-TWISTING MIND GAMES

A few days after Janice's punishment began, the monthly Agency team meeting with Dora was due. I was told this one would be special, as Erik was putting in a rare appearance. Apparently, there was something in particular he wished to share with lowly agency staff.

At the beginning of the meeting, Erik casually introduced himself for the benefit of the new staff. Then bluntly said what he was there to say. "Defence is a blame-oriented organisation," he actually said this with a hint of pride, "and there are certain expectations management have of all staff. There have been queries of late about weight limits." Did he not know there was no legal reason for Defence to be a blame-oriented organisation? Or that such a title could change?

He was looking at Janice now. I held my breath. Janice had not been able to carry full tubs of mail and so had been lightening each load, which meant making extra trips. Sometimes, Brian had assisted her by kindly offering to add her excess mail to his tub to save her the additional trips. But now it seemed someone, probably Con, had reported her to Erik.

"The standard for everyone in Defence is 16 kilos." You could have heard a pin drop. "Defence expects its personnel to be able to carry a weight of up to 16 kilos over long distances if necessary."

What? I was horrified! I felt like screaming at him, 'that applies to strong, young men and women who are going through basic military training with backpacks on! It doesn't apply to sixty-year-old civilian office workers!'

"So I expect all DSA staff to be prepared to carry loads of up to 16 kilos."

DSA staff? We were not DSA staff! We were agency staff! We didn't work under Defence rules or military rules but under civilian rules. He had forgotten that small detail and was applying military regulations to civilians. Was this even legal? Of course it wasn't! Could we say so? No!

"There has been a sudden increase in errors lately, and so there needs to be more attention to detail," he continued.

Wonderful! Now he was making it sound like we were inefficient as well as stupid. Everyone in the room knew the errors referred to had nothing to do with 'attention to detail'. They were not typos. They were ASIO errors. They existed because there were no details to 'pay attention to'. Everyone knew this small fact except Dora, who didn't have a clue, and we weren't allowed to enlighten her.

Erik continued. "Formal training has been overlooked of late. I have introduced refresher training as a quality control measure." Then he concluded, "This training will commence tomorrow."

After Erik had left the room, Dora took up the issue of 'attention to detail'.

"I'm very disappointed there are so many errors being made by this team," she said. "Each one of you was personally referred by me because your skill-set testing results showed you have high visual accuracy, but the number of errors coming through shows you are not working to capacity."

Great! Now let's get lectured for something we're not doing wrong by someone who has no clue what we do. Typical! But we, sadly, were used to it.

We handled it the way we always did. We sat in a circle, listening to Pandora waffle on, saying nothing, and waiting for the meeting to finish.

Before the meeting closed, Con interjected wide-eyed and excited. "Tomorrow's training will confirm which format the ASIO system needs us to use for information to pass through their system successfully. Just what we need!"

TRAINED TO OUTSMART ASIO SECURITY

The next day, as promised by Erik, agency staff were ushered into the conference room for 'group training'. Refresher course? No! This was a first! We were about to be trained, on masse, to outsmart the ASIO database. Although we didn't think of it that way at the time, that is precisely what we were being trained to do.

On the way to the training, a vague hope flashed through my mind. Maybe we were going to be given the list of sensitive database fields I'd previously requested of Jack? Of course, that hope didn't last long. Once the training began, it only took me a moment to realise I was being way too optimistic. There were no lists. There were no procedures. There was nothing in writing. Of course! Silly me! Training was by overhead projector, and nothing much was new. We were still required to enter everything we could from the applications, but when the information was missing, it was implied but never directly stated that we should invent the information. This is where thier training became vague and tricky.

- "Remove incomplete data..."
- "Alter dates...make them match..."
- "When mandatory data is missing...fill it in..."
- "Copy previous information...repeat it..."
- "Don't leave gaps..."

ASIO errors, it appeared, could only be fixed if we added information that wasn't written down, information that didn't actually exist. Ironic that while we were being openly lectured on 'paying attention to detail', we were being secretly taught that errors could only be fixed by doing the exact opposite, *not* 'paying attention to detail'.

There was no mention of unique sentences or code words that could show ASIO the information was unreliable. We were not given special streets, like 'fake street', 'suspect street' or 'unknown street', to enter as red flags. We gave ASIO no warnings at all! I never once heard the word 'workarounds' used. Neither was there any mention of adding comments to explain what we had added, deleted, copied or expanded. We were constantly told that ASIO would pick up any discrepancies at their end. How? We didn't know. And we weren't allowed to ask.

What was impressed on us more clearly than anything else was that from now on, no applications with missing information were to be sent to analysts. "No more yellow stickers!" We could only give errant files to team leaders, but even then, the cases had to be extreme, that is, only when there was a lot of missing data. This instruction was another threat! We were not to hand applications back without very good reason – or else!

The rhetoric on how to 'fill in the gaps' was deliberately vague, but the threats which accompanied it were explicit. Anyone who didn't implement the vagaries would be out of a job. So much for 'intelligence'! This place was a nightmare!

In short, it was made abundantly clear that our job was to just 'fill in all the gaps' ourselves, by whatever means, and get the reports through to the ASIO database, no matter what. The strong implication was that ASIO was aware of this arrangement and would pick up any inconsistencies at their end. How they would pick them up was not explained. Apparently, we didn't need to know. It took me quite a while to realise the information we were entering under orders, according to this DSA training, could never be picked up by ASIO.

I later learned, to my shame, that the false information we were trained to enter into the system had permanently contaminated the ASIO database. They couldn't fix it! The false information we fed into the ASIO database could never be 'picked up' or found and corrected unless it was specifically pointed out! And this could only happen when an applicant entered a new application for an upgrade on an existing clearance.

In hindsight, the harsh reality was agency staff were being deliberately trained to falsify information and lie to ASIO in order to speed the processing of applications for the sake of money. We just didn't know it. I didn't know it!

Though I thought the information given was vague and dodgy sounding, I reminded myself this was intelligence. It was probably supposed to sound vague and dodgy. The 'need-to-know' rule had been drummed into us; we would only ever be told what we needed to know, nothing more. But then I wondered, wasn't this one of those need-to-know times?

There were no answers to these questions. And I wasn't allowed to ask questions anyway. It was all a bit much, really. I had to let it go. Greater minds than mine had made this decision. Who was I to question anything? I was at the bottom of the totem pole. What did I know?

Even though DSA's willingness to flout the rules and thumb their noses at established security procedures was staring me directly in the face, I couldn't see it. I didn't want to believe they would actually do anything opposed to Australia's best interest. That is until my eyes started to open during the lunchtime conversation that same day.

A SHOCKING REVELATION

As usual, Janice, Cassie, Jennifer, Owen, Jim and myself had gathered around the yellow cloth in our tranquil garden oasis, and Janice opened the conversation with an unusual question. "Have any of you received your secret-level clearance?"

"No," said Cassie.

"Nor me," I said.

Jennifer took a bite of her sandwich and shook her head.

"I have," said Owen, with his usual good humour. "It came through this week."

"So did mine," said Jim.

"I'm only asking because I haven't received mine yet," Janice explained, "and I was doing all those top-secret applications."

"At least you have a 'restricted'," said Owen. "I didn't even have a restricted clearance when I first started doing them."

"What?" I was shocked. "No clearance at all?"

"You could have been a terrorist," Cassie joked, picking at her salad.

"Maybe he is!" Janice laughed.

"How did you get onto the Base, Owen?" I asked. My mind flicked back to all those times I'd gone swimming at the Richmond RAAF Base when I was a child. I always had to ride my bike the three miles to the pool alone because my friends didn't have passes. It boggled my mind that Owen had been able to freely come and go onto one of our military bases daily without any form of clearance or pass. I was horrified.

"I was working here for a week before my restricted came through," Owen confirmed.

"Accessing top-secret data, with no clearance at all," said Jennifer, "that's intelligent!"

"How did you get through the gates?" I asked.

"The guards never asked me for my clearance," Owen explained, "I didn't think it was a big deal."

Again I was horrified. I'd grown up around military bases. No one was ever allowed in without a pass. The guards always checked. And now, here I was working in DSA, the centre responsible for those passes, and checking passes was irrelevant? Having them was irrelevant? My brain hurt!

We were all required to have a secret-level clearance to do the work we were doing, and to gain one, we all had to submit to a police check and a detailed investigation of the last ten years of our lives. None of us should have been doing this work without the proper clearance. My mind flashed back to the Army Officer who had given us our IT training. What would she think about all this, I wondered? The minimum clearance for a Military Officer was 'secret', and she thought our clearance was higher than hers. She thought we all had 'top-secret clearances', at the very least. I was dumbfounded, but my personal shock went unnoticed, and the conversation continued.

Janice was making light of it all. "The way I'm going, I'll probably be out of here before my secret clearance comes through."

"You and half the other agency staff," drawled Cassie, smiling.

"I wonder if that means all the work we've done is invalid?" Janice said, laughing.

The question was innocent. Janice was merely trying to make a joke, but the joke was ignored, and her thinking was taken seriously.

"That's a good question," said Owen without his usual smile.

Jennifer was nodding. "I wonder why they want short-term people without clearances entering this data?" she asked casually.

We all stopped eating.

I looked at Jennifer. Her eyes were on me. She *had* noticed my shock and was on the ball as usual. Her question hit the nail right on the head.

The penny suddenly dropped for all of us with a 'kaboom' rather than a 'clink'. Yes! Why did they want short-term people without clearances entering this data?

No one said a word.

Things had suddenly gone from bad to worse. There was nothing specific, just a vague nagging that something was very wrong. I couldn't grasp the logic of it. It didn't make sense. Yet, I was suddenly aware of a strong but imprecise perception that we were all party to something which shouldn't be happening. We were seeing things we shouldn't be seeing, and worse, we could all very well be real live pawns in a deceitful game of chess. I began to imagine a nasty possibility:

- Question by an imaginary high-up official: *"Please explain this inconsistency..."*
- Response by a faceless DSA authority: *"An agency temp did that...didn't know what they were doing...fired for incompetence... a one-off..."*

My mind was going numb. There were just too many questions. Why were we really here? Why was the staff turnover so high? What were they hiding? What were they getting us to do that we shouldn't be doing?

The silence continued. The possibilities were scary. We all knew it. Eventually, with unspoken consensus, we shook off our thoughts and began a totally new subject. After all, we truly didn't know if we were being bugged or not. Any further exploration of this topic would have to wait until we were in a safer place.

> *What does it say about the Department of Defence? They were telling their bosses they were not comfortable with this and their bosses were saying, "Get on with your job."* (ABC 20 Sept. 2011)

Did they really think
they would
get away with it?

CHAPTER THREE

Personal threats? Of course!

Defence and the Recruitment Agency supplying temporary employees to DSA were jointly involved in the deception and mistreatment of agency staff. During the two years false information was being fed to ASIO, Defence called the shots, and the recruitment agency fired the gun.

The question had to be asked, why was a recruitment agency collaborating in this misconduct? Surely they had a duty of care to their employees. These employees were their responsibility. Surely they had the authority to inform DSA of possible breaches of law and remove their employees until DSA management addressed any violations?

DSA management had a clear motive for their abuse and corruption of agency staff; they wanted to cover their deception, which was motivated by money. But what motive could the recruitment agency possibly have to subject its employees to such brutality? The answer again was money. Always money!

The recruitment agency received a portion of each of the twenty or so salaries every week as payment for supplying staff to Defence plus a healthy commission for every single clearance application completed by the agency employees working within DSA. The clearance commissions were where the real money was.

Clearance commissions were so lucrative Dora called them the agency's 'bread and butter'. She made it clear to us that individual employees didn't matter. Agency staff were temporary and not supposed to last, but the clearances were everything! They were keeping the agency afloat. The great push from Dora was always 'more clearances'. What we had to do, or go through to get them done, was irrelevant.

A mountain view of the battleground is grand, but we didn't see things so clearly from the trenches. We were caught in a muddle of not knowing what was going on. We couldn't understand the cruelty and were constantly perplexed by Dora's iron-fisted treatment of staff. Nevertheless, the light of understanding was beginning to break through. There was a glimpse here and a flicker there, just enough to let us know something else was going on, though we couldn't quite work out what that something might be. That was about to change.

THE UNDERBELLY IS SUDDENLY EXPOSED

A few days after the penny dropped with a kaboom, revealing another little flicker of hidden reality, tragedy struck Owen's family. The events which followed changed the dynamic of our little group to the point where it would eventually be disbanded. The days of lunchtime camaraderie were all but over.

On September 29, 2009, Owen's family were caught up in the most powerful earthquake recorded in 2009. The earthquake triggered four swift and powerful tsunami waves, which engulfed the Islands of Samoa, American Samoa and Tonga. Samoa took the greatest hit. There was no time for everyone to get to higher ground. Owen lost thirteen members of his family.

DSA let Owen take leave that day without firing him, but I had a nagging suspicion he would pay for it when he got back. They didn't like us taking time off. They didn't like their victims escaping their control. At this point in time, their hand had been forced, and they couldn't say no. Saying no in a crisis of this magnitude would have been seen as way too un-Australian. Even DSA management wasn't that stupid. Owen was, for the moment, untouchable.

Not so, Janice. DSA was a petty organisation. If they couldn't sack one person, they would sack another just to feel that they were filling their sacking quota. As they couldn't respectably sack Owen, they turned their attention to Janice. As usual, Dora was tasked with her dismissal.

"Janice? I'm just touching base with you to see how you're going." Dora always started her phone conversations with such calculated sweetness it set our teeth on edge.

"Nothing has changed," Janice spoke into the phone, wondering if there was any point saying anything at all, "I still have no desk..."

"Well, that's a moot point now anyway," responded Dora. The sweetness was gone.

"I'm sorry, I don't follow," said Janice.

"Erik has asked for you to be removed."

Janice went cold. This was it. She was being fired. She felt disoriented. Her head began to swim.

Dora continued, "He said you've been complaining and wasting time."

Janice wondered how many times she would have to say it. "I am not compl..."

Dora wasn't listening, as usual, and spoke over the top of her, "I want you to be professional and stay on until I can find a replacement."

What was that? Stay on? This was too confusing. "So, I'm not fired?" asked Janice, perplexed. What was the point of this phone call?

"I will inform Erik of your professionalism," said Dora and hung up the phone.

Fired? Not fired? What? Janice couldn't get her head around it. It was too strange. She wondered why they could possibly want her to continue to work within a secure, secret organisation, even though she'd been fired. That was not intelligent, not even smart! It was absurd! Bizarre! What a twisted, psychotic mess! Janice knew then she needed to deal with this unprofessional behaviour and make a firm decision. She'd had enough.

Lunchtime came around, and we all gratefully escaped to the peace and tranquillity of the beautiful sunken garden. Janice wasted no time telling us what had just happened.

"Why are you still here?" asked Jennifer setting off a rush of encouragement.

"Yes, why don't you just quit?" added Jim.

"You only have to give an hour's notice," said Cassie in her usual calming way.

"Yes, why don't you sack them?" I asked, hoping she would choose to resign because the way they were treating her was too terrible to watch.

"I don't know how you can put up with it another minute!" said Jennifer with genuine concern.

"Well, Janice?" I asked.

Janice gave a wry smile and sighed. "If I'm going to leave Defence, I want to leave on my terms, not theirs. I don't want to be escorted off the Base like a criminal, and I don't intend to be. But I have to sleep on it. I don't know precisely what I'm going to do yet."

The next day Janice resigned. She had decided to work her typical day and give notice an hour before knock-off time. So, in the late afternoon, she began her quitting process. Her first port of call was Doug. "Doug, I am giving my notice. I will not be returning. Are there any papers I need to sign?"

Without saying a word, Doug picked out the paperwork she needed and laid it on the counter in front of her, placing a pen on top of the papers.

Janice signed the paperwork and handed it back. "Goodbye," she said in the calmest voice she could muster.

Doug gave a sympathetic half-smile and a nod but didn't say a word.

Janice visited each of her antagonists and personally said goodbye with a cheery smile and a note of genuine goodwill in her voice. She was leaving as a lady! A Christian! And on her own terms. This terrible experience had not changed her nature or her convictions.

Erik wasn't in his office, so she knocked on Paula's door. "I wanted to let you know I'm leaving today. I just wanted to say goodbye."

Paula looked up. She was so stunned at Janice's effrontery she actually looked directly at Janice's face, her eyes glaring with anger. "You're leaving us in the lurch," she barked.

Janice sighed and replied, "The way I feel now, Paula, you wouldn't want me to stay." Then she turned and walked away.

Just after work, as Janice and I were walking toward the Bus station, Janice's mobile phone rang.

It was Dora. And she was angry! "Con has informed me that you've resigned. How could you, Janice? This is so unprofessional! I guarantee you this; I will not in the future seek any further work placements for you."

"Dora, you told me yesterday Erik wanted me replaced," said Janice

"That was not a certainty!" yelled Dora so loudly I could hear her words.

Suddenly everything became clear to Janice. She realised yesterday's tirade was just part of a game. The sacking wasn't real. It was cruel manipulation. Dora and Defence had only been playing with her, tormenting her, abusing and confusing her - for fun! Now she knew she'd made the right decision.

"Your actions will directly impact your friends! Because of you, management will be watching them carefully." Pandora had no tricks left, and she was savage! The phone made a loud click. Dora had hung up.

Janice closed her mobile and put it in her coat pocket. Her hands were shaking. She wasn't saying anything. This was not good.

We reached the station and went upstairs for coffee. "What's going on, Janice?" I asked gently.

"She just threatened you all," Janice put her head down in her hands, "because of what I did today."

"What?" I was instantly livid! "She threatened *us*?" I asked. I felt a surge of rage. It was not anger. It was more powerful and more controlled. "How dare she threaten us!" I said quietly.

"It's my fault," said Janice, "I shouldn't have..."

"Your fault?" I interrupted. "How can this possibly be your fault? You didn't threaten us!"

"But I resigned!"

"Yes, you did! And you did the right thing!" I knew Janice didn't deserve this final nasty blow.

Then suddenly, the reality of the situation struck me, my fury dissipated completely, and I couldn't help smiling. "You know, Janice, you actually got the victory today. Even Dora can see that. I think that's why she's so angry."

"But they're going to be watching you." Janice was clearly distressed and close to tears.

"Janice," I said, covering her clasped hands with mine, "they're already watching us. They watch everyone all the time. You know that."

Janice nodded but was still not convinced.

"It's an empty threat," I said as bluntly as I could. "You need to show her you couldn't care less about her threats. What can she do to us, really? Fire us? Is that it? So what's new?"

Janice laughed. I laughed. The threat and its fake condemnation had just lost their power.

"As soon as I get home, I'm going to email her, in my most 'professional' manner, of course," Janice was still smiling, "and let her know that I do not wish to remain on her books and nor do I want any further communication from her office."

"Perfect!" I said, smiling back. "You've kept your integrity...and your dignity...you win!"

LEARNING TO PREDICT THEIR GAME PLAYS

Despite my assurances to Janice, I knew the DSA nasties were not going to be merely watching us; they were going to be targeting us. That's who they were. That's what they did.

I was an experienced parent with two married children. I recognised childish games when I saw them. I'd been in DSA long enough now to be able to see through their games, and I was becoming more and more unimpressed by their immaturity.

Like spoilt children, everything had to be done their way. If they didn't get their way, they would throw tantrums. Yet, as every child knows, tantrums are no fun if no one is around to see them. The DSA bullies made sure everyone saw what they were doing. It was their way of maintaining power. How stupid! It seems they didn't understand that employers have power anyway. They didn't have to demean their staff to get what was already theirs. Not intelligent at all!

DSA tantrums were nasty, childish, selfish, insane forms of punishment. Like a child sticking a pin into a captured bug to watch it struggle, the intention of the tantrum was to torture, not kill. That's what they'd been doing to Janice - torturing her! Torture was more delicious than death to these people, and now that we had been targeted, there would be no instant sackings for us, just many threats of sackings. That was more fun!

This same nasty, abusive and unnecessary use of punishment to gain control now flavours the COVID playbook. Australians need to recognise it for what it is - fun - for those dishing out the tortures.

I shouldn't have had to know all this about the management of DSA and their civilian henchmen, but I did. I'd learned by bitter experience.

Owen had been able to escape for a few days on his own terms. Janice had been able to escape permanently, on her own terms. DSA had been thwarted. The next tantrum was coming. Like a cyclone at sea moving towards the coast, I knew it was coming. I just didn't know where it would land or how much damage it would do.

Jack came up behind me and suddenly slapped three files on my desk. I jumped and turned around on my chair. "Jack," I said. "You startled me."

Jack laughed; a hearty, friendly laugh. My heart sank. What now? This was bad! Very bad!

"I've just been talkin' to Erik," he said, "and it seems y're makin multiple errors. He's sent a report to Dora informing her of his dissatisfaction." He pointed to two of the files. "These two have spelling errors in the names."

He was intimating that they were going to sack me and that Erik had already put the process in motion. Now I began to wonder, was this a mere tantrum or the real thing? Hmm - not sure!

I looked at the files. The names were printed by hand in thick black ink. I didn't recognise the handwriting or the names. "Jack, this is not my handwriting," I said.

Jack stopped smiling. He straightened up, picked up the files and opened them, scanning the interior for evidence of the names of the files' creators. He checked one and then the other. "Yes," he said, closing the files and looking sheepish, "These aren't your files." This was the first time I had seen him flustered.

Great! Now I'm being punished for other people's mistakes! I couldn't show what I thought on my face. Any hint of criticism would bring instant dismissal. So, I put my head down and turned my attention to the third file. I remembered it. I had completed the application and filed it in the vault-window room just yesterday. "I remember this one, Jack," I admitted, keeping my tone casual.

"There's a problem with this one. I want y'to go downstairs, retrieve the application and bring it to me," Jack ordered, no longer flustered.

I nodded. This was unusual. I'd never been asked to retrieve a completed application. That had never been an agency role. I sensed a setup, but I couldn't see what it might be. Nevertheless, I still had to do as I was told.

With two of the files tucked under his arm, Jack went to the staircase and bounded up the stairs, taking them two at a time, almost running. That was odd. He never ran. It was obvious he was reporting back to Erik and reporting straight away! But why? The penny dropped. Okay, so this was not a sacking; it was a torture, a silly game! How pathetic!

I went down to the vault-window room, which still always gave me the creeps, and opened the filing cabinet drawer. The application was not there. I searched again. Not there. I looked in all four drawers. Not there. Oh-oh! There were only two filing cabinets I ever accessed in that room. I had just searched one; maybe I had filed it in the other cabinet by mistake. I searched each drawer. Not there. Oh no! Losing a file was definitely sackable. Yet I knew for certain I'd filed it. Well, maybe this wasn't a game after all. Maybe I had really lost a file. Game, or no game, without a retrievable file, it was 'game over' for me.

I dragged myself back up the stairs to Jack's office. He was not there, so I supposed he must still be with Erik. I went back to my desk in Doug's pod, where I was seated while Owen was away. I dropped heavily into my seat, feeling numb, not sure what to do next. I turned my chair around to see the stairwell and catch Jack as he came back down the stairs, dreading the conversation I would have with him. Suddenly this application was everything. Nothing else mattered.

Doug swivelled his chair around to face me. "What's wrong?" he asked.

I nearly fell off my seat. Did I hear right? Was Doug actually speaking to me? He didn't talk to anyone. Not even to Defence staff, if he could help it. He pretty much kept to himself.

"Oh," I said, trying to cover my surprise, "um, I've lost an application. I know I filed it yesterday, but I can't find it today. I've searched both cabinets. It's not there."

Doug didn't seem surprised, but then Doug didn't seem to show any emotion, ever! "Come with me," he said, like someone who had a solution. So I followed him.

He led me back down to the vault-window room. "Show me the two cabinets you searched."

I pointed them out.

He looked at them, reading their paper descriptors and then looked around the room. "Over here," he said.

I was puzzled. I went to the cabinet Doug had pointed out and opened the drawer. There was the file! I retrieved it and looked up at him, amazed. "I didn't file it in here," I said.

"Yes, you did," he replied and pointed to the paper description.

The truth dawned, and my mouth dropped open. They moved the cabinet! They moved the whole cabinet across the floor to a completely different spot! What a setup! Various unsavoury names came to mind, but I didn't voice them. Ladies don't! I felt my anger begin to rise. They couldn't find anything to blame me for, so now they were making it up. Unbelievable! I closed my mouth without saying a word, and my anger deepened. Then I went beyond anger and became very calm.

Doug remained silent. It was clear he had seen this kind of thing happen before. This game was not new to him. He knew exactly what to look for, and he'd chosen to save me. Suddenly I saw the real Doug. He was not like them. He didn't play their games. Now I could see he didn't even like their games. No wonder he kept himself aloof.

"Thank you, Doug," I said, looking into his eyes with heartfelt sincerity, "God bless you."

He met my gaze and smiled, a broad, genuine smile, accepting the blessing. Nothing else was said.

I turned and strode, with purpose, out of that ridiculous excuse for a room, around the vault door and up the stairs to Jack's office. He was there.

"Here's the application you wanted," I said, holding out the paperwork, meeting his gaze, almost challenging him to take it from me.

He looked genuinely surprised. "Oh, you found it," he said, taking it from my hand. He clearly didn't expect me to find the file for his face showed his puzzlement. It was my turn to watch his reaction, read his eyes and answer his unspoken question.

"Doug helped me," I said, knowing I was dropping a mini bomb, and that it would hit its mark. I didn't wait for Jack's response. After watching his eyes register their surprise, I turned and walked out of his office. There was no problem with that application. He knew it. Erik knew it. Doug knew it. And now they knew I knew it too.

I didn't hear another word about it. I'd been right. This was just another torture game. A stupid tantrum! Didn't they care about the psychological and emotional damage they were doing to people? Didn't they know how insane their behaviour was? They were playing with people's lives!

The greatest surprise for Jack that day was Doug. He was supposed to be one of 'them', but he'd shown his true colours. I guessed I wouldn't be sitting in Doug's area for much longer. They wouldn't allow that!

When I got back to the pod, Doug was waiting for me. "Have you ever wondered how many agency temps go through this place?" he asked in almost a whisper.

I shook my head. I still wasn't used to this new talking Doug.

"I've been running some numbers on the agency temps who have passed through here in the past eighteen months."

My, oh my, he was full of surprises today!

"Sixty, in eighteen months," he whispered.

"That's a lot of people," I said softly, taking care not to be overheard. "In any normal business, those figures would be a huge warning sign – 'management in crisis'."

He nodded. "Have you thought about the cost?" He was looking at me intently, trying to see if I understood what he meant.

My eyebrows shot up. I indicated 'no' to him and quickly did a mental calculation of the cost of the two clearances, restricted plus secret, which every new agency staff member had to have, $1700 per head. I couldn't speak the amount out loud. This was dangerous ground.

He was watching me intently. "Now add those who are here at the moment."

I nodded in response. "And how long are we twenty going to last before we are replaced?"

"Around 100 in less than two years," he said and paused...people were coming up the stairs.

$170,000! The unspoken amount hung in the air. He had made his point. All these clearances were short-term. This was wasted money!

We turned our chairs back to our work positions, but the conversation continued in my mind. Who pays for this? The obvious answer was the Australian taxpayer. All these wasted clearances were nothing short of a huge, deliberate and indiscriminate abuse of taxpayer money. Why did Doug tell me this? Why, after all this time, did he suddenly want me to know about the cost?

I was amazed at Doug. This was so unexpected. I felt warm all over. I had won a friend, an ally. In this horrible, dark, dark place, there were still beautiful, flickering, shining lights. And they warmed the heart.

When the coast was clear, I turned my chair around and asked him why he was helping me.

"Which church do you go to?" he said in response and smiled a full, natural smile. His face was alight with life, and his eyes danced.

So...he was a Christian! That explained it!

It is was clear that this quiet man, who barely spoke, wanted me to know he didn't like what he was seeing. As we chatted in covert whispers, he told me he was due to start his long-service leave and would be gone for three months. Ah, so that's why he was giving me this information now. He knew I wouldn't be here when he got back. What an unexpected blessing!

THE DIVISIONS BEGIN TO BREAK DOWN

The next day I was moved out of Doug's cubicle and re-located, like a ping-pong ball, back to Crystal and Linda's pod. Whether it was because of my sudden friendship with Doug, because management was addicted to chaos or because agency staff were moved continuously to keep us aware that we were only temporary and didn't belong, I will never know. But I wasn't surprised.

I was happy to be working with Crystal and Linda again, for, unlike some others, these two women didn't make me feel like the enemy. This time I was seated in Cleo's old seat. It was still hers officially, and all her things remained in place, but she was no longer using them and probably would not be using them again for quite some time. She'd been promoted and moved. She was now a team leader. Did they only pick the nasty ones? This promotion happened just a few short weeks after she had so viciously humiliated Brian, so I guess that incident must have proven she was DSA management material! Thankfully, she was permanently working in a different section.

"Hey Monica, come and join us," Crystal said.

I'd been absorbed in my work, minding my own business, shutting out the chit chat. I was good at that now, I didn't even hear the chatter anymore, but this time my name had been called, so I turned in my chair to give Crystal my attention.

Crystal, Linda and a new trainee analyst, I'll call her Deb, had wheeled their chairs to the centre of the pod as if they were about to discuss something. They were all looking at me expectantly, waiting for me to join them.

This was strange. I wasn't allowed to enter into office things, like gossip, politics, work issues etc., to do so was a sackable offence, and I also wasn't allowed any unscheduled breaks. I'd seen what happened to people who took them. Not pretty! I wasn't even allowed to talk to Defence staff unless they spoke to me first, so I was unsure what I should do about Crystal's request.

I smiled what I hoped was a rueful smile. "I'm not allowed...I'm sorry."

Crystal looked puzzled, "what do you mean you're not allowed?"

Didn't she know? How could she not know? "We're not allowed to talk to Defence staff. We get sacked if we do," I said, wondering how she would take my honesty.

The three of them lost their smiles. They were all silent for a while, and then Crystal spoke up again. "We thought you were all snobs."

"You get fired if you talk to us?" asked Linda.

I nodded.

"But we talk to agency staff all the time," said Crystal, still puzzled.

I smiled. "Yes, I know, but we're only allowed to talk to you if you open the conversation."

"We didn't know that," said Linda.

Deb was shaking her head, showing she didn't know either.

"Well...we are opening this conversation with you now...so therefore you won't get the sack," said Crystal speaking with a logical kind of mock authority. "Come over here." She was waving me over, smiling.

I laughed. I liked this woman. But I still couldn't join them. "It's an unscheduled break from my work. I can get the sack for that too."

"Mad!" said Linda. "What else can you be sacked for?"

I rattled off a short list.

They looked at each other and then at me. Now, unsmiling, all three were shaking their heads, stunned by the news.

"We didn't know," Deb said gently and with genuine remorse.

"We wondered why no one stayed very long," Linda said, joining the dots.

"And kept to yourselves..." Crystal voice tapered off as the reality of my situation hit home.

"You know, Monica," said Linda, "this is not a break from your work. What we want to talk with you about is part of your job."

"Yes," said Crystal, "it concerns all of us."

"Including you," confirmed Deb.

"We have to discuss how we are going to decorate this pod for Christmas." Crystal sounded like she was presenting the perfect solution to all my objections.

"That is neither office gossip nor office politics," Linda confirmed.

"And you are part of this pod!" concluded Deb. They were all nodding and smiling.

I couldn't help laughing. Wow! This was not what I expected. These women were normal! But I had one last objection.

"I won't be in this area for Christmas," I said. "We're moved around all the time."

"Cleo's not coming back," said Linda.

"Well, not before Christmas anyway," said Deb.

"You'll be here!" smiled Crystal.

"Come on," said Deb, "join us!"

"It'll be fun," said Crystal, waving me over.

Finally, I was convinced! I wheeled my chair to the middle of the room. This was amazing! First Doug, and now this group. The strict, deliberately manufactured walls of division between agency staff and analysts were beginning to disintegrate. I was starting to see the softer side of some DSA personnel, and I couldn't wait to tell the others.

During this COVID crisis, a host of deliberately manufactured walls of division have been hastily erected between Australians. State against State, vaccinated against unvaccinated, employed against unemployed, and their carefully designed purpose is to stop the truth from being seen.

TWO DOWN AND FOUR TO GO

It was Owen's first day back, and I was keen to find out how his family were doing. The sky was overcast, and the air felt moist like rain was imminent, but I headed for the garden anyway. So did the others. We laid out the yellow cloth and were putting our lunches on the table when we saw Owen and Jim coming down the path.

Immediately, we all smiled and waved.

"Welcome back, Owen," said Cassie gently.

"Good to see your cheery smile," I said.

"How's your family?" asked Jennifer with genuine concern in her eyes.

"Coping," said Owen. "We've been overwhelmed with all the support. I spent most of my time running around gathering things people were donating to send over there. Truckloads!"

"I saw one of your aunts on TV," said Cassie, "She did an interview. It all sounded so horrible."

"Mum's over there now," said Owen, nodding, "she went over for the funerals. And she's going to stay for a while to help out."

"What about your Dad?" asked Jennifer.

"He didn't go over. He stayed back to look after the family...go to work...you know." Looking around the group, Owen asked, "Where's Janice? Is she working through lunch?"

We looked at each other for a second to see who would tell him.

"She resigned," said Jim bluntly.

"Had enough," confirmed Jennifer.

"She said to say goodbye to you," said Cassie.

"When did this happen?" Owen asked.

We filled him in on the details.

"I'm sorry she's not here anymore, but to be honest, I'm glad she's out." He looked off into the distance, "The way they treated her," he closed his eyes as he shook his head, "disgusting!"

"Well, I have some news," said Jennifer. "I'm leaving too. This is my last day."

We turned to her but didn't say a word.

"I've been thrown a lifeline by one of my old colleagues," she was smiling. "I'll be working with the State Government again in IT - my cup of tea."

"Oh, how wonderful, Jen," I was truly happy for her. She had escaped.

"Congratulations," Jim bowed in mock salute.

"I'm jealous," said Cassie, obviously recalling the 'good times' we girls had shared in our previous State Government positions.

"Normal people!" said Owen, almost wistfully.

"Tomorrow, I'll be contacting the Fair Work Ombudsman's office," Jennifer continued, "people outside need to know what's going on in here. This place is appalling."

"Let us know if we can help," I said.

"If they want confirmation, they can contact me," said Owen.

"And me," agreed Cassie.

"There's another angle to this," I said. "Doug put me onto it."

"Doug?" Jennifer sounded as surprised as everyone else looked. Not only was he Defence personnel, everyone knew he was a man of few words who kept to himself.

I smiled. "Yes, Doug!

I filled them in on the DSA filing cabinet game, how he'd helped me, what he told me about temp stats and how he'd made me think about the cost of clearances.

"Wow!" said Owen.

"That's amazing," said Jennifer.

They were as incredulous as I'd been.

"That's another angle you can put to the Ombudsmen; the high turn-over," said Cassie.

"I don't know how either the Agency or Defence can justify it," said Jennifer. "Agency contractors are only supposed to work on temporary projects. This is not a temporary project; it's permanent. It deals with military intelligence material, and the workloads are increasing. Someone needs to investigate why contracters are being used."

"You go get'em, tiger," smiled Owen, cheering Jennifer on.

"We're going to miss you, Jennifer," I said and meant every word. Jennifer was a sparky little fire-brand, yet logical and clear-headed. She was doing the most sensible thing any of us could do, leave!

"We have to meet up for a visit sometime, Jennifer," said Cassie. "Don't be a stranger."

"I won't!" said Jennifer and gave us each a warm farewell hug.

"Our group is shrinking..." moaned Jim.

"It'll shrink even more if this rain gets us," laughed Jennifer as light raindrops started to sprinkle down.

We cleared the table, ran up the sandstone stairs and past the grassy quadrant reaching the cement building block just as the rain started to pour down in torrents.

THE SECOND OF FOUR SIGNIFICANT EVENTS

Christmas was coming! The decorations were up, and the harsh, sterile atmosphere had lifted a little, but only a little. It seemed not even Christmas could penetrate the sombre atmosphere of this dark place.

"We have to lighten the atmosphere a bit - bring in a little Christmas spirit," said Linda.

"Only three pods are making any real effort. The rest are just giving token gestures," said Deb.

Crystal had a mischievous look on her face. "What about a great big naughty-n-nice list?"

We all laughed.

"That'll put the cat amongst the pigeons," said Linda. "Do you think it's wise?"

"*We* won't choose whose name goes on which list; *they* will," said Crystal. "It should be fun!"

"And it fits in with our "Santa's workshop theme," said Deb. "I'll make the fireplace."

"I'll bring in the tree and some music and nibblies," said Crystal.

"I'll make the presents to stick on the wall," said Linda. When we all looked at her, quizically, she said, "What? There's no room on the floor!"

"I'll make the naughty-n-nice lists if you want." I offered. "Plus the absolutely fabulous list."

They all stared at me.

"Absolutely fabulous list?" asked Deb.

"Whose on that?" Crystal chuckled.

"We are, of course!" said Linda, smiling.

"No one outside our pod is eligible," I said.

"I love it," said Crystal, beaming. "That's a big job. Are you sure you don't mind?"

"Mind?" I said, "You ladies are like life-savers to me - a ray of sunshine in a dark place. I'm happy to help out. Besides - it's Christmas!"

Over the next week, the filing cabinets along the back wall were transformed with plenty of paper and sticky tape into a large fireplace, a baubled tree was given pride of place on the 'mantle' above the fireplace, the wall behind was covered in large colourful cardboard cut-out 'presents', and containers of home-made Christmas goodies took pride of place under the tree.

The entrance to our pod, Santa's workshop, was flagged by two oversized candy canes. And in the corridor, the outer surface of our pod dividers was wholly covered with three 'naughty-n-nice' scrolls; one for the naughty, one for the nice and one for the absolutely fabulous.

Of course, the absolutely fabulous list only had four places, and they were already filled with our names. The decision about who should be placed on the naughty-n-nice lists was left to Defence personnel. Now, all we had to do was wait and see if people would take the bait and play our little Christmas game with us.

My clandestine role was to eavesdrop on the remarks made about the naughty-n-nice list by passers-by, covertly write them down onto yellow sticky notes and form their quips into a 'comment tree' (a Christmas tree shaped yellow-sticker commentary board) which we would display on the wall opposite the naughty-n-nice list. We had all agreed this unseen background role should protect me from construed blame.

Once the naughty-n-nice list was up, it had a wonderful effect on everyone. The atmosphere finally began to lighten. People would come by to find out which list they were on or put their co-workers on one of the lists. There were smiles and genuine laughter as comments were made.

"Why am I on the nice list? I'm naughty!"

"Where's the boss? Oh yes, that'd be right!"

"Don't tell Paula I put her on the naughty list!"

"Doug is on the nice list? This is rigged!"

"I've got Santa fooled..."

Once the comment tree went up, there was even more laughter. Just about everyone who stopped to read the comments would walk away grinning. People I'd never seen smile, and those who had never looked me in the eye, were now looking into my face and smiling genuine smiles as they went past. Wow! What an amazing change!

THE THIRD OF FOUR SIGNIFICANT EVENTS

About this time, I was given a 'special' task. Giving me this task would turn out to be the third significant event that would lead to DSA's demise. While doing this job, I would discover what Defence was trying so hard to hide.

Along with everything else that had already happened and those things about to happen, that revelation would uncover the broad-scale corruption, which was rife but unseen. This 'special' task would open my eyes - completely!

"Monica, I've something new for y'to do; a special job," Jack announced. He was smiling. His tone sounded to me like I had suddenly become his best friend.

Oh-oh! What now? I looked up from my work and raised my eyebrows but didn't say anything. Was this Christmas spirit, or was he setting me up? This approach screamed 'set-up, so I wondered what was coming. He was just too friendly.

"We call these 'quickie applications'," he explained, handing me a sample application. "They're just simple upgrades from 'restricted' to 'confidential' so they won't take you long to enter."

"There's no file," I commented. Upgrades were done on existing applications, which meant there was a file somewhere. We were not supposed to upgrade anything without checking the new information against the information on file.

"We don't have to wait for the files for these; that's what makes them 'quickies'," Jack said. "There'll be thousands of them comin' in over the next few months, and we need to put them through as quickly as possible."

I wasn't convinced. Why was he still smiling? Jack was watching me carefully.

"Come with me," he said and led me to his pod. "Take a look at this." He opened a screen on his computer and showed me a long list of names, scrolling down through thousands of them.

This was a first! Why was he showing me this?

"These applications are just for security guards who work on military bases," he explained. "They all work for private security firms who've done thorough checks. All we need t'do is rubber-stamp the upgrade."

That sounded reasonable to me. Jack knew what he was doing. He'd been around a long time. He understood the system. Maybe there was nothing wrong. Maybe I was becoming paranoid. At that point, I didn't realise he'd taken me away from the analysts to tell me this. He knew they would've jumped on this outright lie straight away.

"The hierarchy has ordered all these upgrades for security guards on bases, so it's simply a matter of putting them through. Just paperwork! Once they're done, they'll be held until the files come in, then attached to the files and sent back to archives."

He was obviously under orders. This is what smarter minds had decided. Okay, I was convinced. I think he could tell he'd convinced me.

"They haven't started comin' in yet," he said, pointing to the application in my hand, "just do this one. See how y'go. Bring it t'me when y'done."

Like a ship on the horizon, heading towards a field of submerged mines, disaster was imminent. The collision course was set. The explosion was inevitable. It was now only a matter of time.

It took a while for the special upgrades to start filtering through, and in the meantime, to my surprise, I stayed in Cleo's seat. The girls had been right; I had not been moved and would probably not be moved now until after Christmas. Amazing! Six weeks in one spot!

As it turned out, keeping me in Crystal's pod was crucial to unlocking the chicanery. If I'd been moved, I would never have seen the deception. If I'd not been able to build a rapport with analysts, I'd never have worked out that I'd been skillfully trained to deceive and mislead.

I was now in the right place (with analysts) at the right time (Christmas tends to break down barriers) and doing the right job (these special upgrades). Only one more piece of the puzzle needed to fall into place before this whole sorry mess could be seen and exposed.

MEETING UP WITH OLD FRIENDS

Even though Jennifer and Janice were now gone from DSA, Cassie and I had a chance to meet with them again a few weeks later. We were invited to the ex-Home WaterWise employees Christmas party on the Kookaburra Queen, a paddleboat steamer that sailed the Brisbane river.

"So, what's happening at that dreadful 'D' place?" asked Jennifer. Defence had become a dirty word to us, so we now only used the letter 'D' when referring to Defence.

"So much to say, so little time," said Cassie.

"It's all still going off like fireworks," I said, not knowing where to begin. "There's just one explosion after another. It never stops."

"One poor fellow only lasted a week," said Cassie in her caring way, "as soon as he was told he would need a secret clearance and have the last ten years of his life exposed to prying eyes, he quit. He objected to having his privacy invaded for a short-term agency job. And then there was George..."

"You would've loved it, girls!" I laughed." He exploded for everyone to hear!"

"What happened?" asked Janice

"He was an older man, so I guess he just wouldn't submit to their bullying," said Cassie.

"He told them they were the most disorganised bunch of people he's ever worked with, that they had no people skills and didn't have any idea how to time manage workflow efficiently. He told them he was doing his work and would appreciate it if they didn't pile his desk with more until he'd completed the tasks already assigned," I said.

"Really?" said Jennifer and laughed.

"That was brave," said Janice.

"What happened to him?" asked Jennifer, knowing no one ever gets away with that kind of behaviour at DSA.

"Nothing!" I said, watching the amazement spread over my friend's faces. "They had meetings at the highest level, thanked him for his input, then appeared to back-off."

"As they do," said Janice referring to her encounter with the Ice Queen.

"I can't figure them out," said Cassie

"No point trying," said Jennifer.

"Meanwhile, all the others downstairs cheered and clapped and congratulated him for speaking up, that is, when the bosses weren't looking, of course. Then a few days later, he was gone," I said.

"We don't know if he was sacked or left of his own accord," said Cassie.

"What a crazy mindless place to work," said Jennifer, shaking her head.

"Yes, well, it gets better," I said. "You know how Owen used to get gout in his knee sometimes?" Cassie continued.

Janice and Jennifer nodded.

"Well, it just suddenly flared up again. His poor knee was twice its normal size. It was huge," said Cassie, using her hands to show the size of his knee. "He said the pain was excruciating."

"He was using crutches to walk," I said.

"His doctor gave him a certificate for two days off, but Dora said he couldn't have time off, even with a doctor's certificate," said Cassie.

"But he had a doctor's certificate, for goodness sake," said Jennifer.

I nodded. "Yes, he did!"

"Anyway, he came to work, and by lunchtime, he couldn't bend his leg," said Cassie, "he was in agony."

"Oh, they're so cruel," said Janice.

"He rang Dora again and told her how bad things were and that he needed to go home," I said, "and do you know what she told him?"

They shook their heads.

"She said she didn't know why he came to work that day since he was so unwell." I watched their faces. The concept was so twisted, so abnormal; it took them a moment to adjust their thinking and remember how utterly absurd conversations with Dora always were.

"What?" said Jennifer. "Oh, she's just mad!"

"Poor Owen," said Janice.

"It gets worse," I said. "Then Dora told him he could have a day off if he got a doctor's certificate!"

"Didn't you just say he already had one?" asked Jennifer.

"Yes!" I said, unable to hide my disgust. "Owen was threatened with the sack if he didn't go to work and then berated for working."

"That place is insane!" said Jennifer.

"What did he do?" asked Janice.

"The sensible thing. He took a couple of days off," said Cassie. "His knee went down, and he is walking normally again."

"But who knows how long it will be before this comes back to bite him?" sighed Janice. "You know what they're like; they'll use it against him for sure."

"They already have!" I said. "He has a bung knee, so they've given him a job that requires him to climb two flights of stairs several times a day."

"Why am I not surprised?" said Jennifer.

"How low can they go?" asked Janice.

"This week, they moved him up to the top floor with me," said Cassie. "Well, not with me," she laughed, "on the same floor. He's now doing top-secret positive vetting."

"Oh, he's joined the elite group, has he?" Jennifer asked.

Cassie and I nodded.

"Do you still meet in the garden?" Janice asked.

Cassie glanced at me, "No," she said gently.

"It's not safe anymore," I said. "My job is being threatened every week. And Owen feels the hammer is sitting just over his head. He doesn't want it to fall. He has a family to support. They have to come first."

"It's just not the same without you two," Cassie drawled with a rueful smile.

Jennifer and Janice grinned.

"So Dora's threat was real," said Janice.

Yes," I said, "they're watching us, but it's not your fault. They were watching us anyway."

"I'm glad I'm out of there," said Janice.

"What happened with the Fair Work Ombudsman?" I asked Jennifer.

"I lodged the complaint," said Jennifer, "but I wasn't given a reference number. They told me to speak to DSA management first. The fellow who rang me didn't appear to understand the problem. He told me that after I'd spoken to management, I'd be able to phone a different number. Useless! There's no point speaking to management if I no longer work there, and if I no longer work there, it seems there is nothing they can do. The whole thing is stupid! There has to be a better way."

A SUDDEN CATASTROPHE

Christmas was lovely, but the New Year didn't go as well as I'd hoped. On New Year's Eve, I was phoned and told a good friend of twelve years, Peg, had died suddenly after a short illness. She lived in a different State. I knew I couldn't miss her funeral but would leaving work for two days cost me my job?

The next day, New Years Day, my daughter-in-law Kristy came rushing through my front door holding my eighteen-month-old grandson.

"Can you watch Jaylan?" she was distraught, "my brother is missing."

I took JJ out of her arms as the story gushed out of her. "We were all at Tallebudgera, swimming in the river - mum and dad, Stephen, my sisters - he was swimming with us. He disappeared! We can't find him."

The Tallebudgera River, on the Gold Coast in Queensland, is a saltwater tidal river. Though a favourite swimming spot for local families because of its calm surface, it is notorious for its undertow in king tides. Kristy's seventeen-year-old brother had epilepsy, and they were afraid he may have had a fit while swimming and been washed out to sea.

"Police rescue has been called in. I have to go!"

"Where's Stephen?" I asked, concerned. I couldn't help but wonder why my son was not with his wife and child.

"He's terribly upset - blaming himself. Heath was right behind him when he disappeared. Stephen's been diving down trying to find him for hours." Poor Kristy, her heart was being pulled in so many directions. Poor Stephen. What a horrible situation. It didn't sound good.

"JJ and I will be fine; you go and be with your family. Do what you've got to do," I said.

"Thank you," she replied. As she moved towards the door, she turned. "I don't know when I'll be back."

"Don't worry," I said and waved her on, "go!"

Police Rescue and Surf Lifesavers searched all day but couldn't find him. It wasn't until the following day after a rescue helicopter was brought in that his body was found wedged against a large sand dune at the bottom of the river.

Kristy's parents were devastated. This was their only son and the youngest of their four children. They couldn't face going back to their home with the Christmas decorations still up, his shoes at the front door, and his Christmas gifts unused. They couldn't face going into his room. They moved in with Kristy and Stephen.

I was glad Kristy had a large supportive family and that she and my son went to a caring church. Even though the weight of her parent's grief and the responsibility for organising the funeral had fallen onto this lovely young couple, the overwhelming support they were receiving meant I could return to my restrictive work routine, knowing that they did not have to cope alone.

Quite aside from all this grief, I was facing a personal dilemma. Two funerals! There was no way I could go to both funerals. It would be hard enough to get time off for one! I would have to choose which funeral to go to. The stark reality was DSA would not allow me to attend both funerals and keep my job. I wasn't even sure they would allow me to attend one.

I knew I had to make a choice. I had to choose friend or family - what a horrible decision. I should have been free to go to both funerals, but DSA and Dora were monsters who loved to torture, so I had to choose. I chose family over friend and found myself in the awkward position of having to tell Peg's children I would not be able to attend her funeral. That was the most brutal phone call I'd ever had to make.

Throughout the COVID crisis, we have seen the same officious, mean-spirited, totally unnecessary, cruel and torturous restrictions placed on loving, kind-hearted Australians who merely wished to say goodbye to their loved ones. Was my need to go to two funerals a threat to National Security? No! Is the COVID cruelty continually dished out by Government leaders and vicious bureaucrats necessary to Australia's biosecurity? No! Absolutely not! It is all part of a nasty elite game!

THE LAST OF THE FOUR SIGNIFICANT EVENTS

I advised Dora of Heath's death on my return to work and requested permission to go to his funeral. The exact day had not been set and would depend on when the Coroner's Office would release his body. I told her I would keep her informed.

Meanwhile, I started on a new pile of the special 'quickie' applications, now coming in thick and fast. I had no file to check the information against, so I just accepted what Jack said, that the information had been approved before we received it.

Even when the names didn't match, for example, if Linus Starlinus (fictitious name) had become Joe Star and there was no change of name certificate, I would assume that one had been provided before the application was sent to us and enter the new details anyway. Likewise, if there were any information gaps, I would re-use information already given, stretching the dates to make them fit the missing timeframes, as we had been trained, with threats, to do.

I'd been told the accuracy of this information was not vital to the clearance process. It was made clear that my job was to get them through the ASIO database without triggering an error report.

This grated against everything I'd ever been taught about applications. All my previous training in Parliamentary service, State Government and private enterprise had emphasised accuracy and the importance of legal proof for personal information. In the Queensland State Government, people couldn't even get a rebate for a purchased garden hose if they hadn't provided original documents to prove who they were, where they lived, and their purchase price. Surely such diligence would be regarded as the standard expectation?

But hey, this was intelligence. They did things differently. I just had to do as I was told. After all, I was at the bottom of the pile, the lowest of the low. What did I know? Still, I couldn't shake the nagging feeling something was wrong, despite being congratulated for the work I was doing.

I was getting through eighteen 'quickie' applications a day, when usually, I was only able to do ten. Not having to check information almost doubled my output. One thing I knew for sure was that these 'quickies' made my stats look good! Real good! Dora and Defence were thrilled.

"You need to provide us with all your previous addresses," Crystal was speaking on the phone to an applicant, "if you can't provide accurate details, we will not be able to approve your clearance."

What? Did I just hear right?

Linda was also on the phone, "You need to tell us where you were employed at the time, sir, and the name of your employer. We need exact dates."

Wait a minute! What were they saying? Accurate details? Exact dates? That's not what I was doing! That's not what I'd been told!

Alarm bells began ringing loudly in my head. Why were the analysts telling the applicants they had to provide these details when I'd been told these details were not necessary or even important?

Deb was requesting a change of name certificate, "You need to supply the original, sir. Until you do, your clearance cannot continue to be processed."

I wasn't allowed to ask questions, especially of analysts, and it seemed I'd been lied to by the team leader, but I wasn't sure. I had to work this out! I kept listening. Maybe they were working on higher-level clearances. I looked at the files on their desks. No, we were working on the same levels. I'd been told my applications were 'special'. Was that true, or not? Why hadn't I noticed this before? I searched my mind to understand, then I realised.

Until I was invited to get involved in everything Christmas, I'd taught myself to shut out all the conversation around me. Being given the job of eavesdropping on every naughty-n-nice conversation while doing my work changed that. When I became involved in their Christmas games, my ears had opened, and now, although Christmas was over, my ears were still open. I was alert and hearing everything.

This was the fourth piece of the puzzle. I was in the right place (with analysts) at the right time (Christmas tends to break down barriers) and doing the right job (these special upgrades), but now, I had suddenly come face to face with correct procedure and was acutely aware that I had been lied to. I had been used as a pawn in a deadly game of deception. The realisation left me reeling. But what was I going to do about it? I didn't know.

Heath's funeral had been set. So I emailed Dora requesting the day off, expecting her to get back to me promptly. She didn't. The afternoon before the funeral, she had still not responded.

This was torture, deliberate and unnecessary. My stomach was in a knot. I wasn't going to get tomorrow off. Still, nothing would stop me from attending Heath's funeral, so I made a firm decision. I was going! Even if it cost me my job!

The moment I made that decision, the knot left my stomach, and peace entered like a balm. Suddenly the game was over. Goodbye job! I decided to say goodbye to my new friends while I had the chance. "Well, girls, it looks like it's my last day today." I'd turned my chair around and was speaking to everyone in general.

Crystal, Linda and Deb turned around to face me. "What do you mean?" asked Crystal.

"I still haven't got permission to go to the funeral tomorrow," I said.

"Just go! You won't get the sack," Deb said lightly like I was worrying over nothing.

I smiled and shook my head. They just didn't understand. "It's been wonderful working with you. I wanted to say goodbye while I have the chance."

"But you're a good worker," said Linda.

"You know the job," said Crystal.

I shook my head again. How could I explain it to them? They didn't have a clue.

"Hello ladies," Con was standing outside the pod with his usual fake expression in place. I wondered how long he'd been standing there and what he may have heard.

"Just letting you know, Monica, that Erik is allowing you to go to the funeral tomorrow."

I raised my eyebrows, wondering why I hadn't heard from Dora earlier. "Is Dora away?"

"Oh no," said Con using his hand to brush my comment away. He looked like he was waving to a friend somewhere off in the distance. "It's just that I wanted to make sure you got the message before you went home, in case you didn't check your emails and decided to come in tomorrow."

Emails? I suddenly saw the gameplay. They had decided to give their permission for me to attend the funeral via email, but so late in the day that I wouldn't see the email before knock-off time. That way, when I came in to work tomorrow, I would see the email and spend all day upset, knowing that it was my own fault that I was not at Heath's funeral. Nasty, nasty, nasty! With difficulty, I stifled the urge to expose their motives. Could these people sink any lower?

"Thank you for letting me know, Con," I said, controlling my tone and my words. He was acting like my friend, but I knew he was the enemy, so why the good deed? Had he overheard my conversation about leaving? He must have; why else would he tell me about the email?

Then the light of understanding dawned.

Of course! Jack was in the next pod. He must have overheard and called Con! And now Con was covering their tracks. How sly! How sneaky! When they found out I was ready to quit, the torturous game they were playing was over, and they had no choice but to make sure I got the message today. What snakes! These people were unbelievable.

"No problem, see you when you get back," Con said cheerfully and turned to leave, but I wasn't going to let him off that lightly. I was angry now, and I wanted him to know I understood the game.

"Con, can you let Dora know I've been checking my emails regularly, for days, waiting for this news, as everyone here knows." I turned to the analysts – they nodded.

I continued, "And also that I had no intention of coming in tomorrow, permission or no permission." The fake smile started to leave his face. "There was no way I was going to miss Heath's funeral, Con, even if it cost me this job. My family comes first."

"Rightly so," he said, but he wasn't smiling. His intention was written on his face. He would run back to his computer and write a report on my attitude. What a ridiculous bunch of people.

At this point, I couldn't have cared less what kind of report he would send back to Pandora and her puppet master. Something had changed in me and was not going to change back. I had already decided to walk away from this pathetic excuse for a job. When I made that decision, I lost my fear. They no longer had any power over me.

I'd heard somewhere that when evil goes too far, pushes too hard, goes beyond the limit of what people will bear, it's at that point that fear loses its power. That's when victims rise up and fight back. Historically, that's why wars are kept short. People can only be pushed so far before they turn on those pushing them. Somewhere deep inside, I knew that Erik, Dora and Con had just gone too far.

I was now not only in the right place, at the right time, doing the right job, and seeing the right procedures, but I also had the right mental attitude to do what I needed to do next.

I had lost my fear.

I was no longer afraid of losing my job.

I didn't know what was about to happen. I was just being led, step by step, by God to see what I was supposed to see and learn what I was supposed to learn. I could've quit like Janice and Jennifer, but I stayed because of the miraculous beginning. My faith was in God and his unseen will. I had asked God every day to show me why he wanted me in this horrible, horrible place, but I hadn't received an answer. So I stayed. And now I suddenly felt strong, bold and ready. For what? I didn't know.

THE DAY THE TRUTH EXPOSED THE LIE

Heath's funeral was beautiful, if one can say that about any funeral. The chapel at the crematorium was packed. Every pew was filled, and the walls were lined with people standing at sombre attention. Yet there were twice as many people outside as inside, standing quietly, giving the service their full attention.

For a young man, Heath had made a lot of friends. He had just finished high school, so his classmates formed a choir and sang his favourite songs, and his closest friends shared their favourite memories. Many of his football mates were Maori, so they performed their traditional funeral haka for him on the lawns outside the chapel after the service. The Surf Lifesavers and Police Rescue members involved in finding him attended, and then there were the people from his church and those from Kristy and Stephen's church, as well as large numbers of family and other friends. He was only seventeen, but he was loved in life and honoured in death.

I returned to work the following day to be greeted with gentle queries about the funeral. Despite the no talking rule, these remarkable women had found a way around it and always spoke first. They made me feel like a human being instead of like a bug that needed to be squashed.

"How was the funeral?" Crystal's eyes were filled with compassion. The other girls had turned and were waiting for my answer, so I quietly gave them a very brief overview.

"But how are you personally?" asked Linda.

I smiled. They genuinely cared. "I'm fine!" I said, "Honestly! "Ready to get back to work." I hoped this was all the reassurance they would need.

It was. They all nodded their agreement, and we settled into our regular routine.

"I'm phoning about your clearance application. I need a few more details." Deb's words reminded me of what I had been thinking before the funeral.

Crystal had answered an incoming call, "Oh, you have that information for me? Great!"

"No, not enough detail," said Linda, "you need to give us specifics."

That did it! I couldn't continue putting these applications through unless I checked with Jack that I was doing the right thing. The trouble was, that was a dangerous thing to do. If I questioned him about anything, I would be sacked. If I told him my reasons for questioning, I would be sacked. If I didn't put the questionable ones through, I would be sacked. Yet if I continued to put them through as I had been directed, I may be doing the wrong thing.

I chuckled to myself, 'doomed if you do and doomed if you don't'. It was time to bite the bullet.

The thing that amazed me was how bold I felt. I was now more interested in hearing what reasons or excuses they would give than in their reaction to me. These people had literally lost their power to make me afraid.

Over the next two days, I put aside the most outstanding problems. One application had no birth certificate; a birth certificate was mandatory information. Another had only three years of employment information; five was mandatory. Still, another had a change of name with no proof the name on the application was the person on our system; a change of name certificate was mandatory.

I had plenty of examples to choose from, for about forty per cent of applications had some kind of missing information, but on this occasion, I wanted to take just a few of the worst back to Jack.

Now that I knew the analysts, who were highly trained in vetting, required this information upfront before they could legally grant any clearance, including upgrades, it followed that what I was being ordered to do was not correct - or even legal.

The ramifications were ugly. I didn't want to think about them, let alone face them. Could it be that I'd been trained to enter data illegally? No! That couldn't be! Could it? I must have misunderstood. The blame must be mine.

But had I made a mistake? Had I misunderstood? Had I been doing things the wrong way all this time? I had no written procedures. Nothing was ever written down. So I had to know. Was this my misunderstanding, or something worse? Had I been deliberately trained to do the wrong thing? Horrible! Horrible! Horrible! I couldn't continue entering data, not knowing...

I decided to lay these applications before Jack and see what he said. His answer would tell me, once and for all, if this was my mistake or worse - that it wasn't!

If he told me to pass them to an analyst to have their facts checked, I would know I had completely misunderstood the process, and the fault would be mine entirely. But, if he told me to put them through anyway, I would know, without a doubt, that I had been deliberately trained to falsify data and pass that falsified data on to ASIO.

I took a deep breath and set off towards Jacks' office, files in hand. Jack was at his desk.

"Jack, I have a few problems here." I placed the three files on the desk in front of him.

He didn't look at the files; instead, he looked up at me. Oh-oh! This was not good.

"One has missing data, one has no birth certificate, and the other has a completely different name to the name on the system with no change of name certificate."

Jack slowly stood up and picked up the files. Turning to face me, he opened the first and scanned the contents.

I'd carefully avoided asking a question, so why did he stand up? Had he read my approach as a challenge?

Looking up from the files, he stared directly, piercingly, into my eyes. Then suddenly, without flinching, he snap-closed the files and handed them back to me, "Be creative!" he said. His eyes never blinked, never left my face. He was watching my reactions intently.

I held his gaze. So! It is deception! The worst of all possible scenarios. I'd been tricked into falsifying data! Lied to! We all had! No wonder they didn't want us talking to analysts!

I tried not to show my newfound knowledge on my face, but I guess I failed because his eyes changed, and I could tell he knew I had worked out what was going on. You could have cut the tension in the air with a knife. His eyes were speaking volumes. Though the expression on his face was inscrutable, his eyes were telling me loud and clear that I had just lost my job.

Neither of us said another word. I turned and left the pod. The lie was exposed. The truth had broken through.

A NASTY, UNNECESSARY FALLOUT

I didn't tell Crystal or anyone else what had just happened. But I had no doubt Jack had gone straight up to the puppet master. Bad news travelled like lightning in that dark place.

"Hello, ladies," said a familiar voice. The smiling assassin! Of course! Right on time! I knew I couldn't be getting the sack, it was already knock-off time, and they were required to give an hour's notice. So why was he here?

"Monica, I want to ask a favour," Con said like we were best friends. "I need to get home quickly this afternoon for an appointment, so I need to use the T2 express lane."

Con lived in the same general area as I did, so his reason was feasible, but I didn't think for a minute he was telling the truth. What was he up to now? Best to face it head-on. "Not a problem, Con," I said pleasantly. "I could do with a lift home."

I said goodbye to the others and followed Con out to his car, a sporty red and black two-seater, reminiscent of a red-backed spider, which I thought suited him to a tee.

As we headed into traffic, his reason for wanting to get me alone became obvious. "Have you heard the news?" he asked, sounding innocent.

So this was it. "What news would that be?" I asked, bracing for the worst.

"About Jim and Owen."

I turned my head to search his face, but he had no intention of looking at me. His head was fixed in the forward position, feigning attention to his driving.

"What about them?"

"They were both let go this afternoon."

"Both of them?" I was shocked. I couldn't breathe. I didn't expect this!

"Yes, both of them."

"But why?" I felt numb. I couldn't grasp what I was being told. "They are such good workers."

"It wasn't about their work. Their work was excellent." Con was dispassionate.

"Then why? Why get rid of good employees?" I said, "It doesn't make sense."

Con didn't miss a beat. "Well, Jim was going back to university anyway."

"Yes, but not for another month."

It seemed Con was privy to all the details. "And Owen was going to America."

What? Did I hear right? Was that their reason? Couldn't they think of anything better than that?

"This is January, Con. Owen's not going to America until March!"

"True, but that was not the only reason."

"What do you mean?"

"Erik wasn't happy Owen had taken so many days off. It's not acceptable."

So, it *had* come back to bite him. Poor Owen had dared to take a couple of days to grieve when he lost thirteen members of his family in one day. He had dared to take a few days off to rest his swollen knee under doctor's orders. What a terrible person he was!

"That was three months ago." I reminded Con, starting to feel a little angry.

"It's still not a good attendance record."

"What about Jim? He didn't take any time off." I said. I was facing him, but he wouldn't look in my direction.

"Well, he was going back to uni anyway," Con responded, this time without conviction. He had lost his fake, excited expression. I suddenly saw that he was out of his depth.

Dora's words to Janice pounded in my ears, "*your actions will directly impact your friends*."

I wondered if this could be regarded as a direct impact. Was this my fault? Was this because of what happened in Jack's office today? Who was behind this? Erik? Dora? Con? Questions tumbled around in my head, but I had no answers.

Why Owen and Jim? Why together? Why this afternoon? It seemed they were sacked so suddenly Defence didn't have time to work out a decent excuse for sacking them. Or maybe it was all just a wild coincidence.

Was it a coincidence that two of my close friends were quickly dismissed the very day DSA management realised I'd worked out what was going on? Was it a coincidence they were bustled out the door before I had a chance to tell them what I knew? Did I believe in coincidences? Not this time. There were just too many.

The saddest thing for me was that I didn't get a chance to say goodbye. In the space of just a few weeks, I had lost four people I'd been close to without being able to say goodbye to any of them, a friend of many years, a family member and now two close work colleagues, and my poor heart was finding it hard to cope.

If I had known at that moment that things were about to get a whole lot worse, I don't know that I'd have found the courage to continue. The ship had struck the mine, but the explosion and its fallout had only just begun.

> *The Inspector-General of Intelligence and Security stated, "there was a wide variation in the use of incorrect data and little by way of documentation. Further, except in limited circumstances, the use of the modified data had not been agreed by ASIO."* (IGIS Report, 2012 page 4)

Did they think
their threats
would keep us quiet?

CHAPTER FOUR

Witnesses? Shut them down!

Defence personnel were not free from the sadistic cruelty which permeated DSA. Public humiliation was standard practice, and it was not unusual for Defence analysts to be loudly berated for minor incidents, like requesting clarification of vetting procedure or asking applicants too many questions. It was not uncommon for female Defence staff to be set upon by multiple team leaders until they reduced them to tears.

Everything was closely monitored and consistently micromanaged. Any mistakes by the DSA analysts in data input, poorly worded sentences in emails or unnecessary questions to applicants during phone calls were picked up within minutes of being done. Then, within a few more minutes, everyone around the person who made the 'mistake' would hear them being loudly berated.

Stress leave was out of the question, but several Defence personnel were forced to use their long-service leave as stress leave because the pressure placed on them by DSA management was intense, yet there was nowhere for them to go to complain about the treatment they were receiving. Official complaints were always reported back to DSA management, who savagely punished the complainant. In the eyes of permanent DSA staff, complaining only made things worse. DSA had all the exits covered. Or so they thought!

Agency staff and Defence analysts alike were generally unaware of the way the opposite group was being treated. The enforced segregation of the two groups was powerfully effective and supported by physical separation as most temps worked on the top floor or in the basement while Defence analysts occupied the middle floor. It wasn't until Owen and I were seated on the middle floor with the analysts that each group began to witness what was happening to the other, and the dividing wall began to crack.

When the dividing wall of segregation developed a crack, it was the beginning of the end. Like the proverbial finger in the dam, nothing was going to prevent the truth from pushing through. Though DSA management did everything in their power to prevent the dam from breaking, their efforts weren't enough. The truth was too powerful.

The only option left to them was to shut down the witnesses. After all, they had worked extremely hard to develop a financially lucrative, though illegal, system of streamlining applications that had so far been undetected by ASIO. They'd been so clever. They were not about to let anyone spoil it. Agency staff were easy to get rid of, but Defence witnesses were not an option.

It's easy to see the same reasoning at play behind the separation politics used during COVID. The walls of division are all the power-mongers have to keep their illicit deals secret. When we bring down those walls, the truth will break through.

EAVESDROPPING AND TANTRUMS

After the revelations, stress and repercussions of the previous Friday, and not knowing what would be facing me on my arrival at work on Monday, it was nice to be greeted with kindness.

"How was your weekend?" asked Crystal with a friendly smile. "You look a little flustered this morning."

"Oh, it's probably because I've lost four people in the last few weeks, and it's a bit much to take." I smiled. "Don't worry about me. I'll be fine."

"What do you mean by four people? I thought there was only your friend and Heath?"

"And Jim and Owen," I said, expecting that Crystal would know DSA had dismissed them.

"They were fired?"

"On Friday. I'm sorry, I thought you knew."

Crystal looked shocked and so sad I wanted to go over and hug her, but of course, that kind of emotional display was out of the question. Nevertheless, I felt for her. She had a soft heart.

"I'm going to miss them," Crystal said with genuine affection, "especially Owen."

"Me too!" I could feel myself getting hot. I didn't want to get emotional, but there was a prickle at the back of my eyes, and I knew I had to change the subject.

I started using my hands as fans to try and cool my face, and as I did, Jack walked past, stopped and stared at me.

I smiled up at him. "It's a bit hot this morning. I'm still getting over the walk from the bus stop."

He was not amused. He could see my face was flushed, and my eyes were too moist, but he didn't say anything. After a few seconds, he continued walking.

It was nearly time to commence work, so I turned my chair around and started my computer. I had only been working a short time when the smiling assassin arrived.

"Good morning, ladies!"

O, I was so over his fake-ness!

"Monica, can I see you for a moment?" He pointed to the front entrance, "In the foyer?"

He called me by my name - not 'sweetie'. This was not good! Okay, so this was it. I was sure I was going to be fired this time. I knew it was coming. It could no longer be avoided - not after last Friday's confrontation with Jack.

Jack hadn't wasted any time! I wasn't even officially at work when Jack walked past, but he'd obviously gone straight to Erik and then to Con. I was on the mat! I just wasn't sure how it was all going to play out.

"Jack has just reported to me that you are 'falling about crying'." He said, using his hands to make elaborate quote/unquote marks in the air.

I looked him square in the eyes. "Do I look like I am 'falling about crying'?" I asked. It was blatantly obvious that was not the case.

He looked at me unconvinced. I was amazed. How could he possibly be unconvinced?

"Is my makeup washed away?" I leaned towards him so he could get a closer look. "Look at my face, Con, can you see any sign of tears?"

"There doesn't appear to be..."

"Why would Jack say something like that to you when you can see it's completely untrue!"

"I think I'm going to have to call Dora."

This was totally unreasonable but nevertheless typical, "why would you need to call Dora?" I asked.

"Because you got upset when you learned Jim and Owen had been dismissed!"

What? How absurd! "Con, you told me yourself on Friday afternoon, in your car, that Jim and Owen had been dismissed. Are you saying that I fell about crying then?"

"No! But I still have to call Dora."

So, I was going to be sacked for being upset about Owen and Jim's dismissal. For goodness sake! I couldn't fathom how anyone could deny logic the way logic was being denied at that moment.

I tried again. "I don't understand this, Con. Isn't it obvious to you I am not showing any signs of distress?"

He looked down at his notes, "Umm - why don't I call Jack?"

"Good idea!" I said and waited while Con disappeared to return a few minutes later with Jack.

This new 'set-up' was not very smart or well thought out. And I was becoming annoyed. So when Jack arrived, I didn't wait for him to speak; I opened the dialogue. "Con tells me you told him I was 'falling about crying'," I said, being careful not to ask a question. "I don't understand why you would say that."

"I thought y'were..."

"I think it is plain I am not."

"And I think it is plain y're upset because Owen and Jim were replaced," Jack stated firmly.

There it was again. My suspicions had just been confirmed. Jack was making an issue of me being upset over Owen and Jim's dismissal, but why?

"And what if I was upset?" I began to feel justifiably angry and decided to take the bull by the horns. "I've lost four people whom I was close to in the last few weeks, Jack, and I didn't get a chance to say goodbye to any of them. Crystal was just asking how I was coping. Is that a crime?"

"Emotional displays are unprofessional..." Jack's words faded as he spoke them.

I shook my head in disbelief and tried again. "I didn't just learn about Owen and Jim's dismissal today, Jack. Con told me about it in his car on the way home on Friday afternoon. I've known about it for days!"

Jack's eyes narrowed. I guessed he didn't know that rather important little fact. He glared at Con.

Con looked embarrassed.

"Well, I must've been mistaken," Jack said and turned and left the room.

"I'll still have to contact Dora," insisted Con, who was now suddenly angry as well.

"What?" I said. "Why?" I was surprised by Con's manner. "Jack has just said he was mistaken. Surely there's no issue here."

"Dora needs to be kept informed of everything." He stood up, looking uncomfortable. "She'll be contacting you." The meeting was over.

If these two wanted to sack me for last Friday's confrontation in Jack's office, they'd well and truly messed it up. I guessed it was now up to Dora to finish the job for them.

When I arrived back at the pod, Crystal looked at me with red eyes and tears flowing down her face.

I was shocked but not game to speak out loud because Jack was in his pod only a few feet away, so I wrote her a note, "What's wrong?"

She picked up her pen and wrote me a return note, "I got grilled by Jack while you were away."

I read her note and mouthed, "Why?"

Crystal scribbled some more, put the note in a file and placed it on my desk. "He wanted to know every word we had exchanged. Every word! He is reporting me to Erik."

"What can he report you for?" I scribbled and returned the file to Crystal's desk.

"I don't know," Crystal scribbled back, "something about the Code of Conduct."

"I'm so sorry," I mouthed, then scribbled, "how can someone be in trouble for caring about another person?"

She looked at me with sad, sad eyes, shrugged her shoulders, and went back to work.

This place was hell!

Nothing good was allowed to live here.

GRILLED TO PERFECTION

Con arrived at about 11am and escorted me to the conference room. Dora phoned me there and 'grilled' me mercilessly via a conference call for more than an hour. Erik had informed her of my conversation with Crystal, courtesy of Jack's interrogation, and was convinced our innocent, caring, and very short conversation had sinister motives.

"You've broken the 'office politics' rule," said Dora, like it was a statement of fact.

"I don't understand. How have I broken it?" I asked. My mind was clear. I had truly lost my fear.

"You had no right to discuss any DSA business with any DSA staff member. This breach brings instant dismissal."

Okay. So it's happening. This is my official dismissal. Good! At least this horror will soon be over.

"You've broken the 'office gossip' rule. In informing a DSA staff member about the dismissal of agency staff, you've entered into 'office gossip'. This breach brings instant dismissal."

Oh, there's a list - and she doesn't want me to interrupt. Okay...

"You've broken the 'criticism of management rule'. By being upset, you showed you disapproved of Defence's decision to sack Owen and Jim, thereby criticising management. This breach brings instant dismissal."

I didn't criticise DSA; well not to Crystal. What a distortion of facts. I'd had enough. It was time to be direct. "Dora, am I being dismissed?"

Silence!

Con was sitting next to me, head down, listening to the call, taking notes, saying nothing.

I continued. "Dora, when soldiers die in battle and their mates take time out to grieve, their grief doesn't show disapproval of the army, it shows empathy with the fallen, and neither does talking about their fallen mates constitute 'gossip', 'politics' or 'criticism of management'. So I don't believe I'm in breach of any of these rules."

"You've broken them all," she answered bluntly, "and they bring instant dismissal."

"So am I sacked, Dora?" I couldn't believe I could not get a straight answer out of her. Did she want me to beg her for my job? That was definitely not going to happen! The job was no longer important to me. Begging was out of the question.

"No one is sacked from Defence. You're merely being replaced."

How lame! Another side-step. Did she want me to quit? Well, that was not going to happen either! I wasn't going to throw in the towel. This ridiculous scenario was going to run its full course. The bottom line was I knew God had put me here, and I firmly believed by now I would only leave when he was ready for me to leave. Besides that, I still didn't know why he wanted me in this position or what he wanted me to see or do. And I suddenly realised that Dora couldn't sack me because I still hadn't worked out why I was here.

I tried again, "so, am I being replaced?"

While I waited for Dora to make a decision, I tried to remember how many times I'd had my job directly threatened in the last seven months, my goodness; it must have been at least twenty times, maybe more, not counting the daily indirect threats. It was all becoming a bit of a yawn, really.

Then suddenly, Dora backed down. "You still have a job, Monica."

I was incredulous. God had done it again! Against all odds and all threats, and though it seemed I had broken every rule that could be broken, I was still employed. I was amazed. God was not letting Dora sack me! But why was I still here?

Then Dora's tone became extremely menacing. "If I hear, even one more thing, Monica, just one more, you will not have a job, and I will not consider you a good candidate for any other position." The phone clicked. Dora had hung up.

I shook my head. Her threats meant nothing anymore. My highest priority now was to find out what God wanted me to do and just do it so I could get out of this place. It was painfully obvious I wasn't going anywhere until I had done his will.

"What happened?" asked Crystal gently when I returned to the pod.

"Are you fired?" asked Linda. They were both concerned and prepared for the worst.

I shook my head and smiled. "I can't believe it myself, but no, I'm not fired, incredible!"

What was it about?" asked Crystal.

Aware that Jack could be listening in the next pod, I decided not to answer her directly. "I'm going to type out what was said while it's still fresh so I don't forget," I said, while with my eyes, I let Crystal and Linda know I'd show them what I wrote.

"Well, something's going on," said Deb, "Con has gone home. He's taken a few days sick leave..."

I spun around and looked at Deb, open-mouthed. I was not only surprised Con had suddenly felt the need to take time off but that he seemed to be the only agency staff member who could take 'a few days off' and not be fired!

"...and Jack has just announced he is taking seven weeks leave starting immediately. Something about stress," Deb concluded.

"What did you do?" whispered Linda.

I raised my hands and my eyebrows and shook my head. Stress? I'd just been through the same events as these two men, and they were putting the pressure on me not the other way around, yet, I felt relaxed and they, it appeared, were the ones who couldn't cope. Interesting! Was this God's protection at work? It certainly seemed so!

"We thought for sure you must have been fired," said Crystal, "you were gone so long."

I shook my head again, stunned at the news about Con and Jack. "Con was with me in the conference room," I muttered, more as a thought than a comment, "he didn't seem to be sick..."

"Well, I, for one, am glad you're still here," said Linda looking like she wanted to know more.

"So am I," said Deb from across the room.

Crystal came up close to me and spoke very softly into my ear. "Defence personnel have a meeting tomorrow, something to do with whether we should be speaking to agency staff or not."

I looked at her aghast, and my mouth dropped open again. So much horror had happened in such a short space of time. I was now continually dumbfounded! Could things actually be getting worse? Apparently, they could!

ORDERED NOT TO TALK TO AGENCY STAFF

The meeting Crystal told me about was held early and was over by mid-morning. Then Crystal did something she'd never done before. She came outside to find me while I was having my morning tea break.

"Would you like to go for a walk?" Crystal asked, wanting to lead me away from prying ears.

"Love to," I smiled, knowing this unusual behaviour signalled bad news.

We put some distance between the other agency staff and us. When we reached the middle of the manicured quadrant, Crystal opened up. She spoke softly, and her voice shook with emotion, but she maintained control. "I can't believe what they've just done."

"What happened?" I asked almost in a whisper, following her lead.

"We've been ordered not to talk with agency staff." As she spoke, tears began to well in her eyes. "I can't talk to you anymore." She looked at me with pain on her face and then looked up at the sky, trying to control her tears.

"Ordered?" I asked. "You can't talk to us at all?" I looked down at the ground and shook my head. Management was unmistakably desperate now. The walls between Defence and agency had begun to crack. They were frantically trying to shore them up before they broke completely.

"They told us that if we talk to any agency staff member, the person we talk to will be fired." Crystal's voice was full of emotion, "They're going to fire you, Monica, and they're going to blame me when it happens because I can't help talking to you." She looked at me with soft, moist eyes, "you're my friend."

I was horrified! So that was the new tactic. I didn't think they could sink any lower. I didn't think this could get any worse. I was so, so wrong!

I needed to double-check what she'd just said. "They're making you think that firing me will be your fault?"

She nodded, wiping away the single tear which rolled uncontrolled down her cheek.

I looked firmly into her sad eyes. I so wished I could tell her everything. "They're going to fire me anyway, Crystal, it's just a matter of when. This is merely another one of their low tactics; a way of punishing you. I'm so sorry you're involved."

I looked firmly into her sad eyes. I so wished I could tell her everything. "They're going to fire me anyway, Crystal; it's just a matter of when. This is merely another one of their low tactics; a way of punishing you. I'm so sorry you're involved."

After all, that was why she'd been interrogated so ruthlessly by Jack; he wanted to know if I'd told her what agency staff had been trained to do. That's also why they'd ordered the ban on communication. They'd been 'found out', and they were trying to contain the damage.

"Well, I'm not sorry we're friends. I'm glad we're friends. This is wrong!" She wiped the tears from her eyes and looked at me with a new resolve, "I'm going to do something about it."

I smiled at her. I loved her fighting spirit. "What're you going to do?"

"I don't know yet, I'm going to talk it over with my husband tonight and see what he thinks, but there must be something we can do."

"Yes, there has to be something..."

"Meanwhile, I'm not going to be able to talk to you, and that's going to be really hard." Crystal started to get teary again.

"Only at work," I said. "They can't stop us from talking outside work."

Crystal laughed, a genuine happy laugh. "You're right," she said, "they down own us; and they can't stop our friendship."

"No," I said, "they can't!"

Crystal checked her watch. "I think I should go back first. I'll see you inside."

As I watched her walk away, I wondered how on earth anyone in Australia thought they had the right to order people not to talk to others or not to care about them. This was outrageous. Sure we worked in 'intelligence', but this nastiness had nothing to do with security.

All analysts and agency staff processing clearances had the same security level. We were accessing the same files, using the same programs and data. There was no 'security' reason for this lasted atrocity. It was a cover-up. Pure and simple!

DSA management was working hard and fast to cover their deliberate and illegal breach of National Security and their blatant deception of ASIO. The truth had been discovered. Now they had to stop the truth from spreading.

Can you see the similarity to the way our leaders are treating all of us during COVID? The same questions are now being asked across Australia. Why do our leaders and government bureaucrats believe they have the right to order us not to talk to each other? Why are they monitoring our emails? Why do they think they have the right to make it impossible for us to care about others?

The callous public orders being dished out by government officials are not about protecting us from disease. Rather, they are a deliberate attempt to cover a carefully planned hidden agenda and stop the truth about it from getting out.

That afternoon I was moved out of Crystal's pod and back to Doug's pod. Doug was no longer there, he'd taken long-service leave, so I was alone.

I no longer had to process 'special' applications; that task had been passed to others - funny about that! So I was back to doing regular secret and top-secret applications, selecting only those with complete information. I would never 'fill in' an empty field again.

Though I couldn't have imagined things getting worse than they'd become, amazingly, they did get worse. The next change happened suddenly that afternoon.

All the lingering camaraderie from Christmas dissipated as if it had never existed. Since Christmas, Defence personnel had made eye contact with agency staff, saying hello in corridors and generally exuding a pleasant demeanour. Now suddenly, that was all gone. There were no more nods, no greetings; there was not even any eye contact. Agency staff had become like lepers, avoided like the plague. And except for spurts of expletive-filled conversations between Defence personnel, the building was as quiet as a morgue.

What a nightmare! This place was hell on earth! An infernal vortex spinning out of control, getting blacker every day. The only thing I knew for sure was that I did not want to come back tomorrow. DSA management was on a diabolical power trip with no end in sight.

"How can they do this to people, God? How can they do it?" There was nothing else I could do now but pray. This whole situation was insane.

That evening during a prayer meeting with my friends, while I was privately talking to God about it, telling him I couldn't face another day, I began to see everything from a completely different angle. And I saw clearly! Suddenly I knew I could handle whatever I had to face for as long as it took. I finally understood why God had brought me here.

I remembered Christ's Commandment was that we love our neighbour as ourselves. That's what I'd been doing, but now care and concern for others had been outlawed. Human kindness had been outlawed. Common decency had been outlawed. Friendship had been outlawed. In effect, the law of Christ had been outlawed.

This meant my faith was on the line. This was crunch time, and I now had to make a choice. Who was I going to obey, God or man? It was clear I could no longer do both.

Most Christians in Australia now find themselves in the same position. The ungodly orders being enforced during COVID challenge our faith and willingness to stand up for God. Whom will we serve?

In DSA, I now needed to consciously choose which law would I obey, the law of God or the law of man. It was no competition, really. I had stood with God for a long time, and I wasn't about to change now. I also knew anyone who ordered me to disobey God's law would find they had God, Christ, the Holy Spirit and all the angels of heaven against them. Not a winning position!

I understood the military needed to teach people to kill, and breaking the law to defend your country was never considered immoral, not even in the Bible. But DSA was not military. We were not at war. And their blatant brutality had nothing to do with defending Australia. This was about money.

Only a few weeks earlier, the head of DSA, Frank Roberts, had travelled up from Canberra to announce that the new Australian Government Security Vetting Authority (AGSVA) would be located in Queensland. This decision was apparently made because DSA Queensland proved they could process applications faster than any other vetting office in Australia.

It didn't seem to matter that those applications were only half done; that information was made up and entered as if it was correct just to get the applications through quickly. It didn't seem to matter that National Security was being compromised or lives were being put at risk. It didn't seem to matter that so many Australian laws were being flouted or that God's law was being flouted. Not a bit!

What did God's law have to do with all this? Only everything! The whole fabric of our society revolves around people caring for others. Without care and concern for others, our society would disintegrate into lawless chaos. Nevertheless, a few greedy bureaucrats had outlawed 'loving your neighbour' for the sake of financial gain.

It seemed that the only thing that mattered to them was that this new deal would save over $5 million in vetting expenses and produce $45 million+ per year in revenue.

Christ's words, "you can't serve both God and money," were never more applicable than in DSA.

DSA management was not only happy to ditch their humanity, but they also had no qualms about introducing the same torture tactics used on military prisoners, like those in Guantanamo Bay, into an Australian Government workplace.

Under their authority, agency staff were isolated, forbidden to speak to one another, continually threatened and kept in a constant state of confusion and disorientation - essential torture tactics! We could not rely on the protection of Australian law, for it didn't apply to anything done within DSA, and so we become people without a country.

Likewise, under the guise of 'health orders', unscrupulous Liberal and Labor leaders, government bureaucrats and their civilian puppets are currently having a lot of fun using military torture tactics on the Australian population. The same torture tactics used in DSAs pre-COVID social experiment have now been inflicted on all Australians. An extreme over-exaggeration? No!

In DSA, the above well-documented torture tactics were our reality! Nevertheless, despite the pressure of the constant psychological abuse being used to force compliance to illegal activity for the sake of money, my choice was to stand for God's law and continue to love my neighbour.

That meant I would need to be openly friendly and speak to whoever wanted to talk to me, no matter what the cost. I found strength in the hope God would one day lead me out of this horror with joy and peace as his dependable word promised he would do.

I finally understood why I was in this wretched place. What a relief! This is what I needed to see; people were being ordered by their bosses, by government officials, bureaucrats and their civilian puppets to disobey God's law. Ordered! This was not his will at all - and never would be! All God needed was someone to be his witness, that is, to witness what was happening and ask him to act. So that's what I did.

Every day from that day till the day I walked out the gates for the last time, I prayed God would tear down the evil which had raised its ugly head in that place. Whenever I needed to get up from my desk and walk around the building, I would claim the victory as I walked. My prayer was simple, "Go, get'em, Lord! Uphold your law! Uphold the victory of your Son!" I had complete confidence that is precisely what God would do. That's why I was in DSA; to witness what was going on and hand it over to him so that he, himself, could act.

From that time on, I felt the victory of God. I had moved beyond freedom from fear. I could see the victory! I was walking on air! It was easy to choose to live by God's law with that mindset. So, every morning I would smile and say hello to all my co-workers, including Crystal, and greet them cheerfully when I passed them in the hallways. They may have been ordered not to say hello to me, but I could still greet them. And so I did!

At first, I was hurt and saddened by their unwillingness to speak to me or even look at me, but now I was no longer offended. I saw their rejection of me as an act of kindness. They didn't want me to be sacked! I could only thank God for them.

LIBERATION! FINALLY! HALLELUJAH!

My day of liberation came two weeks later. The day started like every other day, but then the unexpected happened - always a good sign. And the unexpected came from Crystal. Once again, she did something out of the ordinary. She walked past my pod and motioned me to follow her, indicating she wanted to talk. Wow! She knew the consequences for me and was still prepared to ask me to take the risk, so I gathered this was important news.

I followed her down the corridor and into the long, narrow filing alcove next to the kitchen. There was no room to manoeuvre; it was hard just turning around in there, impossible for anyone to squeeze past. And we were alone.

I entered first, and as I turned to face Crystal, the brightness of her smile almost blinded me. She was beaming! I hadn't seen her smile for weeks.

"I have good news," she mouthed, not quite game to even whisper.

I smiled back at her, followed her lead and used hand gestures as well, "I can see that! I need sunglasses!"

She giggled, not making a sound. "I've just arranged a meeting with Erik, Paula and a few others to talk about the treatment of agency staff," she said in the lowest of whispers while her eyes danced with excitement.

"When?"

"In a few days, would you like to be there?"

"Why would you want *me* there?" I wasn't sure how I could help.

"To back up what I'm saying...be my witness."

I nodded and smiled. "Happy to!"

Crystal almost jumped for joy but then looked concerned. "You know going to that meeting could cost you your job."

I laughed silently, "What doesn't?"

We both laughed, almost uncontrollably, not out loud, of course, but in a muffled, hands over mouths, shoulders shaking, let's not make any noise, kind of way.

"So, you'll come?" Crystal asked when we regained control of ourselves.

"I would be honoured."

Crystal turned to leave, I tapped her on the shoulder, and she turned back. "Thank you," I said, looking directly into her eyes so she would know I meant it with all my heart.

She tilted her head to the side with an unspoken question and raised her eyebrows.

I smiled. "For sticking your neck out for agency staff." I put my hand on her arm. "You don't have to do this!"

"I know," her manner was matter-of-fact, "but it's the right thing to do."

I was humbled. This woman was not only kind, she was also brave. No wonder I liked her.

"I'm going up to see him now," she grabbed both my hands, "wish me luck."

"I'll do better than that," I said and squeezed her hands, "I'll pray for you."

Crystal left the alcove first, and a few minutes later, I returned to my pod.

About an hour later, Crystal came down the stairs with a huge smile on her face and gave me the thumbs-up sign as she went past. Erik had agreed I could be Crystal's witness at their meeting. Wow! That was good news! Well, so we thought...

Neither of us had any idea that within the next hour, Erik would betray his word to Crystal, phone Dora, and give the order for me to be sacked.

Just after lunch, Con came mincing into my pod.

I hadn't seen him at all since our last conversation in the foyer, which seemed so long ago now, nearly three weeks. He was the agency team leader, but he had been skilfully avoiding me, so I knew this sudden appearance could not be good. This time, there was no smile - no greeting - no fake excitement - he was all business.

"This afternoon, you're going to be moved back into your original seat upstairs," Con said. He looked like he wanted to be somewhere else - and I knew why. The scenario was easy to read. They wanted me to resign. I wasn't going to do it! They would have to fire me.

The seat he was referring to was the 'arctic blast' seat, where I'd been positioned for the first three weeks of my employment, the seat where I'd had to wear a heavy woollen coat, scarf and gloves just to do my job. The air was so cold I'd eventually been forced into the untenable position of having to make a complaint. Even though at that time I'd fully expected to be sacked for complaining, God had intervened, and instead of being sacked, I was moved to the middle floor with the analysts and Jack, a move they now obviously regretted.

It didn't take a genius to figure out what DSA management was doing. Their actions were immature, childish and totally predictable; as predictable as those of a spoilt child throwing a tantrum. Pathetic! Someone would have to step up and be the adult here, and it looked like that someone would have to be me.

The reality was the air conditioning had still not been fixed, and everyone knew, including Con, that I couldn't physically tolerate the cold in that position and so would need to make a complaint.

This was so obviously a set-up. If I sat in that seat, I would become ill. If I said I couldn't tolerate the cold, I would be sacked for complaining. I laughed to myself and shook my head. Didn't they know how transparent they were? My decision was easy. No point dragging it out. "You know I can't sit in that seat, Con; the air is too cold for me."

Con didn't say a word. He turned on his heel, sprinted out of the pod and up the stairs as fast as he could, taking them two at a time.

I watched him with detachment. Run! Con! Run! Places to go! People to see!

He returned a few minutes later, "I informed Paula of your complaint, and she told me to tell you to wear a jacket."

Why wouldn't they sack me? Did they just want to torture me? Of course they did! This time I wasn't going to give them the chance. I was over their games. I had no intention of moving upstairs. It was time to finish this. I sat back in my swivel chair. "It's a health and safety issue, Con. You know it is! I know it is." I shrugged. I was totally relaxed.

Con didn't say another word to me. He turned and left the pod.

At 3.15pm that afternoon, I swivelled around to find Dora standing behind my chair.

"Oh, Dora!" I was a little surprised she didn't announce her arrival. "I didn't hear you come in."

There was only one reason for Dora to turn up at this time of day. Russian roulette! Today was my day! Yay! She was late, though. I was supposed to receive an hour's notice. She was supposed to be here at 3pm, so this sacking would be illegal. But I decided to let that go. I couldn't wait to be fired.

"May I see you in the foyer?"

The foyer was not a private place; we would've been better off staying where we were. Nevertheless, I stood up and followed her to the foyer.

"You are being dismissed," said Dora in her usual blunt manner once we were seated.

"The air conditioning?" I asked.

"Yes, you complained."

"It's a health and safety issue, Dora."

She ignored me.

"I want to be clear this is not about your work. From all accounts, your work has been exemplary."

Yes, let's not make it about the work we do – too dangerous. To my knowledge, no one had ever been sacked for work-related issues. It was always personal. Always trumped up. Fabricated! Like everything else DSA management did.

This was my third sacking experience in the three weeks since the actual work-related 'issue' took place in Jack's pod, and this was the most feeble excuse of all, but I didn't care. I knew now why I had been placed in DSA by God, and I knew I'd seen what he wanted me to see. Thankfully, it was time to go.

"It's not your work ethic either," Dora continued. "You've been conscientious and maintained the high expectations Defence requires."

How hollow were her platitudes! I knew she didn't mean a word she was saying, yet she sat there, going through the motions, speaking politely to me in sickly sweet tones as if our previous conversations had not taken place. Diabolic!

Meanwhile, people began leaving work for the day. No one needed to be told why Dora was there; there was only ever one reason. It was clear they felt as uncomfortable interrupting 'the sacking' as I felt having this personal moment exposed to prying eyes. It was frankly humiliating - as planned!

The door opened again, and Crystal stepped in. She summed up the situation in an instant and froze on the spot. All the hope and joy she had felt that morning had just been thrown to the ground and brutally crushed underfoot.

Erik had betrayed her! He had lied to her! He had assured her I could be her witness in the meeting next week, and in the next breath, he'd had me fired, leaving Crystal exposed and vulnerable.

Erik had killed two birds with one stone, so to speak. By sacking me, he had killed the meeting next week. If Crystal went through with the meeting now, it would be to her detriment. She would be squashed like a bug and tortured later. And she knew it. It was written on her face.

I stood up and went over to give her a farewell hug. The air was thick with emotion, but neither of us was free to say what we wanted to say.

"Are you surprised?" I whispered into her ear.

She was too emotional to speak for a moment, and then her simple response said it all. "No."

"You have my email address..."

Crystal nodded and left the room. She couldn't speak. She was devastated. We both were.

There was nothing left now but to gather my things, tidy my desk and leave the premises.

As she escorted me off the Base, Dora became chatty. "You know you stayed longer than most; CML doesn't like people staying longer than five months,"

"CML?" I asked, "who is CML?"

"They're the recruitment group who holds the contract with Defence to supply staff," Dora explained. "Our agency works for CareersMultiList, and you work for us."

"So there's a 'middle-man' involved here?"

Dora nodded. "Yes, they work out all the minute details with Defence."

I was puzzled. I was no longer an employee. "Why are you telling me this?"

"They don't like anyone working longer than five months, but you've been here for seven."

Another lie! I couldn't believe anything this woman said. Did she know how to tell the truth?

"Dora, you told me when I took this job that I was replacing someone who had been here eighteen months. There are at least two agency staff who have been here for two years. If what you're saying is even close to the truth, why weren't we offered a five-month contract? At least that way, we wouldn't have had to face this terrible, sudden death, one hours' notice thing."

"One hours' notice is the law."

"Rubbish, Dora! It's an abuse of the law. One hours notice is the minimum required to be given in exceptional circumstances, like when somebody is caught stealing or doing something they shouldn't be doing. It is not a general rule, and it's not supposed to replace common decency."

"CML insists...our hands are tied."

"Is CML an Australian company?" I asked. "It doesn't sound like it. This is not the way Australian employment works. It doesn't match the rest of Australian workplace law."

"CML tells us how many staff to supply, and they tell Defence how many applications need to be processed to pay for the staff. That's why there is an emphasis on clearances," Dora continued.

"Do CML pay for the clearances for all those throwaway agency staff, Dora, or does Defence pay?" I asked.

"I don't know," said Dora rather sheepishly, "all I know is they pay the bills."

"What I can't understand, Dora, is why Defence is allowing a foreign agency to dictate policy instead of putting Australia's National Security first."

"Oh well, I don't know if that's what's happening."

"I do, Dora! That's exactly what's happening! You have no clue what's going on behind those doors. It's not about processing certain numbers to pay for staff. It's far more serious than that!"

I had no idea why Dora had decided to 'leak' this information to me, probably just shifting the blame for my dismissal from herself to 'them', and I had no idea if what she'd said about a middle man was true. What I did know was that Dora was vicious and nasty and couldn't be trusted. I would be glad to see the last of her.

When we reached the boom-gate, I turned to say my final farewell and walk away when Dora caught my arm. "I would be happy to recommend you for another position," she said.

Cringing at her touch, I stepped back out of her reach until she removed her hand from my arm. After this experience, there was no way I would ever work for this woman again, not in a million lifetimes.

"Have you been able to find work for Owen yet?" I asked. "You remember Owen, good worker, family man, you fired him a few weeks ago, for no reason. Have you found work for him?"

"Oh, I don't think he's back from America," Dora sounded so sweet and innocent, "I'll find him something when he gets back." She didn't know that Owen and I had stayed in contact after he left Defence.

"Owen hasn't left for America yet, Dora," I was trying to keep my tone professional even though Pandora had just been caught out telling another whopping great lie. "He won't be leaving for another five weeks. Meanwhile, he's using up his holiday money to feed his family. If he doesn't get work soon, his holiday will be ruined. Why don't you find *him* a job?"

Dora didn't even try to respond this time. Another lie just wouldn't cover it.

"I'll find my own employment Dora, and I'll send you an email to confirm my wishes. Goodbye."

I turned to leave and suddenly felt as light as air. It was like a great burden, or heavy weight, had been lifted off me. A huge smile broke out on my face, and I felt like singing. I was happy! Happier than I'd been for months. Had I truly forgotten how good it felt to be happy?

I took a long, deep breath of fresh air and spun around on the spot. "What a beautiful day!" I said out loud.

Dora was watching me, so I gave her a great big smile and a cheerful wave and hurried off down the street. I was free!

I couldn't believe how good I felt. I wanted to dance. I wanted to skip and run like a child. I had an overwhelming sense of joy and was so elated I could hardly breathe. All I could think was I was free, free, free! And it felt great!

This sense of sheer joy and profound freedom, I believe, is waiting for all Australians once we depose the amoral government leaders, bureaucrats and civilian puppets who through the use of coercive force are currently destroying lives and livelihoods, businesses, education, our children's future and our nation's hard-won reputation, all in the name of keeping us safe! What a whopping great lie!

> *The Inspector-General of Intelligence and Security stated, "staff expressed a belief that they were, at the very least, pressured into ignoring security concerns, and in extreme cases, coerced into approving clearances about which they held serious doubts."* (IGIS Report, 2012 page 61)

Did they hope
we would
just go away?

CHAPTER FIVE

Official disclosures? Never!

The problem of National Security and the harsh work environment endured by those working within DSA could not be ignored. So in early March 2010, three weeks after I was dismissed, seven people, both current and ex-DSA employees, banded together to begin the process of bringing what was hidden into the light.

By the end of March, complaints about the treatment of staff within DSA had been hand-delivered to Craig Emerson MP in his capacity as Minister for Independent Contractors, Brett Raguse MP, our local member of Parliament, with a request they be forwarded to the Minister for Defence. Emails had been sent to Frank Roberts, the head of DSA, Mike Quinn, within the Defence's Directorate of Fairness and Resolution, and to the agency for breaches of the APS Code of Conduct.

These complaints were forwarded to the Minister for Defence Personnel, Mr Alan Griffin MP, who immediately ordered three simultaneous investigations, two of which were to be done by an independent party, albeit under the guidance and monitoring of DSA. These two miss-named 'independent' investigations were set up to separately address the complaints of agency staff and the complaints of Defence personnel, while the third was to be conducted by DSA into the management practices of DSA Queensland.

Our letters of complaint had produced fallout, but, for the moment, the ship of corruption was still sailing. Some things had changed, but the bullying of Defence staff had increased, and the illegal vetting practices continued as if nothing had happened. Nevertheless, the truth had exposed many problems, our complaints now had to be addressed, and the underlying corruption could no longer be easily hidden.

The irony was, our letters of complaint against DSA would not have been written and the three simultaneous investigations not ordered if the DSA power mongers had not so viciously turned on Crystal after I was gone. These were the same people who thought it was intelligent to put a heavy vault door on a room with windows. To say that these bullies were not too bright could only be regarded as a gross understatement.

CRYSTAL IS TARGETED AS PREDICTED

Around two weeks after my joyful release, I began to have a nagging feeling my involvement with DSA was not finished, and I was also concerned about the outcome of Crystal's meeting with Erik. I hated to think she could be targeted because she had tried to stand up for me and all agency staff, so I phoned her at home.

"How are you?"

"Not doing so well," Crystal sounded defeated. "I spend my time caring about others, and they just come along and squash me."

Oh, this was not good, "What happened?" I asked, feeling like I was being drawn back into a horror story, a difficult adjustment since I was now chronically happy.

"They accused me of bullying." Her tone was matter-of-fact, like this was old news. "They said I'm in breach of the Code of Conduct."

"How on earth could they accuse you, of all people, of bullying?"

"Cleo was at the meeting, and she told Erik you had dobbed me in." I so admired Crystal's honesty. She was always direct. But I wasn't expecting to suddenly be the enemy.

My mouth dropped open. What did she think I'd done? That place never ceased to amaze me! "What? How...um...how?"

"Do you remember the time when we sticky-taped all your stuff?"

Though puzzled as to why she would bring that up, I nevertheless chuckled as I recalled the day. I had come back from lunch to find the keys on my keyboard in different places, my ruler taped to my desk, and my drink bottle secured with glad wrap. It was quietly mischievous! And one of those special things that had grown the bond between us. That little bit of tomfoolery made me feel like I was one of them. Like I belonged...

"Yes, I remember that day," I said, smiling into the phone. "One of the better memories I have of that horrible place. You made me feel welcome."

"Do you remember the email you sent to Cassie telling her about it?"

"Yes!" Suddenly, my heart started to sink, and I didn't feel like smiling. "What about it?"

"They said it was proof I was bullying you."

"What?" Again, I was horrified. "How could that email possibly...?

"They said that when they read between the lines, it showed you were making a complaint about my behaviour. They said I was being mean."

"Oh, Crystal," I could hear the uncertainty in her voice. She was wondering if I'd betrayed her. Those people were so ugly! I had to reassure her. "You? Mean? No Crystal. You're one of the only nice people in that hell hole. You were never mean to me, and I loved what you did that day. It made me feel like I belonged. I certainly wasn't being bullied."

"Well, they're making it official." Crystal said sadly. "It's going on my personal file."

Now I was mad. How dare they! But I knew what to do. It was no mistake that I'd spent the last few days going over the Public Service Code of Conduct. I was suddenly in awe of God again, and how he equips us for battles we don't even know we are about to fight. "They can't make it official if I don't agree with their assessment," I said.

"That's all well and good, Monica, but you're not here," Crystal snapped. "There's nothing you can do." Poor Crystal, she was an emotional wreck.

"Oh, yes, there is," I said firmly, speaking confidently, so she would understand I knew what I was talking about. "I've been reading over the Code of Conduct for the last few days, Crystal, and I know this; for a breach to be formalised, there has to be an official complaint made against you by me - and I haven't made one!"

"But they're going to use your email..."

"They won't be able to use it if I write a Stat Dec stating you've never bullied me." What a pack of monsters! Good thing bullies aren't too bright!

"Can you do that?" Crystal said almost in a whisper. I could hear the hope in her voice.

"I sure can!" I said, "I'll get it done and witnessed and email it to you in a few days. You can use it or not; that will be up to you."

Crystal began to cry with relief. "Thank you, Monica. I'm so glad you're out of here, but I miss you heaps. You know they put me in the naughty corner when you left."

"Naughty corner?"

"Your old seat in Doug's pod," she giggled as she sniffed, "didn't you know that was called the naughty corner?"

I laughed long and hard, remembering the number of times I'd been seated there. "I had no idea, Crystal," I said when I could contain myself, "and I was there quite often!"

We laughed our way through various memories, and it was good to hear Crystal laughing with me. She could do with a good laugh.

"I like the solitude," Crystal continued when the laughter died down, "I don't have to worry about all the stupid games." She was trying to be cheerful, but the sadness in her voice was unmistakable. She was obviously having a tough time. "You know Con hasn't spoken a single word to me since that dreadful day in January."

"No great loss, surely," I said.

She laughed again, "I sure do miss you."

Poor Crystal! They were trying to use me against her. How typical! How diabolical!

That conversation confirmed to me that something needed to be done. And logically, if something needed to be done, then I was the one who needed to do it; there was no point expecting other people to carry the load. If I wanted something done about the breaches of the Code of Conduct and the lies to ASIO, I had to be prepared to volunteer. So, now the big question was, 'how do I go about making an official complaint?'

CHOOSING THE ROAD LESS TRAVELLED

I wrote out the Stat Dec and arranged for it to be witnessed. One of my friends was a Justice of the Peace, so I made an appointment to meet him at a local coffee shop.

"Done!" Barry said and began putting his JP stamps back into their box. "You said you needed to talk about something else."

"Yes, I need your advice," I said, folding the Stat Dec and putting it back into its envelope. "I have a problem, and I'm not sure which way to approach it."

"Is it to do with the Stat Dec?"

"Yes," I smiled. He was on the ball, as usual, "bullying at Defence."

"Well, Defence is Federal, not State, so you might want to talk to Craig."

He was referring to Craig Emerson, MP, Federal Member for Rankin. We both knew Craig well. I had previously been Vice President of one of the local Labor Party Branches for two years, and Barry was a Life Member of the Labor Party. I was not only on a first-name basis with Craig, but he had offered me his personal mobile number for emergencies, which I still carried.

"Hmm, not sure about Craig. I was thinking maybe Brett," I said.

"Well, yes, he's Federal too..."

I knew Brett Raguse MP, Federal Member for Forde, better than I knew Craig. I had previously worked with Brett in the office of Barbara Stone MP, State Member for Springwood. He was easy to work with, efficient, intelligent, tackled problems by looking at them from various angles and always greeted me with a hug. Yes, that was what I needed. A friend with brains and clout!

Barry looked at his watch, "24th February, Parliament is sitting."

"Oh!" I felt a little disappointed, "so they're both in Canberra."

"Stuart Fenech is Brett's Liaison Officer," Barry was a mine of information. He always knew who was who in the zoo, "run it past him, see what he says."

I nodded. "Yes. Thanks, Barry. That's exactly what I'll do."

I relaxed into the high backed leather chair. Suddenly everything was starting to come together. I could see the road ahead, and it was clear, but I wasn't sure I should begin the journey.

When I got home, I did what I usually do when I'm uncertain. I turned to God. I knew a miracle had put me into DSA, and the hand of God had kept me there against all odds until I eventually saw what I was supposed to see and was finally, gratefully, led out in joy, a joy in which I was still living. Now, despite the fact I thought my involvement had finished, doors were beginning to open in front of me, and I couldn't ignore them.

When I read my Bible that afternoon, one verse stood out, almost in flashing neon lights, and I not only knew I should begin the journey but how I should begin and what would happen when I did.

> *Write the vision down, make it plain on paper, so that he who reads it will run with it. (Habakkuk 2:2)*

I was confident this was something I was supposed to do from that moment. I also knew deep down where faith lives that there would be victory at the end of this journey. I had absolutely no doubt victory would be the result because I knew from experience that victory always follows when God tells his people to do something specific.

All I had to do was write a clear and convincing complaint on paper so that those reading it would be compelled to act. I believed God's word and felt totally assured that after I'd done my part, God would do the rest.

It was time to call my friends.

"Hi, Janice," I said into the phone, "how are you? How's the job situation?"

"Still looking for jobs, nothing new to report. What about you?"

"No job but busy as a bee!"

"Well, that sounds interesting." The curiosity behind her words made them sound like a question.

I decided to get straight to the point. "I'm putting in an official complaint...want to join me?"

"Jennifer already tried the Ombudsmen's Office. They're not interested." She was under-enthusiastic, to put it mildly.

I wanted to blurt out all my good news but couldn't. I would have to explain step by step what I'd done. "I'm going through political channels."

"Can you do that?" Janice sounded doubtful but curious again.

"I sure can! I used to be a secretary to a Member of Parliament, remember? I know how the system works."

"What do you mean?" said Janice, now fully curious.

"Well, when a local Member receives a complaint, it's forwarded to the relevant Minister's office for action. After the Minister, or his Liaison Officer, investigates the complaint and makes a decision about it, they send their findings back to the local Member, who then forwards the Minister's response to the person who made the complaint."

"So?"

"So it means that putting a complaint through a local Member is the quickest way to get it seen by a Minister."

"Oh!" I could hear the proverbial penny dropping, "So you mean we should complain to the Minister for Defence?"

"That's exactly what I mean!" Whoo-hoo! She got it! But would she be interested?

There was a pause. I could almost hear Janice thinking. Then suddenly, she spoke. "I'm in! Who else can we get?" Her response was sharp, definite and carried a hint of excitement.

"I'm going to email Owen and Jennifer." No turning back now.

"I could email Cassie," offered Janice.

"Are you sure about involving Cassie? She's still there..."

"Yes, this would get her sacked," said Janice, "and I wouldn't like to feel I was the cause."

"No, neither would I. Let's leave her out of this particular loop."

"Good idea," said Janice. "Who else is there?"

"I don't have anyone else's contact details," I said. When people disappeared from Defence, it was usually so sudden there was no time for goodbyes, let alone phone and email exchanges.

"Well, three or four might be enough," said Janice vaguely, clearly still trying to think of others who may be interested.

Of course! How Scriptural! I chuckled into the phone, "You're right, Janice! Three will be plenty! Our complaints only need to be based '*on the evidence of two or three witnesses'*," I said, knowing Janice would recognise the quoted Scripture immediately.

"How are we going to start this?" asked Janice, curious to know our next move.

"I already have," I said. "You know I used to work in the office of the Member for Springwood."

"Yes,"

"Well, your current local member, Brett Raguse, was working in the same office at the same time. I shared a workspace with him for nearly a year. I know him really well."

"I didn't know that," Janice interjected, "but do go on."

"Today, I phoned his office and spoke to his Liaison Officer about the situation in Defence. Stuart took some details and said he would talk to Brett about it when he returned from Canberra."

"Oh, that's good!"

"It gets better! Stuart didn't wait until Brett returned; he emailed him while he was sitting in Parliament and told him our story straight away!"

"While he was actually sitting in Parliament?" said Janice. "Wow!"

"Yes, wow! Then, to my great surprise, less than an hour after I first spoke to Stuart, he phoned me back!"

"What did he say?"

"He said Brett is happy to take our complaints to the Minister for Defence. All we need to do is get our letters together."

"Oh, fantastic!" Janice was now gushing with excitement. "Oh, this is the best news I've heard in a long time!

Janice's enthusiasm was refreshing after our arduous ordeal. I was so pleased she was onboard. Things were definitely falling into place.

OUR GROUP GETS BACK TOGETHER

Over the next few days, Owen, Jennifer, Donna, Janice, and I began drafting letters that could go through Brett's office to the Minister for Defence. Now there were five of us. Our weakness was that we were all agency staff. It would be better if we could have our stories confirmed by Defence personnel. It was time to tell Crystal what we were doing, so I phoned her.

"So, that's where we're up to, Crystal. Owen, Janice and I have completed our letters. Donna emailed me tonight and said she will finish hers tomorrow, and Jennifer's is in draft."

"I can't believe you're doing this." Crystal's voice was shaking with emotion.

"The five of us alone have complaints so serious the Minister will have to act. We've used words like discrimination, bullying, intimidation, abuse, segregation, isolation and humiliation – not one of these practices is legal. We're all using testimony rather than accusation. It's more effective," I said. I didn't tell her it was a Scriptural principle. Crystal wasn't a Christian.

"If ever there was a good cause..." she broke off. Was she crying?

"Are you okay?"

"Sorry, Monica, there's just so much pent up emotion," she sniffed.

"We don't have to talk about this."

"No, I want to, but it scares me," Crystal blew her nose, "don't get me wrong, this is really important to me."

"Do you want me to continue?"

"Yes, please do," she sounded a little stronger. "I'm okay now."

"In our letters, we've named Erik, Paula, Con and Dora as the main sources of abuse."

"What about Jack and Cleo...and Helga?"

"Yes, and the rest, Crystal! We can't name them all. Well, not yet anyway."

"So, do you think these complaints might actually get somewhere?"

"Yes, I do! With five eye-witnesses, this is already a very strong complaint. The trouble is, it doesn't address your situation."

"No, it doesn't! You are all agency staff."

"Exactly! The final nail in the coffin would come if a Defence permanent backed our claims."

"It would also show the problem is widespread and entrenched," Crystal confirmed.

"Yes, it would! Would you be game?" I knew this was a big ask. I knew how much it could cost Crystal to be involved. There was a long pause.

"I would need some kind of protection." Crystal said quietly. She wasn't sniffing anymore and in her voice was a ray of hope flickering ever so faintly, "They can't know. I still have to work there."

"I might have a solution."

"It'd better be a dammed good one," Crystal snapped. Her tone was sharp, and she immediately pulled herself up, "Sorry, not belittling you, but you're not here anymore. You know what they're like and the way they work. They can quite easily make my life a living hell for a very long time.

"Yes, I understand," I spoke as gently as I could. "But what if you could meet with the Minister for Defence face to face and tell him your story. Would you be interested?"

Crystal laughed in derision, a short, sharp, shocked kind of laugh, "you can't arrange that!"

"No, but I know people who can."

An intense silence filled the phone line. Not even the sound of breathing could be heard.

"Let me tell you what I mean," I said, speaking into the silence. "I went to the office of Craig Emerson, Minister for Independent Contractors and told his office manager I needed some advice on how to make a complaint about Defence. She immediately phoned his Ministerial Advisor. I was on the phone with her for about twenty minutes. The short of it is, his Advisor told me, and the office manager, that as soon as I brought in the letters of complaint and any supporting documents, she would organise a meeting between Brett Raguse, Craig Emerson, the Minister for Defence, herself and us. Now, that is heavy duty in anyone's language, Crystal!"

"No way! When did this happen?" Crystal was almost breathless.

"Just a few days ago."

"I can't believe this!"

"So I figure if you had the courage to come along, we could verify each other's stories. Our combined complaint from both sides, permanent DSA staff and agency staff, would present an impossible situation for DSA."

Crystal began to laugh. And kept on laughing. I laughed with her. It was so good just thinking about the possibility of a solution.

"I know you're going through hell, Crystal. However, this is an open door that goes straight to the top. These MPs want to know what's going on. They're all ears. And they have the power to stop the rot in a way that doesn't cause you any harm. Please think about it."

"I can't believe how much you've done in such a short time."

"Nothing's been done yet, but if we turn on this spotlight together, DSA won't have the power to turn it off."

"The fight will be outside their control."

"Exactly!" Now she was getting it, but would she join with us. I held my breath.

"Look, why don't we get together. My place. Are you free next weekend? Come for dinner!"

"I'd love to, Crystal." I was grinning from ear to ear. Another door had just opened. Amazing!

DEFENCE'S GOOSE IS COOKED

Crystal was smiling her broadest smile as she welcomed me into her home.

After presenting her with a box of after-dinner mints, I followed her to her dining room. The table had papers spread all over it, and someone was standing near the double window, looking out at the lush tropical backyard garden.

"Linda!"

When I called her name, Linda turned to greet me, and the smile on her face was as bright as the sunlit garden behind her. "Surprise!" she beamed.

I looked from Linda to Crystal. They were both smiling like children with a secret and that could only mean one thing. "Does this mean you're in?"

They both nodded, and Linda came over to greet me with a hug. "I think you're both incredibly brave. I don't know how much I can do, but I support you all the way."

I was overwhelmed. All I could do was laugh. We were now seven, five agency and two Defence. This was going to work!

We spent hours going over events, listing incidents, making notes, weighing the damage to Australia's national interests and discussing the best way forward.

"We can't disclose these things," Linda was stating the obvious, "we'll be prosecuted if we say anything about this to anyone."

"Drawn and quartered," said Crystal.

"We can't be prosecuted for talking to a Member of Parliament," I said.

Linda was nodding, "Go on."

I continued, "Parliamentary privilege will make our conversation totally private and secure. You can safely lay it all on the table to an MP, the whole lot, everything we've discussed and more."

"And it can't come back to bite us." Linda smiled. She was on the same page, but Crystal still had doubts.

"I want to see what Jeff thinks." Crystal left the table and went to find her husband. When they came back, we asked his opinion.

"I think you need a few approaches," he said, "agency complaints about bullying," he turned to his wife, "your complaints about bullying," he looked back at our group, "and a combined complaint about security issues."

"A three-pronged attack," said Crystal.

Linda nodded and smiled. "Yes!"

"So, we start with one, and while they're looking at that, we send the second from a different direction. Then while they're busy with those two, we hit them with our main complaint," I said.

We sat back in our chairs. We had a clear and logical plan. We all nodded in agreement.

"We need to organise and coordinate our complaints," said Linda.

"The agency complaints are organised," I said. "They mainly concentrate on bullying."

"I'll help you make your bullying complaints, honey," Jeff suggested, "they can come through my official channels. That way, they'll bypass DSA but still reach the right people." Jeff worked in Defence as well and understood the system.

"So those two areas are covered," said Linda smiling. "How do we go about the vetting side?"

"I'll make an appointment for the three of us to see Brett Raguse," I said. "I know him as well as I know you girls. I worked with him. He'll give us accurate advice about threats to National Security. If there is a way through, he'll find it for us."

"What about seeing the Minister for Defence?" asked Crystal.

"Our main complaint will go to him, but we need to be organised before we contact him," I said, "seeing Brett first will give us our best advantage."

"How soon can you make an appointment with Brett?" asked Linda.

I shrugged my shoulders. I didn't have a clue. "Parliament's sitting - he'll only be in the office a few days this month. I'll see what I can do."

I arranged the meeting with Brett by phone and wrote a letter to confirm the reason. Three days later, when the first two agency letters were completed, I hand-delivered them to the offices of both Brett Raguse MP and Craig Emerson MP. The other three agency complaint letters had not arrived in the mail, so I planned to take them with me to the meeting with Brett, which had been set for the 23rd of March.

Brett put the girls at ease and confirmed the secure confidentiality of our meeting. After laying out everything that had been going on in DSA for years, the recent increase in coercion and the urgent nature of the current threats to National Security, Brett gave us clear direction on how to proceed and the paperwork we needed to provide.

He assured us he would work with Craig Emerson MP to bring this to the attention of the Minister for Defence. In the meantime, he would pass our complaints to the Minister for Defence Personnel, Alan Griffin MP, whom we had both worked with in the past. Brett's advice and offer of assistance had been invaluable.

Like Moses parting the red sea, it seemed that all the obstacles in front of us were being pushed to the side. The way ahead was clear, and nothing was getting our way.

THE HAMMER FALLS ON CRYSTAL

A few weeks after the meeting with Brett, my home phone rang. "I hope you're not busy," I recognised Crystal's voice straight away.

"Never too busy for you, m'dear."

"Which do you want first, the good news or the bad news?" Her voice was emotionless.

Oh no! I recognised the signs. This was not good. "Bad news first, please."

"Okay! Two days after the meeting with Brett, I was ordered into Paula's office and 'grilled' for three and a half hours," Crystal said. "I think they must've got a whiff of what we're doing."

"Oh, no!" I said. Crystal thought Brett had betrayed her. I held my breath.

"Paula was out for blood. She threatened me and let me know well and truly how many people I would be up against if I continue with whatever I am doing, assuming I am doing anything and assuming I am continuing. She was covering all bases." Crystal said.

"It sounds like they know."

"It does, doesn't it?" her voice had an edge to it, and I had to put her mind at ease, somehow...

"If they do, I can assure you, Crystal, it didn't come from Brett's office." I knew Brett and was convinced I was speaking the truth. "Maybe they've heard about our bullying complaints."

"They're coming after me, Monica. Specifically! According to them, I'm the bully. Apparently, I am a terrible bully, and I bully everyone all the time, especially Cleo. Can you believe it?" Crystal said. "They're literally gunning for me and for anyone who tries to support me."

"Ah! So they *have* heard about the bullying complaints," I said. "Are you all right?"

"No," Crystal said simply.

"I'm so sorry, Crystal." Are you able to take any time off? What about stress leave?"

"The doctor gave me a couple of weeks off, but Jeff arranged for us both to meet with someone from Defence's Department of Fairness and Resolution in the middle of my leave. That meeting was at DSA, and it was a waste of time."

I suddenly understood! "Oh! Crystal! That's how Paula found out you made a complaint. The meeting was held at DSA!"

I shook my head. There was nothing 'fair' about their choice of venue! "Paula didn't know what was discussed in the meeting and was fishing for information, like Jack did, to try and get you to spill the beans," I said. "What happened in the 'Fairness' meeting?"

"It was in Erik's office. I explained to the investigator what had been happening, and Jeff pointed out all the laws being broken, but it didn't mean anything to either of them."

"Not even to Fairness and Resolution?"

"No!"

"Well, I suppose that was to be expected, seeing they were prepared to expose you by holding the meeting in Erik's office," I said. "It show's whose side they're on!"

"Jeff's really angry," said Crystal. "He'd only heard what I've told him about the bullying; just second-hand information, but now he's seen it happen first-hand, for himself. With that and the grilling I got from Paula, he wants to put in an official complaint tonight. That's why I called. That's the good news!"

"Oh, fantastic!" I said, "That *is* good news, but I'm so sorry it's taking such a toll on you."

"So am I, but at least now Jeff can see what I have been up against. I'm no longer fighting alone."

"Good on Jeff! The cavalry has arrived!"

"I think they've gone too far, Monica." Crystal's tone had become very calm and matter-of-fact again. "I don't have any choice anymore. I have to fight for what is right, no matter how I feel."

"Just try and catch your breath, my friend, and get lots and lots of rest."

"I will. I have another five weeks holidays owing to me, and I'm taking them now."

It was the end of March, just six weeks since my Departure from Defence. We now had two arms of complaint in place, and Crystal was taking herself out of the line of fire. Things were looking up.

HEADS BEGIN TO ROLL

A lot happened over the next two months, both inside and outside DSA, and we seven remained in constant email contact, with all of us copied in on every email:

- "Did you know? No new agency staff have been hired since Monica left in mid-February? Not one! People are still leaving, but no one is being replaced." Cassie.
- "I was told by my team leader there were no more agency staff coming in because there were not enough qualified people to do the job." Crystal.
- "Rubbish! Another lie! We're in the middle of a recession! Heaps of people need work. However, knowing what I now know, I wouldn't offer DSA to my worst enemy." Monica.

- "Maybe that's the problem. Maybe they're not game to supply any more staff to DSA until this mess is sorted out." Janice.
- "Hey, guys! Did you know that in the Saturday Career's Guide, March 27, the employment agency advertised their Operations Manager position? Wasn't that Dora's position? Has she been fired? Heads rolling - people jumping ship maybe?" Linda.
- "It's good for me. I told Erik I was resigning, and he offered me part-time instead. I guess they can't replace me if I leave, and there's hardly anyone in here now." Cassie.
- "Speaking of jobs, my old boss contacted me about an opening. I put in my resume, did the interview and am now employed again. Back with normal people!" Monica.
- "I received my ADF service medal at a little ceremony this morning presented by an MP. I mentioned a couple of things to him about DSA. He was interested and is going to get back to me. Can't hurt to have a couple of MP's sniffing around, huh?" Linda.
- "DSA has begun their internal investigation. I had my interview today. Very shocked at some things I revealed. They didn't like your Stat Dec, Monica. Too bad!" Crystal.
- "Not sure if Crystal has let you know yet, but big news. The complaints you put through the Minister's Office have reached DSA and have resulted in a fantastic response! Just in the sweetest of time too. The internal investigation seemed to be winding down - and then bammo - your complaints were received. Unreal!!" Linda.

- "The heads of DSA came up from Canberra and called a meeting. They wanted to know if what was in your five letters was true. Everyone was nodding, even Defence staff. No one objected." Cassie.
- "Whatever the outcome, it's been an awesome ride! I'll leave it in God's hands. *Bring down your large hard hand, Lord, and start smacking some butts. Amen!"* Owen.
- "Dora came in today and announced she is resigning. She said someone had complained about her being a bully. She said she couldn't understand how anyone could accuse her of such a thing!" Cassie.
- "Smack! There goes one!" Owen.
- "Ooooh! They must be feeling it now! I would love to be a fly on the wall in Erik's office - as long as I'm protected by anti-Erik spray and can have a very long and thoroughly cleansing shower afterwards." Linda.
- "It'll be interesting to see how the D culprits are handled. Somehow, I don't think they'll be sacked - just moved on to another position. Such is the joy of being a permanent government employee." Jennifer.
- "Just letting you know, Jack was called to Canberra, came back and surprised us all by resigning. He didn't say why." Crystal.
- "Smack! There goes another one!" Owen.
- "Everyone is confused. There seem to be two investigations being run; one for agency and one for Defence. But they are not being explained or communicated. Nobody knows what's going on." Linda.

It was all happening! After receiving Crystal's complaints through Jeff and our complaints through Brett, Alan Griffin, the Minister for Defence Personnel, had ordered two simultaneous investigations, the first into the treatment of Defence personnel at DSA and the second into the treatment of agency contractors working within DSA.

Though these two investigations were called 'independent', they were not even close to independent. They were controlled by DSA management and in typical DSA fashion, Erik and Paula were keeping all staff, both Defence and agency, in the dark about the purpose of the dual investigations being conducted right under their noses. Nevertheless, it seemed our complaints were having an effect. Heads were rolling. Dora and Jack were already gone, and this was just the beginning. We hadn't even been interviewed.

HAPHAZARD HALF-BAKED INVESTIGATIONS

On 1 July 2010, I received a letter from DSA by express mail, dated 23 June, telling me I would be contacted shortly by an investigator seeking to set up an interview time.

I thought sending a form letter by express mail was odd until I received a personal letter from Alan Griffin MP dated 28 June, five days later, telling me he had extended the investigation because DSA told him they couldn't find some of us.

I was astounded! Had DSA just lied to the Minister? Our information hadn't changed. They had every detail of our lives for the last ten years at their fingertips, on their database; our phone numbers, addresses, our next of kin, siblings and parents and their phone numbers and addresses. To say they couldn't find any of us was an outright lie.

The express letter was the first contact they'd made with any of us. There'd been no previous attempts! It was painfully clear that yes, they had lied to the Minister about us before they even tried to contact us!

Why? What was the point of such a lie? Were they deliberately putting us in a bad light? Had they already decided the outcome? Why did they want the investigation delayed? This investigation was supposed to be 'independent' of DSA, but now it was clear that DSA was still controlling everything. This was not good.

The day after receiving my 'overnight' notification from DSA that an investigator would contact me, I was phoned at work.

"Hello, Monica, I am Julie from Robert Brennan and Associates, and I'd like to set up a meeting with you for next Monday or Tuesday."

"Hello, Julie. Today is Friday. Monday or Tuesday is short notice. Are there any other times available?"

"Didn't you receive notification I would be contacting you?" She sounded pushy.

"Yes, it arrived yesterday, and it said you would be contacting us sometime in the next few weeks to make an appointment."

"I am flying up from Canberra on Sunday. I only have Monday and Tuesday for interviews."

This all seemed very unprofessional. "Robert Brennan and Associates, is that a legal firm?"

"We are management consultants."

Management consultants? Not lawyers?

It was clear they had no intention of looking at our complaints, which all involved breaches of the law. I sighed. "Okay, well, as it turns out, I have already arranged with my employer to take Monday off for a dental appointment. Monday morning would be good for me," I said.

"Are you in contact with Donna and Jennifer?"

Whoa! Red lights started flashing! She was fishing! Why did she want to know if we were in contact with each other? Where was this going?

"Why?" I asked.

"It's just that I don't have contact details for them," she responded.

Really? Defence intelligence had told the Minister they had trouble finding some of us, but now, here was the truth – DSA didn't give the investigators our contact details! No wonder we couldn't be located! I shook my head. Would the games never cease?

"I know how to contact them," I said.

"Can you give me their details? I need to speak with them as soon as possible."

You've got to be kidding me! Was this investigator asking me to breach the Privacy Act? Definitely not a lawyer! Unbelievable!

"What if I pass your contact details along to them so they can phone you?" I was starting to get a little annoyed at this woman. Rushed, disorganised, pushy, unaware of basic privacy laws, and now wanting me to do her work for her. Some management consultant! No, not looking good at all!

"I've booked you in for Monday. I will confirm the time via email," Julie concluded.

The following Monday, the interview was conducted in Julie's private hotel room. Another shocking lack of professionalism! I would have expected to be interviewed in a conference room or an office, not a bedroom. It wasn't acceptable, and I felt uncomfortable being there.

"I'm just going to go over what you've written in your letter of complaint," Julie said. "You used the word 'collaborate'. That's a very strong word. What did you mean?"

Was she checking grammar? What about the serious issues? Strong word? Not strong enough! Did she think that word was a random choice? I took a deep breath. "I meant in the strongest possible terms that Defence and the employment agency jointly worked together to bully, harass, intimidate and psychologically torture employees."

"Oh!" she looked back down at her notes, "Can you give me an example of how they collaborated?"

Was this it? Were these the kind of simplistic questions we were going to be asked? "Examples are all through my letter, Julie. Let me refer you to the day of my dismissal." I pointed out the example on the paperwork in front of her. "Basically, Erik said jump and Dora said how high?"

The interview continued along those lines. It seemed the only thing this investigator wanted to do was check that what I'd written in the letter was grammatically accurate. In our meeting, I used strong words like bullying, harassment and psychological torture and yet not one of those words, or their implications, was picked up or discussed. After two and a half hours of explaining 'what I meant by' I was exhausted. It was like sitting for an English exam.

"In conclusion, is there anything about the management style in DSA that you would like to see changed?" Julie asked.

What? I nearly fell off my chair! Didn't she know how unreasonable her question was? The concept wasn't even relevant! How could I possibly give her an answer? It was like she was reading a list of 'management consultant' questions she'd found on the internet. Her questions didn't fit our complaints. I felt like knocking on her forehead and saying, 'Hello! Is anybody home?'

As quickly as my frustration came, it went. What the heck? Julie was only a management consultant and not a very good one at that! She clearly didn't have the legal qualifications to investigate our bullying allegations and probably didn't have the security clearance to investigate the intelligence issues. That meant all she could report on was management style. How typical of DSA! They had carefully misdirected this investigation to avoid our complaints.

"It's not about management style, Julie. Style has nothing to do with it," I said quietly, hoping she would listen and try to understand. "They all need to be sacked! All of them!"

She looked up, dubious and paused her record taking.

How could I explain this to her? "They don't have a management problem, Julie; they have a morality problem! They are very good managers. Over a long period of time, they have successfully managed to break the law, deceive ASIO, destroy Australia's National Security, and manipulate any investigation that comes along. They know what they are doing. It's deliberate! What they need is to be sacked! Removed completely!

Julie was looking at me, stunned. She put down her pen, so I guessed she wasn't going to write what I'd just said in her report. "Well, we are out of time," she said. "I have another appointment to go to over at Victoria Barracks."

Of course we were out of time! We were just getting to the good part! It was clear to me she was out of her depth. I sat back in my chair. I had so much more to say and no way of saying it.

"If you think of anything else, please let me know. Email me, and I will include your comments in my report." Julie was standing now and packing her paperwork away.

"Thank you," I said, a little taken aback by my sudden and somewhat informal dismissal, "I might just take you up on that offer." I stood up, gathered my things, said goodbye and left the room.

DSA MANIPULATES THE OUTCOME

A few weeks after our interviews, we arranged to meet for pancakes at a converted convict-built church in the city. Seated around a long refectory table on backless wooden benches, we soon entered into our own little world. All that was missing was our signature yellow tablecloth. Jim couldn't make it, but Donna came along, and as Cassie was part of our email chain, she also joined us.

"You picture intelligence organisations, and you think they've got it all," said Owen, "James Bond! A well-oiled machine!"

"Well organised and, of course, well dressed," laughed Donna. "What a letdown!"

"In reality, it was more like 'Maxwell Smart' embracing 'Kaos' and working together in the same building," said Janice.

It felt good to laugh at our antagonists and to speak freely. We still couldn't talk about DSA with anyone else. It was good to be together, and we were all aware we had just passed a significant milestone, no matter what the outcome.

"I think we can all be proud of what we have done," I said, and I meant it.

"Three simultaneous investigations is quite an achievement," agreed Janice.

Owen made his 'sorry-I'm-saying-this' face, "I hope it hasn't been a waste of time."

"How can it be a waste of time?" asked Janice.

Jennifer was nodding, "I'm not overly confident with the process," she said.

"So, you think it's a whitewash?" I asked.

"I thought the interview was ridiculous," said Owen. "I was hoping for something more substantial, like some legal discussion about breaches of the Code of Conduct and what could be done about them."

"She wasn't interested in the security issues either," Donna agreed.

"I sent her an email about all that," I said, "I don't know if she will add it to her report or not."

"So did I," said Janice, and smiled a cheeky smile, "copious pages of notes. She'll have lots of choice for her report."

"At the end of the day, she works for Defence," said Owen, "she'll report what they want reported."

"But, they're independent investigators, aren't they?" said Cassie.

We were all very aware that Cassie still worked inside DSA. She didn't know everything we knew.

Jennifer chuckled and said gently. "Really, Cassie? Who do you think pays the bills?"

No one spoke for a moment. The truth was sinking in. Jennifer and Owen were right. If DSA had chosen the investigators, and if Defence was paying them for their services, and if they were reporting their findings back to DSA, then this investigation was not 'independent'. It was nothing more than a covert DSA investigation. A cover-up!

"Yes," nodded Owen, "if these investigators want to be hired again next time, they'll say what DSA wants said!"

It was appalling but true. We knew before we received any notification from the Minister that this had been an exercise in futility. DSA had twisted Minister Griffin's orders and manipulated the investigation into a farce. Our only hope now was that Minister Griffin would notice that our complaints had not been addressed and would order a new investigation. But, would he?

DSA BURIES THE INVESTIGATION

DSA had already forced Minister Griffin to extend the investigation, and now, though the Minister wanted the investigation finalised by 30 July 2010, it had hit another DSA snag - the absence of one vital witness. Erik!

Erik still needed to be interviewed, and yet, just two weeks before the winding up of an investigation into illegal activities in his department, he abandoned his post. Why? An interview only took a couple of hours and could be done over the phone. So why was taking leave being used as an excuse to delay the finalisation of this investigation?

Had Erik not taken leave, the investigation would have been completed on time, and Minister Griffin would have been able to review the report and discover the duplicitous nature of DSAs interference. That was no longer an option. Erik's absence ensured that the findings of the investigation would not be given to Minister Griffin.

A Federal election had been called for the 21st of August 2010, which meant a possible change of Government, with a possible change of Minister. DSA were hoping for a more lenient Minister.

As a result of the federal election Minister Griffin was replaced by Warren Snowdon MP. DSA had the Minister they wanted. Someone who could see nothing wrong with a report that completely ignored its mandate to investigate bullying, harassment, coercion and vetting practices and instead reported on management style. They may as well have presented a paper on office furniture. Either way, Warren Snowdon couldn't have cared less.

By the end of September, our investigation had been brought to a close, and everyone had been notified of the outcome except us, the people who had made the complaints.

> *With regard to the complaints made by Monica Bennett-Ryan, Janice Weightman, Owen Laikum, Donna (surname removed) and Jennifer (surname removed) the investigator was unable to find any evidence of bullying or harassment.* (Warren Snowdon MP - 26 Oct. 2010)

Though the date of this letter was 26 October, we didn't receive our copies until the week before Christmas. Did we believe it had taken nearly six weeks for a letter to get to us? Was Australia Post that slow? No! The delay was deliberate - typical!

Our letters didn't arrive until Government offices were shut down for the Christmas break. Mr Snowdon made sure we could not immediately respond. Did he know what he was doing? Yes! Did he and DSA hope we would simply go away? Yes!

Even though our five original complaint letters about bullying were accompanied by a strongly worded covering letter which emphasised in four dot points our concerns about breaches of National Security, Minister Snowdon's response showed no indication that any of our concerns had ever been queried by him, let alone taken seriously. It seemed his response was merely a 'rubber-stamp' after all.

Erik's ploy had worked!

Defence was off the hook!

Where to now? Where do you go when your elected Ministers willingly support corruption? There was only one place I could think of - the media!

Am I surprised that our current politicians and departmental health bureaucrats are manipulating the COVID crisis to forward their own hidden agendas? No! That's the shallow and predictable nature of politicians! What we, the people, need to do is wake up to their lies and hidden agendas and seek the truth ourselves. Politicians don't right wrongs. That's our job! And they don't have the last say. We do! It's up to us to ensure politicians do what we pay them to do - serve us! If they betray us, we need to expose and remove them.

POLITICIAN pol·i·ti·cian | \ pä-lə-ti-shən

a person primarily interested in political office for selfish or other narrow usually short-sighted reasons | Webster's Dictionary

Now things were
starting
to get interesting!

CHAPTER SIX

ABC Lateline Story? Not true!

In April 2011, three of the original group of seven contacted ABC *Lateline* investigative reporter and producer John Stewart, outlining our situation. He acted immediately, and in May 2011, the story of the abuse of DSA staff, the corruption of data, the deceit of ASIO and the danger to Australia's National Security was aired on ABC's *Lateline*.

The most immediate response from Defence was silence. When queried about the silence, Defence Minister Stephen Smith said we hadn't given him anything 'specific' to comment on.

The next day, he revised his statement by saying he would be taking our allegations seriously. We knew what he meant. The problems would remain. It would only be our allegations about the issues that would be taken seriously. In other words, they would be targeting us - coming after us personally with everything at their disposal.

That same day, before any of our claims could be investigated, the outright denials began. The office of Stephen Smith officially reported there was no evidence to support our allegations. ASIO publicly stated they also took our allegations seriously and would work with Defence as required. Federal Labor Member for Gordon, Brendan O'Connor, announced to the world through the Sky News network that our allegations were 'not true'.

That was a strange reaction. Three people had just openly confessed on television to breaching National Security. Instead of condemning our behaviour, Defence told the media and all of Australia before any investigation of our claims could begin that we had definitely not breached National Security. Their response was unplanned and ridiculous! We had caught them off-guard!

Within a few days of the *Lateline* story, many current and ex-DSA personnel contacted the ABC to confirm our story was true, albeit anonymously. In all, almost one-third of the vetting staff came forward.

Then inexplicably, on the same day Defence publically denied a problem existed, and much to everyone's confusion, the Minister for Defence confirmed the veracity of our claims by announcing that the Inspector-General of Defence would lead a costly, high-level investigation into our allegations.

We had no physical proof for our allegations, but Defence didn't know that. Unlike most whistleblowers, we couldn't provide any paper evidence because all the paperwork was valid. The corruption was in the data entry. Only when information in the database was checked against original applications would discrepancies be seen.

The DSA database was highly secure and inaccessible to anyone without the proper clearance, yet all any approved investigator had to do to see the corruption was check the digital records against the originals. But, would they check them? Or would the Defence investigators only be interested in coming after us? Was this investigation just a trap in disguise? Was it their intention to use it to gather evidence against us so that they could prosecute us? We knew them! We knew that was the Defence way.

As it turned out, that is exactly what they had planned. That high-level investigation was a trap. All we wanted to do was tell the truth. All Defence wanted to do was prosecute us and send us to jail.

THE MEDIA WAS OUR ONLY OPTION

Even though I knew when I received my letter from Minister Snowden that the only avenue of complaint left to us was the media, that option suddenly became impossible. It seemed the door to the press had been firmly closed.

Just after Christmas, in January 2011, massive flooding devastated Queensland, parts of NSW, Victoria and Tasmania. It was recorded as the biggest natural disaster in Australia's history, with an estimated recovery cost to Australians of upwards of $30billion. The flooding was followed closely by a record category five cyclone, 300 kilometres wide, which cut a devastating path across Queensland and finally died down in the Northern Territory three days later. It then became a low-pressure system which caused more severe and widespread flooding across inland Australia.

The army was deployed to rescue disaster victims and hunt for bodies in the most devastated areas, and they worked tirelessly as they always did in such circumstances. Now was not the time to complain about Defence to the media.

People generally didn't know the difference between the Department of Defence and the military, so a complaint against Defence would translate as a complaint against our military. And that just wouldn't be tolerated at this present time. Our selfless military were out there in the muck and mire, serving us - doing the nastiest of jobs on our behalf. Our military were our heroes!

In early January 2011, before the catestrophic flooding began, Janice had written to Minister Snowdon stating our objections to the findings, or lack of them, in the Brennan report and asking him to reconsider the evidence of bullying within DSA along with the serious breaches to our National Security. We received his response at the end of March, confirming his earlier apathy. He just wasn't interested.

The big question now was what to do next? The media was out of the question. The Minister wasn't interested. DSA was becoming old news, yet the problem was still continuing. According to our insiders, bullying was still rife within DSA, and Australia's National Security was still being compromised with false information still being fed to ASIO. Yet, though it appeared nothing had changed, and no doors were open, I continued to have a deep assurance that this was not over. God was still involved, and things were about to change. Who can explain deep-rooted belief? I can't!

A WEEK LATER, THE CHANGE CAME

In late March 2011, the Australian Defence Force Acadamy *Skype Sex Scandal* hit the media. It was a horrible thing to happen, but it opened the doors again. And this time, the doors were open so wide nothing could close them. A young female officer cadet had taken her complaints about sexual abuse to the media, and suddenly there were complaints of Defence brutality and bullying coming out of the woodwork. This was our opportunity, and I was going to take it!

As I gathered the paperwork to review what I could tell the media, I saw something I hadn't noticed before in our latest rejection letter. Minister Snowdon had inadvertently revealed the truth.

DSA had clearly hijacked a taxpayer-funded investigation approved for National Security issues and used it to pad out their pet project - DSAs impending move away from Intelligence and into its own Department, The Australian Government Security Vetting Authority (AGSVA).

> *The firm contracted to investigate the allegations was asked to separately review the management arrangements of the National Coordination Centre (DSA), given its central role in the security vetting process and the imminent move to undertaking vetting for the majority of Commonwealth Departments.* (Warren Snowdon MP March 20, 2011)

According to this letter, Management arrangements were supposed to be a 'separate' investigation to our allegations. But we were only involved in one investigation, and it was about 'management styles'. Our strongly worded complaints about bullying and coercion were *never* investigated! They were completely pushed aside.

No wonder the investigators were '*unable to find any evidence*' of bullying, and National Security issues were supposedly only '*mentioned in passing*'. The investigators did exactly what they had been commissioned to do by DSA - *review management arrangements!* They had used our complaints as a cover while they advised on an entirely different subject. This letter was proof the investigators were corrupt as well! Great!

Shortly after recognising Minister Snowdon's bombshell, I arranged to meet with Crystal and Linda in an out-of-the-way bar for a drink after work one afternoon. I showed them the telling letter and brought them up to date.

Crystal was hopping mad. "Why can't they simply admit they've done the wrong thing, fix it, and move on?"

"That's too easy," said Linda.

"Talk about childish! What do they hope to gain out of all this?" snapped Crystal.

"What will Australia gain?" asked Linda. She looked at us without a smile "or lose?"

"There are too many people in high places who don't seem to care about Australia," said Crystal, "they're only interested in their own personal success."

"I think there could be quite a few red faces when the truth comes out," I said

Linda was on to me straight away. "What do you mean, 'comes out'?" she asked.

I let the question hang in the air for a moment. The girls could see I was teasing them, and I had their attention. "I'm tossing up going to the media," I said.

"No!" said Linda, and her eyes were suddenly dancing with fun, "really?"

Crystal started giggling. I guessed it was a happy kind of shock response.

"There's nowhere else to go anymore," I continued. "I just need to talk to the others and see if any of them want to do this with me."

"And if they don't?" asked Linda

"I'll do it myself," I said. "Want to join me?"

Linda sat back in her chair, ready to listen, "go on," she said, taking a sip of her chardonnay.

Crystal was on the edge of her seat, fidgeting with the stem of her wine glass, deep in thought.

"I don't want to put myself out on a limb," I said, "but someone has to say something, and I can't see anyone else with their hand up."

"If you go to the media, then so will I," said Crystal. She had stopped fidgeting and sounded calm, too calm. Did she know what she was saying?

"Crystal, are you sure?" I asked. These girls were still working at DSA. I didn't expect either of them to volunteer, and I wondered if Crystal should.

"I'm sure!" she replied emphatically, smiling at each of us. She was totally confident. "I can remain anonymous and give supportive evidence behind the scenes," she explained.

"We both can," said Linda, suddenly sitting forward. "Give them my name too."

I sighed with relief. What a perfect solution. These girls were amazing. We poured some more wine, clinked our glasses to seal the deal and settled back in our seats to plan our next step.

"Who are you going to contact?" asked Crystal. "One of the current affairs shows, I suppose?"

"I don't know yet," I said, shrugging my shoulders, "probably all of them."

"Well, now is a good time," said Linda, "with all the allegations of abuse coming through the media since the ADFA story broke."

"Oh, that's right," agreed Crystal. "There are so many bullying complaints Minister Smith announced he would be setting up an external review because there were too many to handle." She turned to Linda, "what was that review called?'

"From memory, 'The DLA Piper Review', I think it's called," said Linda. "It seems they already have over 700 complaints, and they're going to be looking at all the allegations of abuse given to the media between April and June this year."

"That's wonderful!" I said. It was about time we got some good news. "So, let me get this right. If we act now, we will be in that timeframe, which means whatever we allege will be further investigated. Is that right?"

Crystal and Linda both nodded.

"Oh, it would be so good to have this investigated again," I said.

"And this time by lawyers, not some small-time management consultants," said Linda.

"What a rort that was!" said Crystal.

"So, is this what we want?" I asked.

Crystal and Linda looked at each other and then back to me. "Yes!" they chorused.

BECOMING WHISTLEBLOWERS

Over the next few days, I wrote my 'story' letter and researched the news media. Where was I going to send it? This was not a flash-in-the-pan news item. It had the potential to be explosive. It needed to be handled with care.

Could the media be trusted not to exploit the situation for immediate ratings? No! They couldn't! In the end, I chose to limit my contact to the four major current affairs shows via their own websites and waited to see what would happen.

Days went past. Nothing! No response!

That following Saturday morning, I met up with Janice for coffee.

"I guess they're sick of stories about Defence," she said, aware of what I was doing.

"I suppose," I agreed, feeling a little disheartened. "Apparently, it's one thing to contact the media but quite another to have them accept the story."

"Yes, well, I don't think there is anything wrong with the story," Janice said rather sharply. "In fact, I think it is an exceptional story and any reporter worth his salt would see that."

I chuckled. Just when I needed some encouragement, there it was. Janice to the rescue!

She suddenly smiled. "I knew this wasn't over, and I am glad we're taking it further. I just hope a few of the others feel the same way."

"Crystal and Linda are on board for anonymous background information only, and I've spoken with Jennifer and Donna." Then I had to tell Janice the bad news, "but Jennifer and Donna want to sit this one out."

"Oh? Why is that?" asked Janice, with concern for our friends in her eyes.

Donna wants to remain completely anonymous, which is fair enough," I said.

Janice nodded, "and Jennifer?"

"Well, as you know, Jennifer's house went under in the floods, and she's still homeless. She's living with relatives and spending all her free time renovating. She said she doesn't need any extra pressure at the moment."

"That's more than reasonable," said Janice.

"Yes, I agree! I told her we would keep her in the loop."

Janice nodded. "This one is a little bit more public. Oh, by the way, do you think you would want to show your face? Or will you be interviewed 'blacked out' or behind a screen or a big potted plant or something?"

I chuckled. Next, she would have me in a trench coat with a fedora pulled down over my eyes, "I actually hadn't thought about it," I grinned, "what are you going to do?"

"Me?" Janice seemed surprised by my question. "Why would I need to be interviewed?"

"Why not?" I asked, more as a challenge than a question.

"Oh, well," said Janice recovering quickly, "I guess it would give me a chance to have my say."

"And it will add more weight to the story if more than one person is interviewed," I responded.

Janice nodded, "Have you contacted Owen?"

"Yes," I smiled, "he's in!"

"Oh, wonderful!" Janice gushed, almost jumping off her seat, "so there are three of us!"

I nodded, smiling at Janice's reaction. She was far more enthusiastic than I though she'd be. "Owen's super keen. When I told him what I was thinking, all he said was, 'let's do this!'"

"Wow!" Janice said, "so we're ready to go!"

"Yes! as soon as someone from the media gets back to us - if they ever do."

Janice became serious. "There was some talk recently about Defence hiring 'current affairs' journalists to help them with their PR," said Janice, "I know I read it somewhere..."

"Is that so?" I said, again amazed at Defence's subtle manipulation. So, now they were employing television journalists, but not just any television journalists, only 'current affairs' journalists. How deceptive! Did that mean they were buying off the media to control what could be reported about Defence? It sure seemed so!

After that little bit of information was revealed, I was not surprised when I didn't hear from any of the mainstream commercial channels.

Is it a coincidence now, during the COVID crisis, that the mainstream media only report what the Government wants reported? No! Ten years on from the DSA debacle, the Government has had plenty of time, an entire decade, to work out how to control the media.

As soon as the COVID crisis began, the Government opened a financial floodgate of free money for the commercial media channels. They were granted 100% freedom from taxes for the 2020 financial year; the equivalent of $41million. Plus, they received $50million for 'public interest' journalism, that is, $50m to ensure the Government perspective of COVID was blasted *ad nauseam* to the public. And an extra $5million was granted to regional publishers. It's called propaganda. It's called bribery. If you still think the journalists on commercial television today are presenting a balanced perspective of COVID - think again!

Thankfully, back in 2011, there were still a few worthy reporters who hadn't sold their integrity to the highest bidder.

CONTACTED BY THE ABC

Three weeks after we received Minister Snowdon's bombshell, we were contacted by John Stewart, producer and investigative reporter for ABC's *Lateline*, regarded as the hardest-hitting current affairs program in Australia, often creating the next day's newspaper headlines.

John Stewart turned out to be an answer to prayer for us. In all our dealings with him over the next year, he never once broke his word to us or betrayed our trust. Here, at last, was a man of integrity.

His first contact was by email to confirm a few details, and then he phoned. "From what you have given me, I think this is an important story," said John. "Is there anyone else who may want to come forward?"

"There are three of us who are willing to speak with you openly," I explained, "but there are others who will have to remain anonymous."

"Are you all Defence personnel?"

"No!" I took a deep breath. It was hard to go back to square one and explain from the beginning. So much had happened. I had to remind myself this reporter knew nothing about our situation, and it was up to me to educate him. He would need to know the basic set up of agency versus Defence, the treatment of staff and the gist of the multiple fake investigations before he could understand the scale of the story.

"The Defence personnel wish to remain in the background. We three are ex-agency staff, who were contracted to the Defence Intelligence and Security Authority known as DSA."

"Can I speak with them?"

"That won't be a problem, John. I will email your details to them, and they will contact you directly. There are another two agency staff who were involved in the initial investigation but don't wish to be involved in this. They are happy for you to see their letters to confirm what we are saying but want to remain anonymous."

"So when did the falsifying of documents start, do you know?" asked John. His questions were blunt but delivered with courtesy.

"In 2009, I believe, but it could have been earlier. I was employed in 2009, and three weeks after I started in July, the processes suddenly changed. The changes didn't make sense."

"What do you think may have been the motivation for Defence to abort the proper checks and push the clearances through?"

What a question! I was astonished at how quickly John was piecing everything together. I was dealing with a very intelligent man.

"The new AGSVA contract," I said, I knew I would have to explain what I meant, and I just hoped I would get it right. "Defence wanted to set up a centralised vetting agency for the whole of Australia but were not sure where it should be located...in which State...so they sort of pitted the DSA offices in each State against each other. The most efficient State would win the contract.

"Queensland won?"

"Yes," I confirmed. "The head of DSA Canberra announced at the end of 2009 that the new AGSVA would be located in Queensland, and all the DSA Queensland staff would be running it."

"So in order to win, they had to cut corners?"

I laughed. "You've got it in one, John," I said. His questions were so 'to-the-point'!

"When did they start charging money for clearances?"

Another bold question! "I can't answer exactly, that's one of the things which will need to be confirmed by the analysts, but I believe it was just before I started, around the same time the idea of the new AGSVA was being developed."

"How many clearances do you think have been compromised?"

"Thousands," I said, "maybe tens of thousands. I don't know."

"Have any terrorists slipped through the net, do you know?" John's voice was matter-of-fact.

Another bold question! I couldn't help thinking that these were the kinds of questions the investigators should have asked us. But they weren't interested!

"No one has slipped through the net as far as anyone knows, John, but it's only a matter of time. It only takes one. I think the most risky are security guards working on military bases. They're often recent arrivals, new Australians, who may still have overseas contacts which may compromise them."

"They were not checked properly?"

"No!" I said and paused. Was I actually saying all this? "When information was missing, it was just made up and entered into the database as fact."

"How do you know this?"

"It was my job. That's what I was ordered to do!" I was starting to feel embarrassed.

"You made up information about security guards on Australian military bases?" John asked.

When this direct question came out of his mouth, it sounded so very, very bad, yet that was the point - it *was* bad!

"Yes!"

"How many others entered false information?"

"More than a hundred people that I know of - just about everyone," I said, "certainly all the agency staff. We were all lied to, given false procedures, and told certain fields on the database had to be filled in, but the information we put into them didn't matter."

"Was this only for low-level clearances?"

"No, the same applied to secret and even top-secret clearances."

"Why are you coming to the media?"

"There's nowhere else to go, John," I said. "We've been everywhere else. The Ombudsmen's office didn't want to know. A Cabinet Minister didn't want to know. We sent our complaints through the correct complaint channels, both inside Defence and outside. No one wanted to know! When our complaints could no longer be brushed aside, and they had to have an investigation, it was a paper tiger set up to ignore the facts. What amazes me, John, is that you have asked me more relevant questions in this short interview than anyone has ever asked me. No one in authority in Australia, even at the highest levels, wants to know what is going on at DSA."

"Would you be prepared to come on television and say all of this publicly?"

Ouch! This was crunch time! Going public meant possible prosecution for breaching the Official Secrets Act. Once I was 'out there', there was no turning back. I wasn't sure if I was ready. I took a deep breath before answering. "That's a very scary thought, John," I said.

"We could film you blacked out and leave your names out of it, but it would be better if you showed your faces and we could use your real names. It would make the story more credible."

I understood the logic of being completely open. It made sense. But I couldn't make this decision alone. I would have to talk to the others.

"Do you mind if I get back to you on that one, John?" I asked. "I need to talk this over with Owen and Janice and see what they think."

"Sure," John responded. "You know it's highly unusual to find three people who are willing to speak out. That tells me things in DSA were very bad."

"I know so many more would love to speak up, but they're afraid and with good reason."

"If you come forward, the others might also come forward," said John.

"I suppose we should contact a lawyer to find out what we can and can't say," I said. "Prosecution is a reality, so we have to be careful."

"I think you should contact a lawyer," John said, "but I also think there would be so much bad publicity it would just not be worth it for them. It would look terrible for the Defence Minister to be going after someone with the moral courage to speak up about failed processes and security risks to Australia. That's my view, but I'll talk to the lawyers at the ABC and see what they say as well."

"Thanks, John," I said. As I hung up the phone, I felt encouraged. Finally, a good interview!

John was refreshingly professional, but this story wasn't about him or even us. It was about some pretty serious issues affecting Australia's National Security.

My mind flashed to the rash of 'security' advertising being run on television, telling people to alert authorities about anything they thought might be suspicious. Signs were placed on walls in public places and inside trains and buses telling people to report any unclaimed luggage, presumably in case of terrorist attacks. In the light of the farce I'd just lived through, which showed no one in authority actually cared about Australia's security, those warnings were a total waste of taxpayer money. An absolute joke!

A MIRACLE OF PROVISION - FREE LEGAL ADVICE

It was difficult for Janice, Owen and me to find a time and a place to meet. Owen and I were working full-time, Janice was working part-time, and Owen's Saturday's were tied up with church and family. It seemed that Sunday was the only day of the week the three of us could get together. So, we decided to meet for a leisurely Sunday brunch at a coffee house.

"John wants to interview us as quickly as possible," I said. "We need to give him a date."

"Look how hard it was for us to find this little bit of time," Janice responded, "it seems we can only meet on Sundays."

"Does he do his TV interviews on Sundays?" asked Owen.

I nodded. "Yes, he's available anytime."

"I'm going to Western Australia to visit my daughter and her husband in two weeks," said Janice, "so the best Sunday for me is next Sunday. The problem is that's Mother's Day."

"Oh, it is too," I said. I had forgotten completely about Mother's Day. "So that's out."

"Not necessarily," said Owen, "How long do you think the interviews will take?"

"A couple of hours," I said, shrugging my shoulders to show I didn't have a clue. My guess was as good as theirs.

"My family can work around that," said Owen. "We have our big celebration for Mother's Day at church on Saturday."

"I'm not having Mother's Day this year," said Janice, "I'm seeing my mother on Saturday, so Sunday is my day, and both my girls are away."

"Next Sunday it is then," I said. "My children won't mind. I'll let John know."

"Where do we stand legally?" Owen suddenly chuckled. "Jail time doesn't appeal to me. I tend to like my freedom!"

"So do I," I said. "I told my boss this week I was planning to do this, and I could be arrested."

Owen looked stunned. "You told your boss?"

"What did she say?" asked Janice.

"She called the big boss over, and we had a three-way conversation," I said. "They're cool with it. Basically, they are concerned it will be rather stressful for me and gave me the option to take the next day off. All I have to do is let them know when I think the show will be aired."

"Wow! Normal people still amaze me!" said Owen, "I'm not used to good bosses anymore. I always expect the worst. That's what comes of working for so long in a toxic atmosphere. It ruins your perspective."

"There's nothing wrong with your perspective, Owen," I said, "you saw things as they really were."

"Getting back to the lawyer situation," Janice interjected, "I had an appointment this week with a Barrister who worked on the Fitzgerald Inquiry and the Christopher Skase prosecution. He is very experienced in sensitive investigations, and he's offered to help us."

Owen was impressed. "That's high profile! How did you find him?" He paused and then shook his head in amazement. "How does anyone find a Barrister with that kind of experience?"

I laughed. "Incredible, isn't it? It just so happens Janice and this Barrister both volunteer their time at the same Community Centre."

Janice nodded. "Anyway, I told him our problem, and he's given us some advice."

"Excellent advice!" I said.

"The short of it is we can't be prosecuted for anything we've told the ABC because we are revealing lies and deception," Janice explained.

"We're not in breach of the Secrecy Act!" I said, beaming. "The Act was set up to protect Australia and its interests. We're not betraying Australia - we've trying to *protect* Australia. We're not breaking the intention of the Act. That means, we can speak out boldly, even publicly, against corruption without fear of prosecution."

"As long as we don't use specifics," said Janice. "Like correct names or exact places."

"And we can be more direct in what we say," said Janice. "Dayle, that's the Barrister, said we should be clear in our descriptions."

I explained. "You know how we always say 'fudged' or 'manufactured'? Well, Dayle suggests we use strong words which everyone understands, like 'lying', 'misleading', 'deceptive', and 'false'. He said that we should never use just one description if two will fit."

"We can say all that?" Surprise was written all over Owen's face.

We all laughed. This was such good news.

"There's a whole lot more," said Janice, "but I'll email it to you."

"I think if we can speak openly about the bullying being used to cover the falsification of data and the corruption of ASIO records, without being prosecuted, then others might realise they also can step forward without reprisals," I said.

"I'm blown away," said Owen, noticeably stunned. "How much is all this legal advice going to cost us?"

"Nothing! Dale is offering his advice as a community service," Janice confirmed.

"What do you think the odds are of us finding an experienced Barrister, with his particular field of expertise, willing to give us free advice at this exact moment in time?" I said, speaking earnestly.

Janice looked serious.

Owen shook his head.

"This has God's hand all over it," I said, "It's not only a miracle of provision, it has shown us we don't have to worry about hiding our faces. We have absolutely nothing to fear."

"It certainly is amazing!" said Owen smiling. "I'm so happy right now. I'm on a real high."

OUR STORY GOES TO AIR

John and his crew of two arrived at my home at 10am on Sunday 8 May 2011, Mother's Day, and it was action stations immediately. The sound and camera operators rearranged the furniture, found power points and set up their gear. They had so many cords running across the floor; I wondered how they remembered which one went where - the cords all looked the same to me.

John handed out different lists of questions to Owen, Janice and me, and we all went to the dining room to study them and practice our answers. Janice phoned Dayle, who gave us sage advice on the best way to present our specific viewpoints and then asked to speak with John. It was all 'go'.

Four hours later, it was over, and we were exhausted. None of us was nervous about being filmed. Instead, we were consumed with saying the right thing and getting our message across clearly, but it was extremely difficult to tell if we had been able to do that.

We'd answered the same questions so many times and in so many different ways that at the end of the day, it was impossible to know if we'd said the right thing. Plus, we didn't know which versions of our answers John would use for his story. Would we come off looking genuine or like cranks and idiots? We didn't know.

The story would not be aired until the following Monday evening, so we had to wait eight long self-questioning days to see what John would do with the information we had given him.

Meanwhile, John plied Crystal, Linda and me with probing questions via email, sometimes ten a day, checking details and pedantically making sure he was getting every little fact correct. I admired his professionalism. No wonder he was successful; defence investigators could benefit from his example.

The big day arrived. Monday 16 May 2011, a date to remember. Janice was in Western Australia with her family but as nervous and excited as I was. We had all spent a week wading through the options, going over the 'what-would-we-do-ifs'. Now there were no more 'what-ifs'.

Lateline came on, and I held my breath.

- "Defence staff told to fake security checks - orders from the top. They say fake security clearances have left a gaping hole in Australia's National Security. They say that information was invented to fill in gaps on security applications, including top-secret-level clearances sent to ASIO."
- "Sometimes applicants didn't give the city they had gone to in a certain country, so you would just pick a city, sometimes they would write Asia, so then you'd just pick an Asian country and certain things like that." Owen.
- "There was a large percentage of applications that came my way that had gaps - that had problems that needed the applicant to be phoned. About 25 per cent." Janice.

- "Information like where you live, or previous employment - DSA didn't care about that stuff. We were told to just make it up, put in some dates, put unemployed for periods which were missing, addresses, just find a street or make up some information, any information, to fill in those gaps." Owen.
- "I put a few problem applications aside and took them to a manager. Problems with their addresses, their workplaces, or they didn't give information about relatives or didn't supply certificates for a change of name. I was told these words, 'be creative'. Monica.
- "The pressure is on you to process them and get them out quickly, so if you don't meet that pressure and get your numbers up, then you're going to lose your job." Owen.
- "In May 2010, an investigation was conducted, but Mr Snowden said in a letter that the investigator was unable to find any evidence of bullying or harassment." John.
- "I explicitly told one of those investigators that information in top-secret clearances had been fabricated." Monica.
- "Minister for Defence, Stephen Smith, has told *Lateline*, "Defence has in place a rigorous vetting and quality assurance process." John.

It was the main story and took up most of the hour, but I don't remember breathing again until it was over. It was so good, so shocking, so well presented, I was speechless. I looked at my son Martin, seated on the lounge on the other side of the room, gave a big smile, jumped up, threw my hands into the air and yelled out, "Yes!"

John was a genius! A true artist! He had taken a little bit of this and a little bit of that and created an exact picture. He hadn't betrayed us! He hadn't let us down! I felt like dancing!

Janice must have too, because she phoned me almost straight away, in awe of what we had just seen. Then through the laughter, the re-hashing of the program started, and gradually what we had just done began to sink in. Defence was not going to like this story. They were not going to be happy.

NO RESPONSE FROM DEFENCE

We expected Defence to come gunning for us immediately. So did John. But it didn't happen. The day after our shocking allegations aired, there was silence from Defence. Nothing! Not even a squeak! Just after my lunch break, John phoned me at work.

"Thank you so much, John, for the way you presented our story," I said. "It was brilliant! It said everything we wanted said."

"I was happy with it," said John. "But I'm surprised we haven't heard anything from Defence." He sounded disappointed. "It's definitely unusual. They normally respond straight away."

"Nothing? Why do you think that is?" I asked.

"I don't know." He said. "I haven't seen this happen before. This story is important, and yet they are not saying anything. I'm going to ring Minister Smith's office and see if I can get a response."

Okay, so he was warning me he was going to provoke a response from Defence. Strangely, I didn't mind at all. "Let me know what they say," I said, "you know, forewarned and all that..."

"Do your bosses mind if I phone you back at work?" he asked.

He was so considerate. "No, John, they don't, I assured him. "They actually offered me the day off if I felt I needed it." He couldn't see that I was smiling. He didn't realise how much I appreciated working with decent people. "They understand my present situation. Call me anytime."

Later that afternoon, John called me back.

"Smith's office said they don't have any reason to comment," he said.

"You've got to be kidding me!" I was shocked. I shook my head. "No reason?"

"They said you didn't provide any specific examples of clearances being compromised, so there's nothing for them to comment on," said John.

Specific examples? Really? We knew that providing specifics would land us in jail. "Can you understand this hedging, John?" I asked.

"No," he said. "It doesn't make sense. We'll have to wait and see what happens over the next few days. Meanwhile, I have some good news."

I laughed. "Oh, do tell!"

"Have you checked out the online comments on our website? There are plenty, and most of them are 100% behind you three," he said.

"Oh! Wow!"

"That tells me a lot," he said, "it shows your story has touched a nerve."

"People have been crying out for justice for years, decades! Defence never listens, and justice is never done! Nothing ever changes."

"I think they might have to change this time," said John, "too many people are coming forward."

"What do you mean?" I asked

"I've also been directly contacted by quite a few people who claim to have worked with you at DSA, and they are confirming everything you guys have told me," John said. "They've given me their names but want to remain anonymous, and that's not a problem, I'll keep them anonymous," he hesitated for a second, "but I'd like to run the names past you to see if you know them - to see if they actually did work with you."

"Not a problem, John. I won't betray their trust either," I said.

"I'll send you an email. I think there are about eight so far," he said. "When we spoke, I could see they clearly knew what they were talking about."

"Eight!" I exclaimed, more to myself than to John. This truly was good news.

John read out the names. "Yes, I know them. Those people are all Defence staff, John; they're not contractors. I thought they were all against us, but it seems many of them also want the bullying and corruption to stop, even if they're not game to be seen standing up against Defence."

"This kind of story usually gives others the courage to come forward, but that's a significant number," said John.

"I hope their coming forward has made you feel more confident about our story, John."

"Yes, it has. I think we need to keep going with this story, though, or Defence is just going to bury it with some internal inquiry."

"Keep me posted, John," I smiled into the phone. "This is getting good!"

SUDDENLY THE DENIALS BEGIN

The next day the denials began. The first of a series of official denials came in the form of statements from the office of the Minister for Defence as a direct result of John Stewart's enquiries.

- "In response to questions from *Lateline*, a spokesman for the Defence Minister has told us, "There is no evidence to suggest that security clearances have been compromised."
- "The Government takes allegations of the fabrication of information in security clearances extremely seriously." Minister Smith.
- I'm advised these allegations are not true, and that's the advice provided by Defence. Brendan O'Connor MP on Sky Channel.

When I heard we had been publicly called liars, my response was immediate. I laughed long and hard! Far from being crushed or hurt, I knew what they were saying was ludicrous - almost to the point of being stupid.

Minister Smith said there was no evidence, but that was totally absurd. There was plenty of evidence - that is if Defence wanted to find it.

The specifics they had told the media they needed in order to believe us was a whopping great deception on their part. If they could trick us into giving specifics, they could prosecute us immediately. But, we would *not* be giving specifics!

As for paper evidence, it simply didn't exist! And they knew it! The corruption was in the database, which was not open to scrutiny by the public. They were lying, deceiving and manipulating the media into believing we were lying. And we knew it!

The main problem Defence had with our public revelations was that we were not pointing the finger at them. We were confessing what we had done ourselves. We said what we had done was wrong.

We had gone on air and said that we had passed false information through their database to ASIO! We had said publicly that we had broken the law, and then they defied logic and said publicly that we were lying and so *hadn't* broken the law!

This put them in a no-win situation!

The reality was, if they prosecuted us, the corruption would be seen. If they ignored us, the public would smell a rat. They obviously didn't know what to do, which is why they were stalling, using vague and very loud denials to fend off the press while their lawyers worked overtime.

That same day a spokesperson for ASIO also responded to our *Lateline* revelations by publicly supporting the illogical Defence position.

- "ASIO understands claims of inappropriate vetting practices have been reviewed by the Department of Defence and have not been substantiated."
- "ASIO takes allegations such as these very seriously and will work with the Department of Defence as required."

When I saw these statements, I immediately wondered when our claims of inappropriate vetting practices had been reviewed. It was evident from the ASIO statement they had been told Defence had already reviewed our claims. But when did they do that? Certainly not since our allegations were aired just two short days ago. And the previous investigation was about management styles, not vetting practices or national security!

Had Defence lied to ASIO? Again?

That afternoon Minister Smith announced he had asked the Inspector-General of Defence to investigate our allegations of inappropriate vetting practices within DSA.

Hold on! Didn't ASIO just tell the media that very morning that a review had already been done? Then why another one? Could ASIO not see the lie? Hmm, confusing, to say the least!

- "Allegations of fabrication of information in security clearances will be investigated by the Inspector-General of Defence." Minister Smith.

Meanwhile, that evening, Cassie emailed us, and her short and interesting 'insider' view made us all howl with laughter. Vault-window mentality had its advantages for us, that was for sure.

- "We had a meeting on Monday to advise us not to talk to the media. That means everyone became aware there would be something about DSA on the ABC, and because of that, it seems most people at work watched it." Cassie

No wonder there were so many comments from DSA and ex-DSA staff after the program had been aired! DSA advertised it for us! We couldn't stop laughing!

DAYLE GOES THE EXTRA MILE FOR US

The next day I came home from work to find a message on my answering machine from an investigator for public defence with the Inspector-Generals office asking me to contact him. That was quick! The investigation was announced one day and begun the next. Hmm, probably some legal advice would be good.

I contacted Janice, still in Western Australia, and asked her to phone Dayle and find out what we should expect from this investigation. Janice called him immediately, and he was available. Incredible! His short, sharp, strongly suggested advice was not what we would have expected.

"Firstly, congratulations on not being scared to say and do what was clearly right," said Dayle.

"Thank you," Janice replied and got straight to the point. "We have been contacted by investigators from the Office of the Inspector-General of Defence."

"Have you spoken to them yet?" asked Dayle.

"No, they just want to set up a meeting."

"Not a good idea. Not even with an independent third party present." There was no hesitation in Dayle's response.

"Why is that?" asked Janice.

"You're not protected from prosecution. Speaking with them can leave you vulnerable. You've given them plenty of opportunities to discuss these issues, and they have hurled them back in your face each time. The safest place to give any further evidence is in the Senate," Dayle said.

"A Senate Inquiry?" asked Janice. "How do we go about that?"

"Find a Senator who will take this issue seriously," said Dayle.

"Okay, but what do we say to these investigators?" asked Janice. "They want a response straight away."

"Don't speak to them!" said Dayle emphatically. "You interview them!"

Janice laughed nervously. "What do you mean, Dayle?"

"Ask them, 'What is the purpose of your call? What is your rank or public service grade? Do you have the proper clearance? To whom do you answer? Who will see this report? Do you agree to pay all our legal expenses'? And then tell them you have been advised the safest place to discuss these issues is in the Senate."

Janice laughed again, this time with delight. "Not quite what they will be expecting."

"Let me know how you go," Dayle said, winding up the conversation.

"Thanks, Dayle," said Janice, "I will."

It was clear from Dayle's advice we had been walking blindly into a massive trap.

This investigation into our allegations looked so proper, so logical, so correct, yet if we participated in it, we could very well end up in jail. And Minister Smith thought this was a good idea!

The immorality of the Defence machine, and all its little operators, never ceased to amaze me. This ruse was about to fail. But what would they try next? We were on a roller-coaster ride now, and there was no getting off until the ride stopped.

The day after receiving Dayle's warning, we were again phoned by the investigators from the office of the Inspector-General of Defence, so of course, we each took Dayle's advice and interviewed the investigators. When we asked if they would pay our legal expenses, each of us was told the same thing. "Oh, ah, um, I can't make that decision. I'll need to get back to you."

Our response to their hesitation was to tell them they need not get back to us as our barrister had advised us not to disclose anything without Parliamentary protection.

They didn't ring us back. We never heard from them again. It was such a hoot - us interviewing them! What a turnaround!

We couldn't wait to tell Dayle about the outcome of his wise counsel to us, so we asked Janice to phone him on our behalf again and let him know how pleased we were with the result. When she called him, Janice discovered Dayle was doing more for us behind the scenes than we'd thought. He'd been speaking to the Defence lawyers.

"I spent some time on the phone with an internal Defence lawyer trying to establish a workable background to permit you to speak to a Defence appointed review," said Dayle.

"A new review?" asked Janice.

"I haven't seen any terms-of-reference for the current investigation, and I believe in the worst when there is no evidence of a newfound intention to throw a klieg light on the secrets and lies."

Janice chuckled, 'klieg light' what a graphic picture it painted.

"You need someone who is independent and can look afresh at the allegations while ensuring you can never be persecuted or prosecuted for whistleblowing," he said.

"Oh, that's what we need," said Janice.

"If it occurs, it will only be with your consent," said Dayle, "and the consent of each of the persons who may wish to come forward."

"Other people?" asked Janice.

"You should consider identifying to me a group of persons whom you trust, who share common experiences with you, and who can point particular fingers at specific bits of gross impropriety."

"Well," said Janice remembering the large number of vetting personnel who had come forward, "there are quite a few of us now, and certainly some of them can point to specific horrendous examples."

"Good! If you present me with an outline of what they might say, I could ensure your group gets immunity."

"Oh wonderful," said Janice, fumbling with pen and paper, "I'm just going to jot this down."

"Don't worry," said Dayle, "I'll forward an email."

"Excellent," said Janice putting down her pen.

"I have also asked for the right to cross-examine the agents for Defence as part of the mix of evidence before the tribunal or other statutory body empanelled to hear your grievances and requests, if any, for redress."

"Thank you, Dayle." Janice's head was beginning to swim. Legal jargon was not her *forte,* and she was quietly thinking she would not like to have Dayle cross-examining her in a courtroom.

"You may have to figure out what, if any, fiscal redress each of you separately seeks," said Dayle.

"Oh!" said Janice, slightly taken aback. "Well, we have discussed that possibility, but we three have agreed that seeking compensation would diminish what we are doing."

"How so?" asked Dayle.

"People might think we are doing this for the money," Janice explained. "We're not! We're doing it because it needs to be done. So, we don't want compensation to get in the way of the outcome we're working towards. We want to stay focused."

"Understood!" Dayle responded.

"The bottom line is Dayle; this is not about us." Janice continued, "it's about Defence thinking they can treat Australians like dirt under their boots. It's about them thumbing their noses at Australian law. It's about all the Australians they are putting at risk, including our military. I can't see anyone with the courage and authority to pull them into line, Dayle, certainly not our elected ministers. 'Illegal' doesn't seem to mean anything!"

"They *are* accountable to Australian law!" Dayle said as if there was no argument to his statement. "The Department of Defence has no power to act illegally, and to allow it to do so would be a criminal offence."

"Can I ask you a personal question, Dayle?"

Dayle remained silent.

"Why are you doing all this for us?"

"Because I think it's a good cause," Dayle said without hesitation.

"So, we're on the same page," Janice replied. "Thank you for everything you're doing for us, Dayle. I'll pass your comments along to the others."

Dayle was a God-send, another answer to our prayers, no doubt about it. A miracle of protection from God! He was the right person in the right place, at the right time. Taking his advice had literally kept us out of jail.

Now he was 'going the extra mile' for us by expertly convincing the Defence lawyers we needed a forum free from prosecution or persecution. He amazed us! He was not only fighting a not so small battle for us behind the scenes but was offering his usually expensive services free of charge, passing them off as a mere good deed. We couldn't help but thank God for him.

ORGANISED AND READY

Emails became the primary form of 'instant' communication within our expanding group. Some of our anonymous ABC supporters had contacted us, so we included them in our email chain. I asked Janice to convert Dayle's email string to a word document so that we could send it out as an attachment to all those who had come forward.

Within 24 hours, Janice was back from Western Australia, the emails had gone out, and everyone was aware of Dayle's advice and what he was doing for us behind the scenes. No matter what we were about to face, we were organised, and we were ready.

- "Isn't this amazing and wonderful? It really is our time to shine, and the fact Dayle is willing to cross-examine is so cool. This is so overdue. Someone up there is looking after us." Crystal.
- "Dayle has confirmed our suspicions. Of course there are no 'terms of reference'. Why would Defence pay a legal team thousands of dollars to find out what *they* have done wrong? They know what they've done wrong! This is just another 'internal investigation' dressed up as something else, and we've all already been through one or more of those." Linda.

- "Kate contacted me, and she is in contact with Leah. They have both spoken to John. I've passed on Dayle's advice. I will get in contact with Jim, our good friend in the DSA saga, to see if he wants a piece of the action and also Rosie. Do you remember her? She worked in the basement and never stopped smiling. Can you think of anyone else?" Owen.
- "Jade told me that when she saw the news story, she just burst into tears and cried all the way through *Lateline* - she thinks you are all heroes. Doesn't that just break your heart?" Crystal.
- "I just wanted to personally write and say you three have taken a huge step which I hope will help a lot of us! You have started something I was just too scared to start myself, but something I have thought of often. You have my full backing when the time comes." Jade.
- "Moira has also spoken with John, asking to remain anonymous." Crystal.
- "It's amazing how many have jumped on board. It's also good to hear about the legal help you're getting. Keep me posted of further developments." Jennifer.
- "The best news is that Crystal, Linda and Jade have all spoken to John, asking to remain anonymous, but confirming our story. Linda is rounding up others as well." Monica.
- "This is AWESOME!" I so would like to talk to this independent inquiry to tell our stories, pending, of course, when Dayle negotiates the terms by which we can speak without persecution or prosecution." Owen.

- "We're not pressed for time. It is all rather early stages at this point, and Dayle is still checking things out and making enquiries; whether it is a review or a Senate inquiry - the more of us, the merrier. This is a BIG learning curve for us all." Janice.
- "I'm jumping out of my skin. This is amazing, and you have no idea how I feel. I so hope it also includes the bullying and harassment eventually - as that is how they got us to do what we did, and some of us have paid so dearly for it." Crystal.
- "I've decided to explore the Senate angle. I've just made an appointment to see Senator Clair Moore's assistant, Meredith Newman, at 8am on Wednesday. She's local, and I've been told she cares about the treatment of workers in the workplace. Does anyone have any questions you think I should ask her about a Senate Inquiry?" Monica.
- "Can I come too?" Crystal.
- "You don't have to ask. I'll meet you there at 7.30am. See you Wednesday." Monica.

Wednesday came around quickly. It was good to see Crystal's smiling face again. It had seemed such a long time since we had sat in the bar and agreed the media was the way to go. In reality, it was only a few months, but here we were again, face to face, planning another mission, and our friendship was echoed in our silent hug.

"The best thing about today is seeing you again," said Crystal with genuine warmth.

"For someone going through the mill, you look pretty wonderful yourself!"

"Will we need to give proof upfront?" Crystal sounded nervous, "you know we can't do that."

"They know that too," I said, trying to reassure her. "Remember what it was like with Brett?"

Crystal's hands were trembling, and I knew she was desperately trying to overcome her fears. She took a deep calming breath. "Okay, let's do this."

Poor Crystal! She was afraid she would be betrayed and punished again. My poor terrified friend. She'd been at DSA way too long! Linking arms, we headed for the Senator's office.

After we gained the information we needed about Senate Inquiries, Meredith took the meeting in a different direction, turning her attention to Crystal's ongoing bullying situation. She was so concerned about the number of horrendous accounts just tumbling freely, without emotion, from Crystal's memory, that she asked permission to personally contact the Minister's Office that day to ask why nothing had been done in response to Crystal's formal requests for protection.

Crystal handed over copies of her formal complaints about bullying and was so grateful for this little bit of support she was flat out holding back the tears.

We left Senator Moore's office content we had done what we needed to do. And after a brief hug and fond farewells, we both headed off to commence an otherwise normal working day.

Our visit to the Senator's office may have seemed insignificant in the scheme of things, but the timing was perfect. We didn't know it, but everything was coming to a head - quickly!

In just one short week, Defence's 'terms of reference' free investigation had been exposed, the witnesses refused to cooperate, a barrister was asking questions, the ABC was asking questions, and now a Senator's office was also asking questions. The pressure was well and truly on Defence!

The whole situation was volatile, all it would take now was one little spark, and the entire thing would erupt into flames.

Suddenly, the spark appeared in the form of a real-life example of what we had been warning about - a clearance gone wrong!

Only God could have provided such perfect evidence at the right time and in the right way. For us, it was another miracle.

It suddenly came to light that one of the men guarding the highest official in Queensland, the Queensland Premier, Anna Bligh, a man with unlimited access to every room in the Queensland Parliament building, had actually been wanted by Interpol for seven years. Wow!

Yet, despite being a wanted criminal, the security guard clearance process, which gave him unlimited access to the Parliament and Parliamentarians, didn't pick it up. And, because of the clearance process, ASIO didn't pick it up! It was shocking! And it was all over the news!

Kaboom! The whole thing erupted! What an incredible mess!

> *A man wanted across the world has been found guarding Premier Anna Bligh and the offices of the most powerful people in Queensland."* (Courier Mail, May 2011)

Defence was
beginning
to back-peddle!

CHAPTER SEVEN

Undeniable proof? Cover it up!

The investigation by the Inspector-General of Defence into our allegations must have been one of the shortest high-level investigations in Australian Defence history. It was abandoned after nine days.

Since we three whistleblowers would not speak with the investigators, they had no other choice but to abandon it. They had no one to investigate! Those nine days were not wasted, though, and in that short time there was so much evidence uncovered that proved what we had said on *Lateline* was true, the Minister for Defence, on the 25 May 2011, announced via the ABC that further action would need to be taken to redress the security breaches they had discovered.

Stephen Smith's humiliating public admission that our allegations may, in fact, have substance was followed by a second admission that there was evidence Defence had previously been told by us about the problem some twelve months earlier but had overlooked the importance and truth of our statements, which he said they now regretted.

These admissions, together with a few uncomfortable questions from Senators, prompted two new investigations. Minister Smith ordered an immediate internal review of DSA, while the Prime Minister, Julia Gillard, took the investigation of our claims out of the hands of the Inspector-General of Defence and gave it to a truly independent body.

The Prime Minister asked the Investigator General of Intelligence and Security (IGIS), Dr Vivian Thom, to conduct an *'inquiry into allegations of inappropriate vetting practices by the Defence Security Authority and related matters'*. This independent investigation was announced in the Senate on 30 May 2011, just two short weeks after our first appearance on *Lateline*.

Defence was in trouble, but they were not going to go down without a fight. At the same time as the new IGIS investigation into our allegations was announced, the Assistant Secretary of Defence, Stephen Merchant, disclosed to the Senate that Defence had only been checking the applications 'touched' by 'those' whistleblowers. He made us sound like criminals, like saboteurs who had deliberately damaged applications to cause embarrassment. They were admitting there was a problem, but now it was clear they had intended, through their investigation, to focus the blame for their problem onto us. No wonder our savvy barrister had warned us to avoid them.

MINISTER SMITH ADMITS THERE IS A PROBLEM

The news that a Queensland government security guard, who had been on Interpol's most-wanted list since 2004, had nevertheless been guarding the offices of Queensland Parliamentarians was received as a shocking kind of wake up call. It showed that what we had been saying all along was true. Checks were not being done as thoroughly as they should have been.

The big question people were beginning to ask was, 'how many more are there out there?' How many had 'slipped through the net'? Could there be others? Could there be terrorists? These were questions no one could answer.

Defence had no choice now but to admit there was a problem. But would they? As long as I had been alive, I had never seen Defence back down. They always held their ground until their opponents either gave up or died, proving the accepted idiom, "no one wins against Defence!"

At the end of May 2011, the power of that old saying was broken. The unthinkable happened. Defence capitulated! Minister Smith contacted the ABC and made a shocking public announcement. What we had said on *Lateline* was true! Unbelievable! Finally! How wonderful!

I first heard about Stephen Smith's humiliating announcement from John Stewart. He phoned me at work just after lunch and told me the good news.

"Stephen Smith has just announced that you guys weren't lying!" said John. His voice was more animated than usual. This news had surprised even a seasoned investigative journalist.

I couldn't believe what I was hearing, "What do you mean?" I asked.

"He's just gone on air and admitted there are problems with the clearances," said John.

My mouth dropped open. "No!" I said, shocked, "He's admitted it?" This was incredible news. I was stunned.

"He admitted to two of your three allegations," said John. "He also said Defence knew about it last year and didn't do anything about it."

"He's backed-down?" I still couldn't believe it. "Defence never backs down!"

John laughed. It was the first time I'd heard him laugh. "I want to do another story tonight."

"You said they admitted to two out of three. What didn't they admit to?" I asked.

"That it's still going on," said John, "they say it was confined to DSA and hasn't carried over to the new AGSVA."

Now it was my turn to laugh. "Well, we know that's not true!"

"Do you think you could do another interview for us tonight?" John asked. "I think we need to respond to these admissions."

"Not a problem, I can do that," This news was overwhelming. "Do you know what this means, John?"

John was silent, waiting for me to continue.

"We can't be prosecuted!" Laughter began to bubble up from somewhere deep inside, and I knew I would not be able to contain it. "Defence can't prosecute us - ever - because of these admissions!" I began to laugh. This was just the best news ever!

"I will try to get a TV crew to your place tonight, though it might be a problem because of the State of Origin football coverage," John said, "there may not be any crews available."

"I'll see if I can round up Janice and Owen. They're going to whoop for joy when they hear this. I'm so elated, John. Nine days? They backed down in just nine days!" I was laughing again. "That's got to be some kind of record for Defence."

"Look, I just want to say congratulations," John's tone was sincere. "This is an unusually good result. I certainly wasn't expecting them to back down, and to do it so quickly means they must have found a truckload of evidence to prove what you're saying is true."

I suddenly felt emotional and found it difficult to respond, but I needed to let John know what I wanted to say that night, so I took a deep breath. "Crystal and I visited Senator Moore's office this morning, John, to get some information on how to start a Senate Inquiry," I said. "That was Dayle's suggestion, and he seems to know the best way for us to proceed. So tonight, I'd like to take the opportunity to call for a Senate Inquiry."

"Not a problem," John responded.

I gained permission from my bosses to go home early so that I could go over the transcript and work out my responses. They were wonderful, as usual, and had no problem with me leaving work early. When I arrived home, several emails from John awaited me. He couldn't get a crew. We would have to be interviewed at the studio. I had never been inside a television station before, so this would be a new experience - and a little daunting!

At the studio, I had my makeup done by a professional, a definite improvement, and was then positioned at a spare news desk with a green screen behind me. It was almost surreal. John asked questions through a speaker connection as he was still in Sydney, and it felt strange giving my answers to a fixed position on the blank computer screen in front of me. I answered questions for about ten minutes, and then it was over. How exhausting! But it was worth it!

This program was even better than the first one. It was explosive!

- Minister Smith had said only Defence personnel clearances were affected. We said this was not so as we were also doing clearances for civilians.

- Minister Smith said it was an old DSA problem that didn't carry over into the new AGSVA. A current DSA worker said AGSVA was now worse than DSA by double.

Janice and I watched the show together, and we both gasped with surprise when we heard that! John backed up his statement by showing a letter of complaint written to the Minister about AGSVA just two weeks earlier, stating how bad it was. We didn't know about that complaint - this was someone outside our group - wow! This didn't look good for Defence *or* Minister Smith!

It was all so amazing to us. It was becoming a bit of a blur, really. It was like we were in the back seat of a limo, watching everything outside flash past. Who else could have brought all these various loose ends together simultaneously, so neatly, so perfectly, but God? We were on cloud nine! This was fantastic! We were enjoying the ride.

The next day the emails began again. This time they were all about John. Minister Smith had not liked his interpretation of events, and so John was now in the firing line as well. Yet, he had the courage to continue standing with us. We thought he was wonderful.

- "John, *Lateline* was great! Stephen Smith actually admitted to the bullying and harassment and what Monica came in and said afterwards was fantastic - about our only avenue being a Senate inquiry - and fairly said not said in an intimidating way. This is something they just will not want, but what other option is there?" Crystal.
- "I thought overall, it was better or had more punch than the first one. I am waiting to see what happens from here." Linda.

- "John, I was on such a high last night and did so appreciate the brilliant way you put it all together. Keep up the good work because we SO need your voice to get the truth out there!" Janice.

- "John, that was excellent. You put it together beautifully. I loved it. You are so good at what you do!" Monica.

- "I got a hard time from them yesterday. They reckon I took the Minister out of context. They said his statements related to clearances only, not bullying." John.

- "We know the context was correct, John! I believe, eventually, they will have to admit we've stated the truth about everything all along." Janice.

- "This is just another example of the Minister not getting his facts right. How many are there now, John? So many! If anyone has taken anything out of context - they have! Defence has taken our complaints about discrimination and constant bullying way out of context, dismissing them as mere management troubles. Not so!" Monica.

- "I want to keep talking to people ex-DSA. ASIO reckon they have no problems with DSA. That is laughable." John.

UNCOVERING THE SOURCE OF THE PROBLEM

The following Saturday morning, I met Crystal for coffee in a small out of the way pastry shop in the inner city. She was still nervous about being seen in public with me, so we took a table amongst swaying palms in the brick-wall enclosed tropical garden out the back.

"Can you believe this week?" I asked, slicing a warm honey and almond pastry in half and sliding the halves onto the two separate plates provided.

"I was blown away by the Interpol story," said Crystal coming straight to the point.

"It couldn't have come at a better time..."

"John asked me if DSA did his clearance," said Crystal, giving me a seriously meaningful look.

I understood that look. The analyst look! The look you give when you know it is entirely unethical to comment. "What did you tell him?" I asked.

"That I couldn't tell him even if I knew."

I nodded. "I told him the same thing."

"I think it's hard for him to understand there is still a line we can't cross," said Crystal. "But the good thing is there are things we *can* talk about."

"And need to..." I agreed.

"You, know, Monica, four years ago it was not like this," she said. "Four years ago, we could ask questions, learn, and everything was transparent. That has all changed. Now, to have the Minister sitting there and publicly saying the change has not carried over to AGSVA is a disgrace."

"Why did it all change four years ago?" I asked, "do you know?"

"It all suddenly happened to go pear-shaped just before a review of all the vetting agencies was done in 2008, which led to the new clearance processes being introduced," Crystal explained. "The review found DSA didn't have the structure, focus, skills or capability necessary to meet Australia's security needs."

"But it had up until that point?" I asked.

"Yes," said Crystal. "Everything was going smoothly. Vetting was being done on time, and there was no bullying. DSA was a genuinely nice place to work."

"What happened?"

"We got a new CSO, and he wanted to rid DSA of its vetting services and pass them off into one centralised agency."

"AGSVA!"

"Yes! That review was used as the basis for arguing we needed AGSVA, a centralised vetting agency for the whole of Australia."

"Hence the competition, to see which State would be chosen as the central office," I said.

"That's when everything started to change, the new procedures began to be introduced, and the bullying started. It was slow at first, but by the time you came, it was in full swing," said Crystal.

"This explains everything," I said.

"Don't take my word for it," said Crystal, "I have an article here," she handed me an old newspaper clip, and I scanned it as she kept speaking.

> *Under the new CSO, DSA would become largely a policy, threat assessment and security advice coordination agency, with security clearances off-loaded to another agency.* (The Australian, 30 Aug. 2008)

"Was this when DSA started charging for clearances?" I asked. "That was a question John asked me, which I couldn't answer."

"Yes. We didn't charge for clearances before that review," said Crystal.

"So, that's when the middle-man got involved."

"What middle-man?"

"Dora told me that a company - I think it's a foreign company - set up the new clearance process for Defence. Every clearance that goes through agency staff earns them a commission."

"So, that's why they brought you all in and all but took vetting out of our hands," said Crystal.

I nodded. "And that's why they wanted to keep us separated - so you analysts wouldn't find out."

"And that has led to all the bullying," said Crystal with a deep sigh.

I shook my head. "All this brutality and sleight of hand has been about making money."

Crystal looked at me with big, sad eyes. "So, that's why I think it's all being rubber-stamped at the highest levels."

Now we both understood.

"And yet the Defence response through Stephen Smith is to feign ignorance of the problem," said Crystal. "They know the truth - they just refuse to be honest about what they're doing."

"And they call *us* liars!" I said.

"On that subject, I got a call from his office yesterday." Crystal looked like she was saving the best for last.

"Smith's office?" I smiled. "When were you going to tell me this little bit of news?"

She smiled back at me. "I'm telling you now!"

It was now lunchtime, so we ordered more coffee and a light lunch. Had we actually been talking for two hours? It felt like ten minutes.

"Why did the Minister's office phone you?" I asked while we waited for our order.

"About my complaint of 'unacceptable behaviour'," she said. "We were on the phone for a while, and I told this fellow plainly that the bullying of staff was continuing, not just towards me but towards a lot of other staff as well."

"Were they interested?" I asked, "or was it just a 'we-have-the-Senator-on-our-back-so-we-have-to-look-like-we-care' call?"

Crystal laughed. "You got it in one," she said. "I gave him enough detail to get him interested, told him about agency staff being moved if they talk to Defence personnel."

"That's still happening?" I asked.

"It's never stopped, Monica. Even a few heads rolling hasn't made any difference," Crystal said. "Anyway, the guy from the Minister's Office told me that kind of behaviour was not acceptable."

"Which means nothing, of course..."

"Then he told me I'd made some serious allegations," said Crystal, "you know how they say it like it's a threat, and you're going to be in serious trouble for making any allegations at all, well that's how he sounded."

I shook my head, "They want their brand new, bright and shiny, money-making AGSVA, Crystal. But it's not bright and shiny - the rot continues..."

"He asked if the illegal falsification of documents is still happening, even after the move to AGSVA, so I told him it was worse, but I didn't give him any details."

"And?"

"He wanted to know more, but I wouldn't tell him," said Crystal, "I said the only place I will feel comfortable talking openly is in a Senate Inquiry."

I nodded. "Good on you, Crystal! Now they know why you've been to see a Senator. They know you mean business!"

Our lunch arrived, and we turned our conversation to more pleasant things. But I couldn't help wondering just how obtuse Defence could pretend to be and for how long. How could the Minister's office continue to deny the problem while the Minister himself was openly telling the media the problem existed? What a farce! It was evident that, despite public admissions, Defence had no intention of doing anything to stop the rot.

I remembered Dayle's words, '*The Department of Defence has no power to act illegally, and to allow it to do so would be a criminal offence.*' Minister Smith would know that, yet despite everything that had happened, it was clear that under his hand, the breaches of the law within DSA would continue, without abate! Our only hope was the Senate!

THE SENATE STARTS ASKING QUESTIONS

Two days later, our claims were being discussed in the Senate. When we found out, we were stunned! How does one have a Senate Inquiry without having a Senate Inquiry? The Senators themselves were inquiring! They were asking the hard questions and forcing the issue. Amazing!

Apparently, the Senators wanted to know if Australia's security had been compromised, and more personally, if their individual safety had been compromised. They spent thirty to forty minutes discussing the problems facing Defence because of the issues we had raised on *Lateline*, which had been highlighted by the real-life example of the parliamentary security guard wanted by Interpol.

This would have been a great outcome for us to boast about if we'd been able to plan it, but, of course, we didn't plan it. None of us had prior knowledge that the Senate was discussing DSA until John phoned me at work after the meeting and told me what had happened.

"Hi Monica," I recognised John's voice as soon as I answered the phone, "have you been able to watch the Senate Estimates?" he asked.

"Hi John," I responded, "no, I haven't. I'm at work and don't have access to television."

"The Senators put a bit of pressure on Defence today," he said, "they asked some good questions."

"So, what was the mood?" I asked. I was sceptical but nevertheless hoping John would give me some good news, "were they for or against?"

"I think the Senators were pretty strong actually," John explained, "and it seemed to me like Defence was trying to play it all down."

"What kind of questions were they asking?" I tried to sound casual. I didn't want to seem pushy.

"They wanted to know if DSA was doing checks for ministerial staff," said John, "They said that in the light of what has happened recently, there seems to be good reason to ask questions about the security process."

I started to laugh, a happy sort of chuckle, "So the right people are starting to ask the right questions."

"You should download the transcript off the net. I think this is important," said John.

"You don't have a transcript, John?" I asked, knowing he would pass it on if he could.

"No, I only have a video copy," he said, "I'll have to wait for the Hansard to become available."

"Okay," I said, "I'll ask Janice to download it."

"It might take a few days for it to appear on the Senate Estimates website, but when it does, it will give you a lot of detail about the response from Defence. It goes for about thirty to forty minutes. There is quite a lot there."

"Oh, excellent! Are you doing another story tonight, John?"

"Stephen Merchant, the acting Secretary of Defence, did most of the speaking for Defence. I'm going to run some of his comments on *Lateline* tonight. Just a brief mention."

"Let me know if you want me to respond."

"Thanks, Monica," John said. "I think Defence know there are big problems at the AGSVA, and they are trying to fix them before the Inspector-General of Intelligence and Security finds out."

Hello, what was that? A new investigation? "Hold on, John, before who finds out?"

"The Inspector-General of Intelligence and Security is now doing the inquiry," John repeated, "not the Inspector-General of Defence. You didn't know about this?"

"No, it's the first I've heard."

"They are not Defence," said John, "they're an independent authority, so it will be interesting to see what they find."

"John, I'm in the dark here," I was painfully aware he was looking for information from me, but instead, I was the one receiving the information. "I need to read the transcript; otherwise, I just don't know what to tell you."

"No worries, Monica, I'm only doing a brief mention tonight. We'll talk again after you've read the Hansard."

"Thanks for the 'heads-up', John."

When I got home that evening, I did an internet search to see what I could find out about the IGIS. What I found out was impressive.

The Inspector-General of Intelligence and Security (IGIS), Dr Vivienne Thom, and her small, hand-picked team of investigators were Australia's Intelligence Agency watchdog. Her office was superior in authority to Defence and all of Australia's security organisations, including ASIO. Her authority came not from the elected Government but from the Attorney General, and her reports were for the Prime Minister's eyes only. If the Prime Minister chose not to make any particular IGIS report public, it remained a secret document.

Dr Thom's role as IGIS was elite, so elite her job had its own Act, the IGIS Act, which gave the Inspector-General of Intelligence and Security immense power to compel people to appear before her, equivalent to that of a Royal Commission. This was great news for us! It meant we could speak openly and honestly without fear of prosecution.

Suddenly, we had everything we wanted. It had only been two weeks since our first *Lateline* appearance, and things were moving super fast. Senators were enquiring, and the Prime Minister had intervened and set up an investigative forum with the power to hear our claims, order changes and protect us from prosecution. Things were definitely looking up! This was fantastic news! The only problem was Defence didn't like it!

DEFENCE MUDDIES THE EVIDENCE

When I watched Lateline that night and heard Stephen Merchant's comments, I realised Defence was not going to simply admit they had done the wrong thing and fix the problem. Oh no! That would've been too simple! Instead, they would try and save face - by putting the blame on us!

Defence couldn't claim that we were lying anymore or that the problems didn't exist because their own cursory examination of the files had shown the problems were there. On top of that, a real-life example meant they couldn't brush it under the carpet. But neither could they face the embarrassment of admitting they had made such a colossal mess of Australia's National Security! So, they had to find a way to dodge the inevitable bullets, and they found it! Or so they thought!

In the Senate, they strongly implied the damage was limited to the clearances handled by three incompetent people. We three whistleblowers!

> *From the examination of the packs that were touched by the three contractors who appeared on Lateline, we estimate that about 1,500 clearances were touched by those contractors.* (Stephen Merchant, Senate, 30 May 2012)

How predictable! How transparent they were! We had seen this coming way back in the garden when we were sitting around the yellow cloth, wondering why Defence wanted to hire extremely short-term agency staff to do the work we did. There had only been one answer then, '*so that agency staff could get the blame if something went wrong',* and that answer had just been proven correct. It was only theory way back then, but now it had become a reality.

Didn't they know how see-through they were? If a few lowly contractors, who were literally the 'bottom of the pile' in DSA, could so easily see through them, how breezy would it be for Australia's enemies to use them? This was not a good look for the Australian intelligence community!

Stephen Merchant's carefully chosen words were derogatory and highly offensive to us and were supposed to be! 'Touched' was a colourful word when used the way it was used against us in the Senate. It made us sound dirty - as if anything our vile hands 'touched' would be tainted. It conjured up a picture in my mind of investigators wearing white coats, face masks and protective gloves, picking up our filthy clearances with tweezers so that our germs wouldn't contaminate them. It also made 'those contractors' sound like we were different from all the other contractors and somehow creepily contagious. Good one, guys!

Yet, the only thing different about us was that, of the one hundred and fifty or more agency staff who had passed through DSA during 2009 to 2011, we were the only three who had publicly admitted the problem existed. We were doing Australia a massive favour by sticking our necks out, but here we were, being crucified for coming forward.

The emails began to flow again, mainly from John, who was full of questions and keen to gauge our response to Mr Merchant's statements.

- "They are basically arguing the only clearance packs which need to be re-checked were packs done by you three. I asked Defence Media if those 1500 checks included other staff as well. Their official written response to the ABC was, *The 1500 clearances are those which Defence records show were 'touched' by the three former DSA contractors."* John.
- "I think it's pretty obvious they are coming after us now, John...want to say we are the only ones who 'filled in the gaps' and falsified documents since they are only looking at the ones we 'touched'." Monica.
- "Blaming us...I guess that is to be expected... but can't they see the writing on the wall? They are going to look so stupid when the truth finally comes out." Janice.
- "Defence said they only needed to re-check the clearances done by you three...not by anyone else. Were there only 1500?" John.
- "There were tens of thousands, John. My estimate would be at least 40,000, maybe more. Looks like they're still just trying to water it down...cover it up." Monica.
- "So why are they only checking the ones done by you three?" John.
- "No one else has gone public! There weren't any faces to the statements about AGSVA and the confirmation letter that you read out on 25th, John, so they are completely disregarding them!" Janice.

- "They don't know who the others are, John, or how many. So, of course, they're going to point the finger at us! Very cowardly of them, though, it takes courage to admit when you're wrong. It's terrible for us to see just how lacking in courage our Defence bureaucrats are - what hope Australia?" Monica.
- "The number of affected clearances is too high to be blamed on just three people. The proof is in the database." Janice.
- "Do you think it could be just classic Public Relations - damage control?" John.
- "Definitely damage control. I think they are running - but running around in circles. Have you ever heard of a high-level investigation being ordered one week and cancelled the next? Just laughable!" Monica.
- "But do you think the new inquiry might be better than the last one?" John.
- "Yes, I do. This is a statutory body - the forum we have been waiting for! No fear of persecution or prosecution! Completely independent and answerable only to the Prime Minister - not to Defence! It's good news for us, John." Monica.
- "I checked with Dayle...he agrees." Janice.
- "It's entrenched behaviour, and systematic corruption, John, and all the clearances were affected. When you calculate the number of applications done over two or three years, you'll find the number that needs to be re-checked. It's not rocket science!" Monica.
- "Is that why Merchant is saying, 'I think it's important we don't jump to worst-case conclusions here...'?" John.

- "Absolutely! They already know...they just don't want anyone else to know they know... including the Senate, obviously." Monica.
- "The Defence advantage is that no one wants to believe it...not even the staff who still work there...most of them still can't believe they've been doing anything wrong...they believe it's okay to falsify documents as long as they are just following orders." Janice.
- "Defence are very good at convincing staff that lying and deception are a normal part of their job. Here's hoping the Senators will see through the lies. We certainly need them to keep asking the right questions. We need a Senate Inquiry!" Monica.
- "Thanks, guys." John.
- "No probs, John." Monica.

CONTACTING SENATOR DAVID JOHNSTON

When the Senate Hansard proof became available a few days later, Janice downloaded it and sent a copy to me. Before I had a chance to read it, she phoned.

"We've found our Senator!" she sounded as if she had just won the lottery.

Her excitement was contagious, but I had no idea what she was talking about, "What do you mean, Janice?"

"It's in the Hansard," she explained, "there is one Senator who is asking all the right questions."

I still didn't know what she was talking about, so I opened the Hansard document on my computer screen. "What page number are you looking at?"

"Page 32, I looked him up. He's not just a Senator; he's the shadow minister for Defence!" said Janice, sounding very pleased with herself.

As she was talking, I was reading, and I liked what I was seeing.

Senator Johnston's questions were clear, direct and to the point, but more than that, he sounded keen to get answers and was quick with further comments when he didn't like the answers given. "Great find, Janice. I think you're right!"

"I know he's the Shadow Minister, so he's obliged to ask questions, but I think there's something more." Janice continued.

"I can see what you mean," I agreed. I was reading his questions and comments. It may have been his role to play 'devil's advocate', but that was precisely what we needed. "He certainly gets to the point, exactly what we need! What State is he in?"

"Western Australia," said Janice.

"Too far away for an introductory visit..."

"I was thinking of sending him an outline of everything that's been going on." Janice continued.

"Okay, but our approach has to be in line with his portfolio," I said.

"What do you mean?"

"He can only act within the bounds of the authority afforded by his office," I continued. "We can't throw everything at him because he won't be able to use most of it."

"Can't we just ask him to lead a Senate Inquiry?" said Janice.

"No, it's not that simple," I said. "We have to give him something he can use, something which will help him do his job, and I think that something is in the Hansard. Have you noticed the answers that were given to his questions?"

"Yes, not entirely accurate," said Janice. "Reading them made me quite angry."

"Exactly!" I said. "They're lying to the Senate! They don't want the Senators to know the truth."

"I thought it was an offence to lie to the Senate," said Janice.

"That's our reason for writing," I said.

"To let Senator Johnston know he's been lied to?" asked Janice.

"Yes! Maybe we should put the whole sorry saga into a report," I said, 'there's so much of it."

"That would be a mighty big report," said Janice, chuckling.

"Not if we limit it to the questions and answers written in the Hansard," I said. "We could do two reports, yours and mine, two different viewpoints of the same pack of lies."

Janice agreed, "yes, let's do it."

Over the next few days, we each went over the Senate transcript with a fine-tooth comb. Senator Johnston had asked some probing questions, but the answers given by Stephen Merchant and the DSA Chief Security Officer (CSO), Frank Roberts, were not accurate at all. They were, in fact, totally misleading. Yet how would the Senators know Defence was lying to them unless someone else came along with proof of those lies?

So, that was the information we decided to collate and send to Senator Johnston; proof that what the Senators had been told was not true. When our reports were done, we met for coffee.

"I've been thinking that before we send these reports, we should 'test the waters' with a short letter," I said.

"I've already written one," said Janice. "I sent it off a few days ago. I got so 'hot under the collar' when reading the lies, I couldn't help writing straight away."

"Did you get a response?"

"Yes! Not from Senator Johnston, but from his Media Advisor, Rebecca," said Janice, "just a general 'thank you for your email' response."

"Excellent, Janice! He doesn't need both of us writing to him, so it would probably be best if we followed the same procedure we used with Dayle."

"Do you want me to be the 'front' person again?" asked Janice.

I nodded. "Yes, you're good at that kind of thing. And you've already got the ball rolling."

Janice beamed. "I have, haven't I?"

THE IGIS INVESTIGATION BEGINS

The following week, we were each personally contacted by Dr Vivienne Thom, Inspector-General of Intelligence and Security, first by letter informing us she would like to interview us, and then by phone to invite us to speak with her about our concerns. Her tone was so nice, so pleasant and so professional, it was hard to imagine just how much power and authority this one woman had.

As soon as I found out there was an IGIS Act, I read the Act. So, when Dr Thom phoned, I was well aware of the legalities attached to that simple phone call. Dr Thom's formal powers included the authority to 'compel' people to appear before her. In reality, once we had been notified of a meeting, it was an offence to ignore the notice. The Act was very clear; six months jail and a $2,000 fine for anyone failing to appear once they had called to appear.

In short, if any of us now failed to meet with Dr Thom as planned, we would be arrested and jailed. No questions asked! Wow!

The interview would be conducted under oath and, though less formal than a courtroom, the Inspector-General had far more power than a judge. Being interviewed by her was akin to giving evidence before a Royal Commission.

Though we welcomed the freedom to speak openly about everything we had experienced, we were each well aware of her immense authority.

"Do you think the IGIS will try to muzzle us? Confidentially and all that?" asked Owen. We were standing in the car park outside the Springwood Community Centre. It was nearly time for our 'pre-IGIS interview' appointment with our Barrister.

Janice nodded. "I was wondering the same thing. Once we tell them what we know, we might not be able to talk about it to anyone else."

I shook my head. "No! I don't believe they could do that. We can check that one with Dayle, but I don't believe they could stop us from telling our story. This is our story! These are our complaints! If we don't like the way this is handled, then we are free to take our complaints elsewhere. *We* have requested this, not the other way around!"

"Well, that may be true, but I'm still glad I have sent everything through to Senator Johnston," said Janice.

"Have you sent your report yet, Monica?" asked Owen.

"No, not yet, it's finished, all fifteen pages, but I am still rechecking the facts. I'll get it to him before the IGIS interview," I said, "that way, if the IGIS freezes our interview information, at least we'll know we can still quote what we told the Senator."

"It's nearly time," said Owen referring to our interview with Dayle, "do you think we could pray before we go in?" He didn't have to ask twice. We needed Godly guidance now, more than ever. There in the car park, we took a moment to pray.

The truth is we were not sure what to expect from the IGIS. Up to this point, all we had seen from any government authority was lies, deception and trickery. Ministers were covering things up as a matter of course, the law was being broken daily, and no one in authority wanted to know about it. The top people in Defence and Defence Security were lying to the Senate, and legal traps were constantly being laid for anyone who wanted to say, 'hey, this is wrong'. On top of that, the stark reality was that Defence was currently setting the three of us up to take the fall for their mess.

It was not so far fetched for us to believe the only reason we were being asked to appear before the IGIS was so we could be forced to stop talking to the media, and everyone else, about the gaping hole in Australia's National Security. Furthermore, we were not sure whether our meeting with the Inspector-General of Intelligence and Security would take the form of interview or interrogation.

We honestly didn't know what to expect. So, prayer was our most sensible course of action. It kept us focussed and calm and got each of us through the next few days.

If the small-scale social experiment we lived through seems hauntingly like the 'new norm' for people currently questioning government over-reach during the COVID crisis, you would be correct. It's not just similar. It's a large-scale replica!

Now, ordinary Australians crying out against enforced experimental drug therapies, questionable laws and restrictions, and excessive brutality to enforce illegally imposed government mandates are made to look like criminals only fit for prison. Where do you go when your government is your enemy? The current government has ensured the unvaccinated can't work or leave the country!

A LIGHT IN THE DARKNESS

Thankfully, not everyone in power is the enemy. Mercifully there are always people who respect our Constitution, and when we find them, those people are like a light shining in the darkness.

Dr Thom was one such light. She was not our enemy. Her manner was both professional and kind. What a contrast to the brutal horror we had become used to when dealing with Defence officials. Our individual, two-hour interviews with one of the most powerful people in Australia came and went. We were grateful it was not an interrogation!

Though I am still under oath not to reveal anything discussed in that meeting, I was assured by Dr Thom and Dayle there was no confidentiality clause. We were all free to continue speaking about our concerns to each other and to the media, albeit within the bounds of established law.

Finally! Someone who was playing according to the rules! It was a bit of a shock, really. At first, I was not sure how to handle it. It took me a while to just relax and trust that Dr Thom was on the straight and narrow and would not be using her power to promote or cover Defence corruption.

DEFENCE TRIES TO BLAME US - AGAIN

While the IGIS investigation was in progress, things were quiet. Everyone, it seemed, was waiting to see what the IGIS would find. Everyone except Senator Johnston!

In September, Senator Johnston sent out a media release insisting that Minister Smith immediately make public the findings of the previous investigation - the 'nine-day' wonder - done by the Inspector-General of Defence.

- "The Parliament needs to get to the bottom of this. In Senate Estimates, in May, the committee was assured by Defence officials and the government that this was a bit of a storm in a teacup, but it is clear I was misled."
- "This is not what I was told by a whistleblower, but I took the evidence of the Defence officials at face value."
- "The Minister needs to explain exactly who is being held accountable for this unbelievable set of circumstances where Defence has potentially left our bases and embassies vulnerable to security breaches."
- "The security breach is now so serious that the Minister has recommended the Prime Minister refer the Inspector-General of Defence's report to the independent Inspector-General of Intelligence and Security for investigation."

During those few quiet months, it had gradually become apparent to everyone involved, Defence, the Senate, Ministers and the media, that the scale of the problem was so widespread and had been going on for so long it could not possibly be attributed to three short-term contractors.

The Minister for Defence, Stephen Smith, now had no choice but to finally admit publicly that there were serious problems, affecting a massive number of clearances.

We had said all along that there was an extreme risk to Australia's National Security. We had said that tens of thousands of clearances had been corrupted. Now, finally, Minister Smith was publicly agreeing with us.

> *I don't want to put a figure out to alarm people, but as a general rule of thumb, the security vetting agency will see in any year somewhere between 40,000 and 50,000 security assessments done. So we are not talking about every assessment, we are only talking about those affected by deficiencies in procedures.* (Minister Smith, ABC Sept. 2011)

He didn't want to alarm people? The numbers were huge! He was only giving numbers for one year, yet the problem had been going on for at least two years and possibly three years. He was talking upwards of 100,000 to 150,000, possibly compromised clearances! And the only way to tell which clearances had been corrupted was to check each paper application against the information stored on the database. In other words, 150,000 clearances would need to be rechecked - by hand!

We knew the ratio of affected clearances was about 40% of the total, so the number of corrupted applications would probably be around 20,000 per year, as we had suggested, translating to approximately 60,000 corrupted files over three years. The problem was enormous!

Nevertheless, to our gob-smacked amazement, Defence continued to try and play it down. The facts were impossible to hide, they couldn't deny the risk anymore, and they could no longer prosecute us for breach of the Secrecy Act, so they came up with yet another angle with a completely new tactic, which would put the blamed back onto us - again! Unbelievable! Why couldn't they simply admit they had caused this problem and fix it?

At this point, Defence began to downplay the seriousness of the problem. They didn't want the media to focus on 60,000 security breaches, so instead of assuring Australians they would get on top of the mess, they belittled our part in the clearance process, making our role sound so trivial and insignificant it could not affect the end result. This made our allegations seem naive and unwarranted, despite the confirmed size and seriousness of the risk to National Security.

Their turn of phrase made us seem like we were too stupid to understand the complete process and were unaware of secret 'workaround' agreements with ASIO. It didn't seem to matter that the workarounds they mentioned didn't actually exist. Who would know? How could the media check?

- "I think it is important to understand that the errors made were essentially errors at the beginning of the data entry process, and there are very many layers to the security assessment." Stephen Smith.

It was like we were banging our heads against a brick wall. We knew that the 'errors' could only happen at the end of the process. But the media didn't! So the media became the focus of the Defence manipulation. They fed them outright lies!

Has the government been doing the same thing to their paid media puppets during COVID? Have they been using the media to lie to the Australian people? Why else would they pay them?

Stephen Smith made the ASIO database rejections sound like simple clerical errors made by inept contractors at the beginning of the process, which more experienced staff could correct later. He took the focus off the glaring reality that the errors were still there! Again, the Minister for Defence was deliberately spreading public misinformation.

From the very beginning of this totally avoidable debacle, all levels of Defence had continually misled the Australian people about the seriousness of DSA's breach of security. Yet, in all their frantic activity, they forgot one very simple thing; they were supposed to be serving Australia's interests, not their own.

- We had said many security clearances were compromised, riddled with false data, or approved despite missing information. Defence representatives told the media what we were saying was not correct. Then (oops) evidence was found that many security clearances had indeed been compromised.

- We had said we told a previous investigation about the risk to Australia's National Security. The minister told the media we had only mentioned it 'in passing'. Then (oops), both the media and the Senate were shown we had detailed our concerns in writing and had been completely ignored.

- We had said security guards were a definite risk. The minister told the media we were wrong, that the security risk was extremely low. Then (oops), a criminal wanted by Interpol for seven years was found working as a security guard for the Queensland Parliament. And people began to ask, "How many more are out there?"
- We had said there were multiple thousands of corrupted clearances. Defence told the media and Senate they would only need to check the clearances 'touched' by 'those' whistleblowers. Then (oops) a thorough investigation showed the number of corrupted clearances was so high they were afraid to tell the Australian public the truth.
- We had said there were multiple thousands of corrupted clearances. Defence told the media and Senate they would only need to check the clearances 'touched' by 'those' whistleblowers. Then (oops) a thorough investigation showed the number of corrupted clearances was so high they were afraid to tell the Australian public the truth.

Thankfully none of the Defence rhetoric had fooled the astute reporters at *Lateline* for a minute, and they continued to ask probing questions, questions the Minister for Defence could not answer. "How worried should the Australian public be?" How worried indeed! Good question!

> *Minister Smith, we're talking about serious maladministration; at this point, a remedial process is only just getting underway, checks which are only just starting. How worried should the Australian public be?*
> (Ali Moore ABC Lateline, 20 Sept. 2011)

Did they really
think they
could deceive ASIO?

CHAPTER EIGHT

ASIO fooled? Nup! They knew!

During the gap between Senate meetings, May to October 2011, 'workarounds' became the new media buzzword. Instead of talking about ways to plug the gaping hole in Australia's National Security, Defence told the media that there was nothing to see; that fabricated phrases like 'Fake Street', 'Green Street' and 'Unknown Street' were used to fill gaps in information as a matter of course.

They gave the strong impression there was nothing wrong with 'making things up' and implied all workarounds used had been approved by ASIO.

Ironically, this very tactic proved our point! We had said DSA staff had been deceived into believing 'making things up' was okay; that it was standard procedure. And now Defence was using the same deception on the Australian people, telling the Senate, the media and everyone else, very convincingly, that it was okay to 'make things up', it was procedure. ASIO, however, was not amused!

ASIO denied any knowledge of the 'Fake Street', 'Green Street' and 'Unknown Street' style of workarounds supposedly approved by them for use within DSA, stating they were not aware of them, and no such approval was documented.

The ASIO denial of the publicised DSA workarounds had a profound effect. Defence had been caught in a lie.

In September 2011, just four short months after we had first appeared on *Lateline,* it was announced via *Lateline*, that both the head of DSA, Frank Roberts, and the acting Secretary of Defence, Stephen Merchant, had taken the unusual step of writing to the Senate revising their statements about workarounds. They had both admitted the procedural workarounds they had referred to when questioned did not officially exist.

That same night it was announced that Stephen Merchant had suddenly resigned his position as Deputy Secretary of Intelligence and Security and, despite his 34 years with Defence, would not be seeking any future position within Defence or the Intelligence community.

A few minutes later, on the same program, when questioned in a live interview, Stephen Smith, Minister for Defence, claimed he had no knowledge of this high profile resignation.

The ship was sinking, no doubt about it. There was nothing left to do now but jump ship or drown. Drastic career choices were being made, and the IGIS investigation had not even been concluded, let alone released.

THE CORRUPTION CONTINUES UNABATED

On a beautiful, sunny midwinter's day, the original four gathered for a catch-up picnic. I pulled out the yellow cloth and threw it over one end of a rectangular picnic table. We all smiled. The memories were bitter-sweet.

Jennifer opened the subject, "So, how are things in DSA land, Cass?"

Cassie smiled, a rueful kind of smile, "Nothing has changed," she said, "well, not for the better."

"What's going on Cass?" I asked.

Cassie didn't answer straight away. We knew she wasn't trying to be evasive. We understood it was difficult to go from not being allowed to talk about work at all, to talking openly. It was a completely different mindset, and she would just need a moment to adjust.

"It's been so confusing lately," she said, "I don't want to sound paranoid, but I think they have been deliberately mean to me."

"What did you do?" asked Jennifer. "You must have said or done something they didn't like."

A rueful grin slowly spread across Cassie's face, "Yes I did, actually. I stood up for you guys." Seeing the inquisitive looks on our faces, Cassie explained. "A few weeks ago the CSO, Frank Roberts, came through and asked the agency staff if we had ever filled in the gaps on clearances or been bullied by Defence staff. He said we could see him privately if we didn't want to speak openly."

"So you went to see him?" I asked.

Cassie nodded.

We all groaned.

"When I went to see him, he asked who had told me to fill in gaps with 'fake street', 'green street' etc. and if we were ever given any printed procedures. I told him I'd never heard of those streets and that agency staff had to fill in gaps, and it didn't matter what we used to fill them. I also told him how you guys were bullied and about other bullying I've seen."

"Oh,"he wouldn't have liked that," said Jennifer.

"Oh, no, he was nice," said Cassie, jumping to his defence, "he didn't know about any of this."

We all laughed and shook our heads. "He knows everything Cassie," I said, "He's known about all of it, right from the beginning."

"He's the top cocky, Cass, he's the one who ordered it and wants to cover it up," said Jennifer.

Cassie shook her head. "No, he's not like that."

"He's currently lying to the Senate and the media about workarounds, Cassie," I said, "he's fishing for proof that the workarounds were official."

"Oh, that makes sense," Cassie said, with understanding dawning on her face.

"What do you mean?" asked Janice.

"I guess that's why the Defence staff are all running around like chooks without heads trying to find old procedure notes. I thought it was just because the CSO wanted copies." Cassie was finally beginning to see.

Janice and I glanced at each other and grinned. This was excellent news! We had written to the Senate via Senator Johnson about the non-existent workarounds, and now the Senate was obviously asking the right questions.

"They won't find anything," Janice said.

"The thing that tickles me is the irony!" I said, "DSA never write anything down, and that's the problem now! It's because they don't write anything down that they don't have any proof for their own statements!"

"Without documents," Janice continued, "the Senate will know they've lied."

"Not very bright, for an 'intelligence' organisation, are they?" said Jennifer.

We all laughed. It felt good to laugh at the ineptitude of our antagonists.

"Well, I'm glad I'm out of there now!" said Cassie, dropping a bombshell in her own quiet and casual way.

We stopped laughing and turned to face Cassie. "When did this happen?" Janice asked.

"Yesterday! I came in, and someone else's purse was on my desk." Cassie continued. "They told me desks were reserved for permanent Defence staff, not agency. So, I didn't have anywhere to sit."

Janice nodded, "sounds familiar..."

"Did this begin before or after you spoke to the CSO?" asked Jennifer.

Cassie's eyes registered understanding, the penny had dropped. "It was just after..." she said, slowly realising the CSO had betrayed her confidence. Betrayed *her*.

"So what's been going on Cass, what have they been doing to you?" asked Janice.

"Well, I was officially told by email from the agency that I'm regarded as an underachiever because I'm not reaching target," she stopped and smiled. "The target is now twenty per day."

"Twenty a day!" gasped Jennifer, "no one can do twenty a day! I was flat out doing ten!"

"So, you don't check information against the previous file anymore?" I said, remembering my eighteen per day record - only possible because I didn't check anything at all.

Cassie shook her head. "That's the new rule, we don't check anything, all we do is push them through and send the ASIO report," said Cassie.

I was flabbergasted, "they're up to their ears in investigations, being scrutinised from every angle, and they're still doing this?" I couldn't believe they could be so impervious to decency. "What's wrong with these people?"

"And Con, fixes all the errors!" said Janice. I wonder if he knows how much trouble he will be in when this all comes out into the open."

"I have a confession to make Cass," I said, "I already knew you had resigned. Crystal emailed me last night and told me Defence staff were officially informed you were let go because you had been speaking to Defence personnel without permission."

Cassie's relaxed smile disappeared as she realised they had not just betrayed her confidence and deceived her, but they lied about her as well.

"Are they still enforcing that?" asked Jennifer, "after all that's happened?" She shook her head. There were no words.

"Horrible, horrible, place..." said Janice.

THE MEDIA FINALLY CATCH ON

Cassie had just confirmed to us the bullying of staff and corruption of data was still continuing, even after all the complaints, all the media coverage, even after multiple and continual, tax-payer funded, investigations. It was beyond understanding – simply mind-boggling! Her personal experience showed that both the bullying and corruption of data was now, in fact, even more intense within the new AGSVA than it had been in DSA.

On top of that, the head of DSA, Frank Roberts, the man who took control of DSA in 2008 and announced he didn't want security clearances done by DSA anymore, the man who, alongside Stephen Merchant, had lied to the Senate about the corruption of data, this man was still pretending to agency staff that he was ignorant of what was happening in regard to bullying and the corruption of applications.

What was it going to take to stop this corruption? Didn't these people care about the security of our military who were putting their lives on the line, trusting that the people around them were also trustworthy? Didn't they care about our bases, our airports, our embassies? Didn't they care that ASIO was being fed so much miss-information they wouldn't be able to sort the truth from the lies?

The worst thing about this whole mess was the knowledge that it was absolutely, disgustingly, blatently and without a doubt, deliberate!

At the same time he was pretending to the DSA/AGSVA staff he was ignorant of the problem and 'innocently' asking if anyone had 'filled in gaps', the head of DSA, Frank Roberts, was being quoted in the media as saying workarounds were a monitored and acceptable part of the security process.

As you would imagine, the media came knocking on our doors to find out if we agreed with the official Defence position. We didn't!

- "Contrary to statements made to the Senate by Mr Stephen Merchant and Mr Frank Roberts, 'workarounds' were not discussed with agency staff during the time of my employment," said Janice to Dan Oakes from the Sydney Morning Herald pointing out the fabricated data was unsupervised and haphazard.

- "The Minister for Defence, Stephen Smith said whistleblowers had only been involved at the beginning of the clearance process." Dan Oaks said, more as a question than a statement.

- "That's the very point!" Janice responded, "When the early stages have errors, errors that haven't been flagged by previously accepted workarounds, how can anyone working in the following stages recognise the error and follow them up? If ASIO is looking for agreed workarounds and not finding them, how can ASIO know what is right and what is wrong?" (SMH July 14, 2011)

  The headlines began to roll:

- Govt ignored faked security clearance claims!
- Fake data used to rush 'top secret' clearances!
- Defence led up 'fake street'!
- Illusory entries were workarounds!
- Contractor challenges Defence testimony!
- Years of faking of Defence security clearances!
- Thousands of security clearances compromised!
- Defence admits need to re-check clearances!

The ABC radio reporter, Michael Edwards, was also asking about 'workarounds' and interviewed Senator Johnston and me by phone on live radio.

- "We were not told about 'workarounds'. The information we entered, whether it was true or false, once introduced, couldn't be checked by anyone else down the line unless it was flagged as a problem. We didn't flag anything." Monica.

- "Opposition Defence spokesman David Johnston says he's almost too frightened to think about the possible ramifications," Michael Edwards.
- "We have embassies, foreign dignitaries, all coming to Australia, all being the subject of people with security clearances doing fundamental jobs like servicing the aircraft and doing all these sorts of things, it is very concerning that this problem has come to the point that it has because it was ignored for so long." Senator Johnston.

Despite the media coverage, the questions from the Senate, and an investigation being conducted under the authority of the Governor General, Defence continued to bury its head in the sand, and Minister Smith continued to publically support the false testimonials to the Senate of both Stephen Merchant and DSA CSO, Frank Roberts.

> *A spokesman for the Defence Minister, Stephen Smith, says that Senator Johnston's assertions are baseless and the Government has taken the matter very seriously since the allegations were first raised.* (John Stewart ABC Lateline, 19 October 2011).

The Department of Defence was so bull-headed! It was determined to betray Australia and Australians. When was it going to end? How was it going to end? Incredible!

For those who hope that our leaders and government bureaucrats, who are currently lying to us about the COVID crisis, will suddenly come to their senses, listen to reason and tell the truth, you are living in a fools paradise. They will not back down until they are forced to back down!

ASIO BACKS AWAY FROM DEFENCE CLAIMS

While the media was running with Defence's 'ASIO knew about workarounds' propaganda, the reality behind the scenes was that ASIO was not amused! The ASIO heads began to distance themselves from the Defence claims by making direct statements, not to the media, but to the IGIS and the Senate.

Prior to the completion of her investigation, and because of the statements made to the media by senior Defence officials, Dr Thom directly asked ASIO to forward relevant documentation to her and to answer a few direct questions like, "Was ASIO aware of the workarounds and, were they documented?" The response from ASIO to Dr Thom was swift and very clear:

- ASIO has not now, and has not previously, agreed to such workarounds."
- "ASIO's position now, as in the past, remains that full and accurate information is required to undertake its security assessment role."
- "Further, because the prescribed workarounds were not known or agreed to by ASIO, ASIO was not in a position to know that modified information was being sent and therefore that it needed to be 'corrected'."
- "ASIO's advice is that the impact of many of the workarounds described is 'potentially significant'." (IGIS report, 2012 page 46)

From this information, Dr Thom concluded, *"There is little doubt the integrity of the data passed from the DSA to ASIO during the period 2008 to 31 August 2011 has been undermined."* (IGIS Report, 2012 page 47)

Despite all the Defence denials, side stepping, accusations and game playing, the truth was beginning to break through. The October Senate Estimates Committee Meeting had now become pivotal. Everyone involved was waiting with bated breath; Senators, Defence, ASIO, the media and, of course, we whistleblowers, to hear when Dr Thom would release her full and final report.

The Prime Minister, Julia Gillard, had to read and approve the report for release to the Senate and public via the media. As the days passed, it became clear the Prime Minister would not be receiving the IGIS report in time to read it, evaluate the contents and decide if it should be made public or remain a secret document, prior to October Senate hearing. Nevertheless, the Senate hearing would tell us when and if Dr Thom thought the IGIS report could be completed and released.

SUDDENLY THE GAME IS OVER

The phone rang at work, and a familiar voice greeted me, "Hello, Monica, is this a good time?"

"Hello, John." How casual we had become, like old friends. "Perfect timing, how can I help?"

"There's been a bit of a breakthrough," John sounded like he was holding back information, and finding it hard to contain his enthusiasm, so I knew our story was going to air again, "Both Stephen Merchant and Frank Roberts have retracted their statements to the Senate about workarounds."

I gasped. I didn't see this one coming! "They admitted they lied?" I nearly fell off my chair.

"They each put it in writing," he spoke in a casual tone, but this was huge! "We have the letters, and we are going to air tonight."

"Both of them?" I couldn't get my head around this, I was astounded! "Together?"

"It's good for you guys," John continued, "everything you've said is being validated." He paused then continued, "if this were a game of chess, this would be 'checkmate'."

I laughed, a quiet, sort of stunned laugh. "This is...this is unbelievable John!"

"Merchant wrote...here, let me read it to you," said John. *'On May 30th, I advised the committee that process 'workarounds' used by DSA to overcome the inflexibility of computer applications were documented and managed. However, contrary to my understanding at the time of the estimates hearing, there was no single document or instruction that recorded all of the 'workarounds'. The controls in place to manage and record the process by which data was adjusted by staff were regrettably ineffective and in some cases non-existent.' "*

"Frank Roberts was similar. *'On 30 May I advised the Committee that contractors used accepted entries; "Green Street, Fake Street and Unknown Street". Subsequent investigation indicates that the use of these entries was not agreed either internally in the vetting centre or with ASIO.' "*

"Finally!" I was almost dumbfounded. Almost! "John, what happens when people in responsible positions get caught lying to the Senate?"

"I guess we'll just have to wait and see." John was non-committal, as usual; he was an excellent reporter and very rarely gave a personal opinion. "We're just going to be interviewing Stephen Smith tonight. I want him to comment on these high-level retractions and the real effect of a lack of workarounds on the ASIO data systems."

Wow! What a story! Though I was pleased I was not going to be before a camera again, I knew this was not just a 'heads-up'. John was after information.

"Without workarounds, John, there is no way ASIO can possibly tell the true information from the false. Totally impossible! These admissions show the false DSA data couldn't help but corrupt the ASIO database!"

"From what we are reading in these letters, ASIO didn't know about the workarounds."

"Exactly as we have been saying, John, we didn't know about them either, seems they were so secret, nobody knew about them!" I couldn't help laughing at the absurdity! How stupid! How vault-window mentality! How DSA!

"Senator Johnston is now asking how many clearances ASIO has approved based on false DSA information."

"Good question, John! The cold, hard reality is that if the false data entries had been mere 'workarounds', none of the DSA clearances would now need to be re-checked. Workarounds would be recognised as workarounds, and there wouldn't be a problem."

"That makes sense," said John.

"The fact that Defence has ordered clearances to be re-checked means they *know* there weren't any workarounds. They know! And it also means ASIO now knows they've been sent a whole lot of false information."

"So, we only need to know how big the problem is, how many clearances need to be re-checked," said John, like he was thinking out loud.

"Yes, well, how do you go back and re-check every clearance done over two or three years? Do you know how much that is going to cost, John? I don't even know if it's possible."

"So they won't be able to be done in six months, as stated?"

I laughed again. "Absolutely not, John! We're talking a minimum of two years of clearances hurried through the process by a full staff, which means, proper re-checking of all those clearances will not be able to be physically done by a handful of people in just six months. Maybe if they were only checking the applications we three whistleblowers did, those few could be completed in six months - but the rest - no. Impossible!"

"Have you heard when the IGIS report will be released?" asked John, "will it be made public?"

"No, not a clue," I said, "I'm waiting, like everyone else, on the Senate Estimates hearing and hoping the Prime Minister will approve it for public release."

"Thanks, Monica."

John didn't tell me he had inside information that Stephen Merchant had not just apologised to the Senate but resigned his position as Deputy Secretary of Intelligence and Security. After 34 years with Defence, he had suddenly, inexplicably, chosen to quit his senior intelligence position and find employment outside Defence.

That night, on public television, when Minister Smith was asked by Ali Moore on *Lateline* to comment on Stephen Merchant's sudden departure, he claimed to have no knowledge of the Deputy Secretary's resignation.

- "I understand Stephen Merchant, the Deputy Secretary for Intelligence and Security, who indeed referred to workarounds in those Senate Estimates hearings, I understand he's announced he is leaving his job. Was he told to leave?" Ali Moore.
- "Well, that's...I don't have that advice. I met with the Deputy Secretary of Intelligence and Security today. I've been working closely with Mr Merchant on this matter, and I have not seen..." Minister Smith.
- "But will someone be held accountable? Will someone be held responsible?" Ali Moore.
- "I've had no discussion with Mr Merchant about his intention or any suggestion that he would leave Defence. He's the Acting Secretary of Defence, and he seems to me to be very comfortable and keen to continue his work." Minister Smith.

Two days later a spokesman for Minister Smith announced to the media that Mr Merchant was stepping down from his high position as Acting Secretary of Defence, but said his resignation was unrelated to the security clearance furore.

Of course! Checkmate!

The harsh reality is that only the truth will set people free. It works every time. That's why Defence and all their hangers on tried so hard to cover up the truth.

It's the same with the COVID crisis, today. The propaganda machine is working overtime, fuelled by bribery and corruption at the highest levels of government. But, in the end, the truth will break through and the gross nature of the malfaesance will be seen. It's inevitable!

OUR CHECKMATE VICTORY CAME QUIETLY

There was no official recognition. No public announcement of any kind. All we had was the knowledge that Defence had totally run out of excuses. They had no more moves! They could no longer deny the problem. They could no longer blame us. They could no longer diminish our roles. They could no longer hide from the truth. Their only course now was to face facts and deal with the problem. It was game over. Checkmate indeed!

On public television Defence had admitted total liability for tens of thousands of compromised clearances, senior Defence officials had apologised for misleading the Senate, and the Acting Secretary of Defence had resigned.

Senator Johnston had taken up the reigns and was carrying our fight forward in the Senate, and the IGIS report, which we trusted would also confirm everything we had said, was due to be completed any day. Our fight was over! We had thoroughly and completely won!

We had started our battle with the understanding that no one wins against Defence, yet against all the odds, three ordinary people had done the unthinkable, we had won our battle not just against Defence, but against Defence Intelligence.

Their multiple denials of the problem had not only been shot down, they had been smashed to pieces, and in such a short space of time! Had it had only been six months since we first aired our concerns on *Lateline?* It seemed like a lifetime.

So many things had come together for us in such a short time, things totally outside our knowledge and control that we could only be in awe of our God and his amazing power!

The emails flowed, and the phone rang continually; friends, family, and acquaintances all contacting us to tell us how proud they were of us and how wonderful to see our victory. When the phone calls ceased that night, I emailed John and thanked him for the impressive way he had handled our story. This was his victory as much as ours.

Even now it is hard to put into words the kaleidoscope of feelings which whirled continually that evening; shock, realisation, laughter, tears, amazement, humility, joy, thanks and gratitude mixed with memories of people, places, events, threats, betrayals, surprises, disappointments, prayers and of course victory. So much to absorb! No wonder everything felt so surreal.

The next day, despite my mental elation, physical exhaustion hit me like a brick. I wasn't expecting it. I couldn't control it. Yet it completely enveloped me, so that I couldn't even speak.

I didn't know I was so emotionally exhausted until I arrived at work and people who had seen the *Lateline* program were coming up to me beaming and congratulating me on what we had done and the surprising outcome. Instead of beaming back at them, I was so overwhelmed with their good-will I couldn't respond. I couldn't even say 'thank you'. I tried to smile, but instead, my eyes filled with tears which quietly rolled down my face, despite the fact I felt happy, overjoyed, and so appreciative of everyone's kind encouragement.

My bosses took me aside. "We want you to go home, Monica. Take a couple of days off, you need a bit of time for yourself."

"I didn't realise it would hit me like this," I said, tears still flowing, "I'm so sorry."

"No, don't apologise," said Jodie, who had been my supervisor for many years before I went to work for Defence, and who had opened the door for me to return to State Government work after I left Defence, "it's a big thing you've done."

I let out a grateful sigh, "we've been fighting this for nearly two years, and now suddenly we don't have to fight anymore. We've won! Nobody wins against Defence! But we did!"

"Is the investigation finished?" Jodie was being practical, an excellent antidote to the emotional.

I shook my head, "No, not yet, but I'm sure it will only confirm how bad the deception has been."

"Will there be any more TV interviews?" I think Bernie was concerned that I may not be able to handle another one.

"I guess there will be a little mopping up to do involving Senator Johnston and the IGIS report, but I think the ABC stories will centre on people in authority now more than on us. I am happy about that because they should be taking responsibility and explaining to the Australian people how it is all going to be fixed." I suddenly stopped talking, sat back in my chair and chuckled. The tears had stopped. I was back. And I was on to them...

My bosses were watching me intently.

I gave them both a look which acknowledged I understood what they had just done and they both grinned at me like Cheshire cats.

"Well," said Bernie to Jodie, "I think she's ready to go home now, don't you?"

"Indeed, I do," smiled Jodie and rose to give me a hug.

The hugs were genuine. It was so very nice to be around normal, decent people.

THE END OF AN ERA

Two days after our 'checkmate' victory was announced to Australia via *Lateline*, I woke to an early phone call. "So you are home," said a familiar voice.

"Crystal," I said hearing, the smile in her voice. "You saw *Lateline*..."

"Yes, it was awesome! You three should be so proud of what you have achieved."

I have tossed up whether to go public, and a few others are thinking about it, but I know I can't. Even now, it will still cost me my job." Crystal's voice began to shake with emotion, "you three did what we couldn't do. You made it all real."

"Crystal, your behind-the-scenes confirmation was pivotal. Without it, I don't know if we would have been able to achieve such a resounding victory."

"Monica, things have finally changed because of all of this." Crystal became a little guarded. Her tone had become professional, which told me she was not able to communicate with me as freely as she used to. I understood. I had lived through the old regime with her, but I no longer held the security clearance to know about the new changes.

"It's almost back to the way it was before everything got so screwed up and the correct procedures are beginning to be enforced again. Too many heads have rolled. Dora, Jack, Erik, Con, Stephen Merchant, plus two more you don't know, head people at Canberra DSA. One has just resigned outright, and the other has suddenly taken holidays just before a critical Senate Estimates, a bit unusual, so no one expects him to come back."

"Sounds like he's doing an Erik!"

"They know what's coming," said Crystal.

"Yes, and it's about time," I responded. "This is only the beginning, Crystal."

"The IGIS investigation has got the hierarchy scared. The leaders are walking on eggshells." Her tone was matter-of-fact. "Even after the investigation is finished, everyone is expecting AGSVA will be monitored for quite some time. They can't keep doing what they have been doing, and they know it."

"This is a good result, Crystal."

"It is! It really is! Let me know if anything else happens," Crystal said, winding up the conversation.

"I will," I responded.

As I hung up the phone, I felt so proud of all the people who had risked so much to achieve this victory, especially Crystal who had steadfastly gone the distance within Defence, knowing the cost, and personally paying it continually for over eighteen months. In my lifetime, I have never met anyone as brave as Crystal.

Our friendship needed to change now. She was no longer free to speak to me about her work in the new AGSVA. I understood, but her bravery, honour and kindness, even in the face of adversity, were etched into my mind and onto my heart. I couldn't admire her more.

SENATOR JOHNSTON QUESTIONS DEFENCE

The Senate Estimates hearing of October 2011 finally began, and it was announced that the IGIS investigation had not been completed and would need to be extended for another month.

This was a good sign. There was apparently too much evidence of corruption for a short investigation. No wonder Defence staff were shaking in their boots and jumping ship.

It was clear the information from ASIO had reached the Senate, for the Senators were aware that ASIO considered the workaround fiasco to have had a 'significant impact' on National Security. The spokesperson for Defence was still Stephen Merchant who was required to face this hearing despite his resignation, and Senator Johnston did not spare him but continued asking all the right, through very uncomfortable, questions.

- "The Minister, on 21 September, almost a month ago, said: 'Allegations about poor security processes were first raised in passing in the course of an investigation into harassment and bullying.' Is that entirely correct?" Senator Johnston.
- "I think that...was a reference to the fact that it was raised in an indirect, in passing way, in the report we received from Miss Trent." Stephen Merchant.
- "Three Ministers were told of these practices." Senator Johnston.
- "I readily concede, and the Minister has said this, that it was unfortunate that ah, that ah, and it was not right that we did not follow through appropriately to that reference in Miss Trent's report." Stephen Merchant.
- "Not only did you not follow through, three Ministers did not follow through on matters which require us to now re-do 20,000 plus vets...of security that is of significant importance." Senator Johnston.

- "The first that came to my attention, about the fact that there were inappropriate practices being alleged in the vetting process, ah, was actually the *Lateline* program of 16 May this year. And that, of course, has initiated all this subsequent action." Stephen Merchant.
- "Well, you can see my problem. It's good enough for the producer of a television program to elicit the matters, but when they are directly taken to three Ministers of this government, and everybody sits on their hands and does nothing, and here we are today with a massive administrative issue. One has to say and ask the question, 'Does it take a television program to get anything done, or to get any attention to these sorts of matters?'" Senator Johnston.
- "Senator, I'm not aware they were raised in such explicit terms to Ministers." Stephen Merchant.
- "I'm told on the 23 June 2010 that a letter to the then Minister Griffin specifically made that Minister aware of these security issues, together with the bullying, but specifically of these issues. I'm told Miss Trent's report adverted to these security issues in 2010. I'm told that on 7 July a letter from Minister Griffin to Mr Raguse, the then member for Forde, indicated he was aware of the matter. A letter from Minister Snowdon, on 26 October, indicated that he was aware of the matter. Now it strikes me that these Ministers are aware of the matter, and here we are today with this problem, and it's been sitting around waiting for a television program." Senator Johnston.

- "Senator the references in my recollection were about the awareness of allegations of inappropriate management practices, ah, at the vetting centre...it is my sincere wish that we would have got onto it much earlier." Stephen Merchant.

The problem could no longer be denied by Defence for it was obvious the Senators had been advised our allegations were true. It was also obvious that neither the threats to National Security nor the bullying had been taken seriously by Defence for both had been fobbed off and treated as 'management practices'.

At this stage, no one knew how big the problem was, how many years it had been going on, or how many clearances had been compromised.

Though Defence had downgraded the annual figure of 40,000 to 50,000, announced on *Lateline* by Minister Smith, to a single 20,000 by the time it got to the Senate, it was apparent the actual figure was closer to 60,000. That is, 20,000 per year over two to three years and Defence was playing down the extent of the damage to save face.

Only the long-awaited IGIS report would be able to shed much-needed light on the real size of this great betrayal of the Australian people.

> *We are going to find out from the Inspector-General of Intelligence and Security the depth and length and breadth of how severe this problem is, and I think it's very severe.* (Senator Johnston, Lateline, 19 Oct 2011)

An enemy
could not have done
a better job of sabotage!

CHAPTER NINE

Accountability? Yeah! Sure!

When the IGIS Report was finally released by the Prime Minister, Julia Gillard, in February 2012, it was beyond severe. It was scathing! It not only confirmed everything we had said but proved we whistleblowers had only seen the tip of a huge and deeply buried iceberg. According to the detailed report, the corruption was so widespread and had been going on for so long that much of the damage done was now unfixable.

The IGIS report recommended thirteen sweeping changes to Defence security vetting, but the first recommendation surprised us. Defence, which for the past eighteen months continually publically painted us as either lying, stupid or criminal, had been ordered to apologise. The Secretary of Defence wrote a two-page letter to each of us, stating that what we had said about the corruption of data from the beginning was true.

ABC's *Lateline* was the first to air the details of the IGIS report and opened their program by announcing to Australia that we three whistleblowers had been vindicated. Their leading story was that an independent investigation had proved our allegations to be true. They reported that the Inspector-General of Intelligence and Security had found the integrity of the data in the DSA and ASIO databases had been undermined, if not compromised, just as we had said.

The next day, in an address to Parliament, Senator Johnston publically honoured the service we had done for our Nation. He told the Parliament Australia owed us a debt of gratitude for coming forward. Finally, our efforts had been acknowledged!

Shortly after that, the results of the DLA Piper investigation into the bullying culture in Defence was released, and it was damning. The Government immediately announced a $40 million compensation package for victims, which they pointed out was to come out of the Defence budget.

With a barrage of bullying complaints coming from every angle, Stephen Smith finally capitulated and did what had never been done in Australia's Defence history. On behalf of Defence, he publically apologised to the Nation for the bullying culture within Defence, promising reform. The media labelled that day 'an historic day'.

Not long after that, and well before the coming Federal Election, the Minister for Defence, Stephen Smith, suddenly announced his resignation. He told the media he would be leaving the political arena at the end of his term and would not seek re-election to any public office in the future. Heads were rolling. Defence could no longer hide its dark side. The truth was breaking through.

THE IGIS REPORT IS RELEASED

On the morning of 8 February 2012, we three whistleblowers were individually notified that the Prime Minister, Julia Gillard, had decided to approve the official release of the full IGIS report. It would be made public, first to Parliament and then to the media the same day. This notification came by phone via an AGSVA agent.

"Am I speaking to Monica Bennett-Ryan?" The emotionless male voice was unreadable. "This is agent Jones from AGVSA, letting you know the IGIS report is being released today, and a copy of the report will be hand-delivered to you before the release."

I was taken aback. We had been waiting for months to hear when the IGIS report would be released, and now suddenly, on the morning of the release, we were being rung and told we would each need to be available for a sudden hand-delivery.

"Hand-delivery?" I said. Though I wondered why the report would need to be hand-delivered, I knew I couldn't ask the agent. He wouldn't tell me. "Where is this going to take place? When?"

"I can bring it to your place of work at around 3pm this afternoon," the agent remained emotionally non-committal. "I also have a letter for you from the Secretary of Defence, which needs to be delivered at the same time."

The Secretary of Defence? Why would he be writing me a letter? While my mind wondered, I continued the conversation. "I'm afraid you can't bring it to my place of work," I said, remembering what I had previously been told by my bosses about conflict of interest, "you will have to bring it to my home, and I won't be there until 5pm."

"5pm it is!" he said and hung up the phone.

As I replaced the receiver, I realised I hadn't given AGSVA my new work number, yet they not only knew where I worked but my current in-house phone number as well. I smiled to myself. It wasn't long ago they had told a Minister they couldn't find some of us. Did anyone ever believe anything they said? Mad if they did!

I wondered if John Stewart knew about the report's release, so I opened my email to send him a 'heads-up'. Too late! There were already several messages from him asking me to contact him about another interview from my home that evening.

The phone rang again. It was John. I filled him in on my conversation with the AGSVA agent and let him know I would be available for him. "I'm going to ask my bosses to let me off now, straight away, John." I was making an executive decision, and I wasn't an executive, but I knew they wouldn't object. They understood how important this report was to me and how long I had been waiting for it to be released. "I should be home in less than two hours. Do you have a copy of the report, John?"

"No, not yet! I can't get my hands on it! I was hoping you would have yours."

Poor John, how could he ask the right questions without a copy of the report? "I won't have mine until 5pm, but maybe Janice will receive her's earlier."

"If I can get hold of a copy, I'll send it to you."

"Likewise, thanks, John, talk later." I could hear from his tone he was under pressure, a breaking news story, but no facts to report, no questions to ask, no time to develop a response. Hopefully, Janice would receive her report earlier and send him a copy.

I didn't have to wait long to find out. Half an hour later, John phoned back and told me that neither Janice nor Owen would be receiving theirs in time either. "Don't worry about rushing to prepare for an interview tonight. I've run out of time. I'll just run with Senator Johnston's official response."

"Okay, John."

I hung up the phone and let out an involuntary sigh of relief. No interview! All I needed to do now was go home a little early and wait for the AGSVA agent to hand-deliver my copy of the report and the mysterious letter from the Secretary of Defence.

DEFENCE WRITES AN APOLOGY

The agent arrived at my home at 5pm as arranged. After checking I was the intended recipient, he handed me a copy of the IGIS report and a sealed envelope and departed. I closed the front door, walked over to the lounge, sat down and stared at the two items in my lap. What were they going to say? Which one would I open first? Defence had not been kind to us, so I put aside the letter from the Secretary of Defence and opened the IGIS report.

It was sixty-four pages long, so I did what most people do to fast track their understanding of a large document. I went straight to the recommendations. There were thirteen, laid out over two pages, and as I read the first one, my mouth dropped open in shock. For a moment, I couldn't quite grasp what I was seeing. It was not what I had expected. Not even close!

These recommendations were not mere suggestions, they were akin to enforceable orders. They had to be obeyed! Knowing that, this first recommendation left me speechless.

> Recommendation 1: *The Department of Defence should write to the three Lateline complainants and acknowledge that their allegations in respect to data entry were true.* (IGIS Report, 2012 page 6)

Understanding slowly dawned. Ah! So that was what was in the letter from the Secretary of Defence. After all Defence had done to us, the denials, the false accusations, the traps, the slurs and the attempted public humiliation, the Secretary of Defence had been ordered to put in writing to each of us that what we had said from the very beginning had been true all along. How wonderful for us! How humiliating for them!

I closed the IGIS report and picked up the letter. My hands shook a little because I still didn't trust them. Would they actually obey this direct order? Or would they word things in such a way that we would still be able to be blamed for something? I opened the letter.

> *"Evidence provided to the Inspector-General's Inquiry confirmed that the substance of your claims was true: both contractors and the Australian Public Service Employees working in the vetting centre were entering incorrect information into the vetting process. Further, this corrupted information was then used by ASIO to conduct its security assessment checks. The Inspector-General concluded that the integrity of the data in both DSA and ASIO had been undermined if not compromised."*

It had started well, but then came the inevitable and expected put-down.

> *"The security vetting process involves a range of other subsequent checks including personal interview, multiple referee checks, financial checks, a police records check and often a psychological interview for high-level clearances."*

Really? How many times did we have to tell the authorities in Defence the same story, over and over again? *We* did the paper checks, the financial checks and police record checks. They were not done 'further down the line'. *We* did them! That's why we blew the whistle! That's why this was all so very bad! There were no more data-entry checks after they left our hands! That was the whole problem! How could it be that the Secretary of Defence, even after all this time, still didn't get it? I was angry now, but the final comment made me wish I had never opened his letter.

> *"It is regrettable that it took your appearance on National Television to bring attention to these inappropriate practices."*

So, there it was; they were only sorry that we had made it all public! How embarrassing for them! Poor dears!

Apparently, there were no regrets about the enormous amount of damage that had been done to individuals, to Australia, to the military, to National Security or to ASIO's records; damage which would take years to fix. No regrets at all!

And no regrets about the tremendous waste of time, effort and tax-payer money so willingly squandered by Defence. It seemed their only regret was that we had made it public.

I folded the letter, put it back into its envelope and firmly resealed it. Then I opened my filing cabinet and put it into the very back file. Out of sight, out of mind. As far as I was concerned, that official insult and ridiculous excuse for an apology could stay there forever and rot. I never wanted to look at it again.

The whole tone of the letter seemed childish and out of keeping with the authority carried by such a high office. It reminded me of a typical playground scene: A child is forced to apologise to another for doing the wrong thing but doesn't want to apologise. So he puts his head down, shuffles his feet and grumbles' sorrrrr-eeee' with a nasty undertone. Everyone around him knows the child is not sorry. They know he's only saying the words because an adult is making him say them. And everyone also knows that until the 'sorry' is genuine, it doesn't mean anything.

It was clear from the tone of the letter that the only reason the Secretary of Defence had acknowledged the truth of our claims was because he had been ordered to do so, yet the ongoing Defence 'attitude' towards us had clearly not changed. His apology was not worth the paper it was written on!

Why was it so difficult, I wondered, for leaders in Defence to simply say, "Thank you for coming forward. Thank you for what you've done." Unbelievable!

Accountability takes courage! It's one of the first rules every new military recruit is taught: 'own your mistakes'. And yet, in the hierarchy, there was no courage to be seen. It was so disheartening for me to witness such blatant cowardice being displayed by so many Defence officials throughout this whole sorry saga. Pathetic!

AUSTRALIA WIDE PUBLIC VINDICATION

That night to my surprise, *Lateline* blasted our vindication across Australia. The story that went to air was about how we three whistleblowers had been vindicated. I was stunned. How typical of God. When he vindicates, he goes all out!

Australia was told, in no uncertain terms, that we three whistleblowers had told the truth right from the very start, that the problems we pinpointed were not easy to now fix, and that Defence had been ordered to implement immediate changes to their vetting practices. I was in awe! I watched the program in stunned silence.

- "Three whistleblowers who claimed thousands of Defence security checks had been compromised have been vindicated after an official report found their allegations to be true. John Stewart reports."
- John Stewart: Last year, three whistleblowers told *Lateline* thousands of security applications had been fabricated to speed up the checking process. They said that information was invented to fill in gaps on security forms, including checks on private security guards working on Australian military basis, Australian staff working in embassies overseas and air marshals and senior public servants with access to sensitive information.
- At first, the Defence Department denied the claims made by the three whistleblowers. But today, the Inspector-General of Intelligence and Security found, "Evidence provided to the inquiry confirmed that the substance of the allegations was true."
- The Inspector-General also found that some security databases still contain fake information. "The Inspector-General found that the integrity of data in both DSA and ASIO had been undermined if not compromised. Modified data entered the databases, and some persist today."

- Senator David Johnston, Opposition Defence Spokesman: Given that 5,000 of the 20,000 are top-secret security clearances for embassies, members of Parliament and other sensitive areas, one would not be able to sleep at night confidently given that the Inspector-General has completely savaged the process and those participating in the process.
- John Stewart: The IGIS report recommended sweeping changes to Defence security vetting and told the Defence Department to write to the three whistleblowers and acknowledge that their allegations about false data entry were true.

The phone rang. I knew it would be Janice. "Well, did you see it?" she said, abandoning her usual greeting.

"I am in awe! How amazing! This is so much better than I thought it would be, and I haven't had a chance to go through the report yet."

I could feel the joy breaking through, and I realised I had been a little emotionally numb. "What did you think?"

"Loved it!" said Janice. "I think it's very nice to be publicly vindicated, but it's rather strange that those telling the truth and wanting to put a stop to the corruption are the ones who need vindication, while those doing the corruption and lying about it are not even reprimanded!"

"True!" I nodded, chuckling at Janice's astute observations.

"This feels so good, Monica," Janice said. "It's over! It finally is over!"

"I'm going to give the report a thorough read tomorrow. Senator Johnson said the report had 'savaged' the vetting process, so I can't wait to see what the IGIS found. I haven't emailed our thanks to John yet," I said, "so I'll do that tomorrow, as well."

"Are you working tomorrow?" asked Janice.

"No! My bosses have given me the day off." I chuckled again. "I guess they remember my last 'day after' experience.

Janice laughed. "Yes, well, I imagine we will be on the phone most of the day...lots of congratulatory phone calls...and people to thank."

"Yes, I think we will be quite busy," I laughed. But my mind was still re-running the Lateline report, and my heart was thanking God. What an amazing, fantastic, stupendous result!

A SHOCKING AND UNEXPECTED NUMBER

I was too awake to sleep, so I opened the IGIS report and began to read. Senator Johnson was right, the IGIS report was scathing! It had also savaged the entire DSA/AGSVA vetting process.

What the investigators found was widespread disorganisation and chaos. Processes that didn't exist, workarounds that didn't exist, lack of training, lack of qualifications, poor management skills, inadequate agency contractual arrangements and inadequate system upgrades.

The investigators had gone over everything done in DSA since 2008 and every accusation made by us with a fine-tooth comb. They were thorough! They shone the light into every little dark corner and, in doing so, had found that the problems were far worse than even we could have imagined.

Defence had given the Senate a generalised total figure of 20,000 possibly compromised paper applications which they said were now beginning the long, slow process of being rechecked. Yet that whole concept was a ruse. Just another lie - that was about to be exposed.

The IGIS investigation revealed the shocking news that checkable paper applications were not the only applications compromised! They were, in fact, only half the problem!

The number of paper applications reported by Defence did not include the high number of electronic applications (paper free), which now could *not* be re-checked or corrected! Adding these applications almost doubled the number of affected clearances. This huge mess had now become the greatest intelligence scandal in Australia's history.

- "Potentially the most significant outstanding issue is that remediation will not resolve all data issues – particularly those relating to the unauthorised and unaudited access to the current electronic vettee packs (ePacks) where it seems likely that it will not be possible to identify the missing or inaccurate information."
- "I was advised that DSA staff have access to a password reset function, intended to be used when an applicant loses their password."
- "It was apparent from some staff interviewed that this permission was neither sought nor documented."
- "Over half of the ePack2 submissions may have been modified in this way."

- "The use of this practice is of significant concern in that it bypasses all security and audit controls."
- "The range of data changed via this method appears to be unidentifiable and, given it occurs at the first step of the vetting process, has the potential to significantly undermine the remainder of the process."
- "These changes cannot be picked up via a comparison of the paper and electronic versions" (IGIS report 2012 page 58)

This was shocking indeed! Besides the corrupted paper applications, at least fifty per cent of all electronic applications had also been changed somehow, and now no one was able to tell how they were modified or who modified them! In short, they could neither be found nor fixed!

I was horrified at the amount of false information which had been fed to ASIO as truth on a regular basis over so many years - information the IGIS report confirmed could not be picked up as inaccurate if it was not flagged as inaccurate.

I wondered how any intelligence organisation in this country could do its job of protecting us from terrorists when the information they were relying on to be accurate was nothing more than a honeycomb of fantasy.

As I kept reading, my shock slowly turned to anger. Even though the people directly responsible for this unspeakable betrayal of Australia and Australians had been identified and named in the report by the Inspector-General of Intelligence and Security, they were nevertheless not going to be officially held accountable.

While I have found that a significant contributing fact to these problems was lack of management oversight, I have decided that there is no evidence of sufficient weight that any person was guilty of a breach of duty or of misconduct to justify referral to the Secretary of the Department of Defence. (IGIS report, 2012 page 52)

What? Did I read that correctly? Was the person responsible for dishing out the discipline for these atrocities The Secretary of Defence? That meant that while he was away, these matters would need to be dealt with by the Acting Secretary of Defence, Stephen Merchant - the same person who had just been caught out lying to the Senate and had subsequently resigned. Could no one else bring these people to justice? What a twisted mess!

Was this why Stephen Merchant had stepped down? Was it because he was one of the people who would need to be investigated by the person occupying his position? Could he investigate himself? No! What do you do when your politicians and leaders are this corrupt?

I couldn't get my head around it! The inner workings of the greatest intelligence scandal in Australia's history had been exposed for all to see, and yet those who had been found responsible would not be held to account! There was no system in place to prosecute those in high positions! Unbelievable! Shocking! Totally immoral!

Everything we had said had been proven to be true, and yet the people who planned all this, organised it, and ruthlessly enforced it were not going to be held accountable in any way. I couldn't believe it! This was too twisted! Too diabolical! I couldn't take it in!

As it turned out, a corrupt system was only half the problem! Dr Thom had told us many times that she did not have a mandate to investigate bullying. And now I knew why.

The exclusion of evidence of bullying from the IGIS investigation was significant. If the bullying, harassment, intimidation and coercion of DSA/AGSVA staff had been investigated, the deliberate nature of the maladministration would have been seen, and criminal prosecutions would have followed. Importantly, those in high positions would not have escaped.

In hindsight, it's easy to see that if the bullying, coercion, segregation, threats and intimidation had been prosecuted back then, a precedent would have been set that would have prevented our current government and its bureaucrats from using those tactics in a broadscale manner on the Australian people in the name of COVID.

> *While not the direct subject of this inquiry, it has been difficult to untangle the allegations of inappropriate vetting practices from the accusations of bullying and harassment at the NCC, as well as poor management in general. The report would be incomplete without some observations in this area.* (IGIS report, 2012 page 37)

The IGIS investigation found it difficult to untangle corrupt vetting practices from the coercion that enforced them. However, because coercive bullying was not part of the 'terms of reference' for that investigation, there was no evidence of sufficient weight, which would have justified criminal prosecution against those responsible. Who defined the terms of reference for the IGIS investigation? The Prime Minister, Julia Gillard!

The previous comment from the IGIS should have been enough to open an investigation into the bullying culture prevalent within DSA, but that never happened. Such an investigation would have revealed a minefield of evidence of deliberate corruption ordered by those in the highest places within DSA and Defence. Yet, the gathering of evidence of criminal coercion, which would inevitably lead to prosecutions, was excluded even from the highest investigative body in Australia.

The IGIS report itself was welcome, thorough, and honest to the point of shredding forever Defence excuses regarding the corruption of clearances but was structured to avoid prosecutions. Without evidence of coercion, the criminal nature of the callous treatment of staff to enforce illegal and corrupt practices would never come to light. Can a government get any more immoral than this? Sadly, the answer is yes!

I didn't know then that I was living through a social experiment that was testing the willingness of Australians to live under totalitarian rule.

In the pre-COVID experiment, 30% of DSA staff objected to the corruption, while 5% openly opposed it! Was this useful information? Absolutely! The percentages during COVID have proved to be about the same! The government knew that around 70% of the population would buckle under, accept their totalitarian rule and join forces with the bullies against those with integrity. Their biggest challenge would be shutting down the other 30%, especially the 5%.

In DSA, we whistleblowers were the 5% and we won! But, none of us knew that our fight for justice would be used as a tool to gauge the gaps that needed to be closed before the government could unleash their COVID brutality onto all Australians.

At that stage, I couldn't see the full picture but what I could see, made me furious. What do you do? Where do you go for justice when you live in a country whose highest officials, though they see the corruption, can't or won't punish those who promote and sustain that corruption with brute force? I was so angry, I couldn't even speak.

TELLING JOHN WHAT I THOUGHT

I couldn't speak about my feelings, but I could write them down. As late as it was, I sat down at my computer, opened an email and began a letter to John Stewart. I was hopping mad, and so I just let my emotions tumble out onto the page in front of me. It was like a relief valve had been opened.

When I finished, I felt better knowing I had been able to express some of my anger, but I also knew enough not to send it to anyone until I'd calmed down. At least I could now go to bed and sleep. I had vented, so I wouldn't be up all night, pacing the floor, tossing over all the arguments, events and let-downs. There were just too many.

The next day, after re-reading what I had written, I decided to send it, unchanged, to John Stewart with a copy to Senator Johnston.

Hi John,

When I wrote this I was angry. So I put it aside, calmed down and re-read it. You can hear the anger - but it still says what I want to say. I don't know if it will be useful to you or not, but you can always delete it. :) Here goes...

You are always asking me if there is any terrorist who has slipped through the net. I'll tell you who slipped through the net, John. The people who have done this...

- *They have lied to Ministers!*
- *They have lied to the Senate!*
- *They have perverted investigations!*
- *They have lied to ASIO!*
- *They have lied about ASIO!*
- *They have falsified people's personal data!*
- *They have ignored Australian workplace laws!*
- *They have forced staff to lie to ASIO!*
- *They have forced staff to falsify personal data!*
- *They have completely ignored Parliament approved procedures for vetting!*
- *They have compromised Australia's security in such an effective way it will take up to a decade to undo the damage!*
- *They have broken multiple laws!*
- *They have thumbed their noses at every authority in this land! And...*
- *They are not being prosecuted!*
- *They are not even being sacked!*

Instead, they are being patted on the head and told: "there, there, it's all right, you're not to blame, no one is - we understand - it just happened."

Maybe this should now be the defence used in court for every criminal act committed in this country from this time forward...

- *You murdered someone? Don't worry, we understand - no one is to blame - it just happened - this is Australia - we don't care about the law.*

- *You want to rob a bank? No problem! Steal a car? Of course - you won't be Robinson Crusoe!*
- *You want to be a terrorist? Come to Australia. We make it easy for you!*

Law? What law? Where are the people who are supposed to uphold our laws?

To work with DSA, I had to endure a ten-year check of my personal life to prove I was an upstanding Australian citizen with a clean criminal history. Then the first thing they did when I passed their test was force me, through the use of threats and deception, to break the law and betray Australia, to enter unwittingly into their criminal activity, falsifying people's personal data and lying to ASIO. Without even touching the rampant bullying side of it, this is a clear breach of the law. A criminal act!

> *A corporation shall not, in trade or commerce, engage in conduct that is misleading or deceptive or is likely to mislead or deceive.*
> (Trade Practices Act - Section 52 [1])

DSA broke that law! I was misled and deceived, and I was forced to mislead and deceive (and I am only one of hundreds). ASIO was misled and deceived. Every applicant whose data was corrupted was also misled and deceived by DSA/ AGSVA. They trusted them with their personal information, and they were betrayed.

The law was broken, deliberately and continually, over and over and over again for years. And now, they beg innocence through ignorance? If they are not prosecuted, lawlessness wins.

How can terrorism destroy our society any more than this deliberate act of betrayal?

What are our government officials afraid of - a compensation lawsuit? If every affected person in this scenario entered into a class action, there would be 30,000, 40,000, 50,000 people or more. That number is not reasonable or even desirable as far as compensation is concerned.

Instead, what every one of us would want to see, I believe, is justice. This is why we have laws! The law needs to be upheld and applied to those who have done this to us and to Australia. Everyone involved in this needs to see that the law actually counts for something in this country.

- *The Ministers who turned a blind eye need to be removed from office, have their benefits terminated and be forced to repay what we paid them while they were betraying us.*
- *The heads of DSA/AGSVA need to do jail time.*

What is the point of laws if they are not upheld? This is not a small matter. And a slap on the wrist just won't cut it.

The law is the net, John. They are the big one, and they're getting away...

Thank you for all your help. Monica.

A few hours later, Senator Johnson's media advisor, Rebecca, responded to my email, requesting my permission to use some of my sentiments in the Senator's address to the Senate that afternoon.

I gave my consent. I was honoured. It was nice to know that even in my raw emotional state, my opinion had some value and had been taken seriously by a person who had the authority to effectively use some of what I'd written. Nevertheless, I was still grieving for my country. My heart was broken.

HONOURED IN PARLIAMENT

When Rebecca emailed the Senate Proof of the Senator's Ministerial Statement to the Senate dated 9 February 2012 I was utterly taken aback, honoured and humbled. Though I was at work and reading it on my work computer, I gasped out loud several times.

I was so shocked at the sheer volume of praise Senator Johnson was laying on we three whistleblowers, that his comments took me completely by surprise.

- In March 2010, three whistleblowers raised the issue of corrupted vetting practices. Defence's response and the response of the Members of Parliament was to simply ignore them.
- It was not until the *Lateline* program, in May 2011, raised these issues that the whistleblowers were taken seriously.
- These whistleblowers were treated with contempt. They were derided and treated as cranks. They have now received the Inspector-General's report.
- The first line of that report is that there should be an acknowledgement that what the whistleblowers said from day one was true and correct.
- We owe them a debt of gratitude.
- These three might have been in breach of the law disclosing what they disclosed.
- The parliament owes these three brave people a great debt of gratitude for coming forward in the circumstances.

- The simple question that we all must ask is: who is accountable? Who is responsible? There is nobody that this government has pointed to as being responsible. It is always a review, adverse findings and 'we'll fix it now'. Nobody is accountable. This is an absolute disgrace.

When I finished reading my face was dripping with tears, and again I couldn't speak. I thought of so many other whistleblower horror stories that I'd heard about over the years, and all I could think was I had never known of any whistleblowers anywhere in the world who'd been honoured the way we had just been honoured, in the highest forum in the land. I was overwhelmed.

We had fought the good fight. We had won the race. We had painstakingly brought everything we had uncovered in the dark out into the light.

I remembered again what Dayle had told us right from the very beginning:

> *The Department of Defence is accountable to Australian law! It has no power to act illegally, and to allow it to do so would be a criminal offence.*

How many people in the highest places of government, I wondered, just from this one scandal, remained criminally accountable for the breaking of Australian law? Too many!

I was so naive back then. I thought it was only the Labor Party Ministers that were corrupt. I thought that when the Liberal Party was voted in, the corruption would cease. Silly me! I didn't know then that both the Liberal and Labor Parties had the same agenda and were working in tandem to bring about the same result - a totalitarian republic!

I THOUGHT IT WAS OVER. I WAS WRONG!

The following year, in the Federal Election of 2013, the Liberal Party ousted the Labor Party and installed Tony Abbott as our new Prime Minister. To our great surprise and delight, Tony Abbott chose Senator David Johnston to be the new Minister for Defence, who promised an immediate overhaul of the entire Defence organisation.

It seemed that people now in authority in this country were taking responsibility, and making all the right decisions. So it looked like, finally, Defence was going to be made to bow to Australian law and accept accountability for their illegal activities.

I was way too optimistic!

Within two years, Prime Minister Tony Abbott was stabbed in the back by his own party and replaced by Malcolm Turnbull, the founder of the Labor approved Republican Movement. The new treasurer and Mr Turnbull's right-hand man was Scott Morrison. Meanwhile, David Johnston was unceremoniously removed after he dared question a massive $1 billion deficit in Defence spending. Clouds were once again building on the horizon...

Where do you go
when your own government
becomes your enemy?

CHAPTER TEN

COVID! Crisis or opportunity?

In the eight years following our triumph in 2012 to the beginning of the COVD crisis in 2020, there were two significant developments.

First, there was a sudden flurry of new 'whistleblower protection' Acts proposed for both Federal and State jurisdictions. These sounded progressive but, in reality, were not progressive at all. Their stated protections were generally supposed to give whistleblowers more freedom to speak out without being penalised or sacked, but in effect, they stifled whistleblowers, corralling them within the bounds of their employers reporting systems and discouraging any reports to 'external agencies' like the media or Members of Parliament.

Though the publicised emphasis was on the heavy financial penalties awaiting employers who penalised whistleblowers, the reality was that the new laws held a maze of hidden traps for those with the moral courage to try to expose corruption. In 2019 a Federal Court Judge, Justice John Griffiths, slammed Australia's new whistleblower laws as "technical, obtuse and intractable".

> *JUSTICE GRIFFITHS: "The outcome is a statute which is largely impenetrable, not only for a lawyer but even more so for an ordinary member of the public or a person employed in the Commonwealth bureaucracy."* (Michael Inman, ABC News, 12 June 2019)

Second, in 2017, the most highly acclaimed, accurate, hard-hitting and in-depth current affairs program in Australia was inexplicably taken off the air. Despite 28 years of leading the news and often creating the front-page headlines for the following day's newspapers, the ABCs *Lateline* was suddenly 'cancelled' and replaced by chat show journalism. From then on, the quality of news reporting throughout Australia began to slide dramatically down into a murky pit.

For a while, a few shining lights remained on the *Sky News* Chanel. Like *Lateline*, they pulled no punches and asked all the right questions. However, in 2021, one of the brightest of those lights, *Alan Jones*, was 'cancelled', and another bright light, Rowan Dean's *Outsiders*, was pushed back to late Sunday night. So, it seemed that any journalists who dared ask penetrating questions or buck the system were reined in, removed or restricted.

As a result, all the Australian public was fed from the beginning of 2020 was a steady stream of COVID slurry. What is it called when you are drip-fed the same unquestioned information, the same news story, from the same sycophantic viewpoint day in and day out, hour after hour, mind-numbing second after mind-numbing second for years without any let-up? It's called torture! It's called brainwashing! It's called propaganda! But, that's what government money and influence demands from the media in this country.

The DSA pre-COVID social experiment had uncovered two powerful loopholes that could derail the government's future plans - freedom to blow the whistle on government corruption and unfettered journalistic investigation. Used together, they had proved to be a dangerous and volatile mix, so, those two 'loopholes' needed to be closed. And they were!

HOW DID IT COME TO THIS?

Decent, ordinary Australians shake their heads at the idea that our government could be so devious. We don't want to believe it! Yet, the evidence has been right in front of our eyes all along. We just didn't see it. We didn't see that, for the last thirty years, right under our noses, government positions have been systematically filled with republicans who want to bring us into a totalitarian, Chinese-style dictatorship. No way! We say. Unbelievable! We say. Well, it's not so unbelievable when we take a hindsight look at the slow and deliberate steps taken to bring us to this point. To do that, we need to go back to the Keating era, when the push for a republic began.

When Paul Keating was Treasurer under Prime Minister Bob Hawke, he introduced superannuation, eliminated tariffs, reformed taxation by adding capital gains tax, fringe benefits tax and dividend imputation, and was most famous for introducing to Australia the first *'recession we had to have'.* That forced recession was purposely and successfully used to change the entire structure of our society.

Prior to that, men on a single wage could support their families, everyone could afford a home, and jobs were plentiful. But Keating's recession forced interest rates so high that overnight a single income was not enough to pay a mortgage, and many families lost their houses. Women were forced out of the home and into the workplace, and as a result, teens began to roam the streets after school and crime and homelessness increased dramatically. Our society went downhill from there.

When he became Prime Minister in 1993, Mr Keating introduced privatisation and began selling off government assets, like Qantas and the Commonwealth Bank, to overseas interests.

Notably, he opened the door to the active promotion of a republic by setting up the Republic Advisory Committee. He appointed Malcolm Turnbull as the Chair and charged him with finding a way to move Australia from a monarchy to a republic. That began a thirty-year push for a republic!

Today, all Labor Party and Green Party members are republicans. And because Malcolm Turnbull embedded himself in the Liberal Party, most Liberal Party members are republicans as well. Tony Abbott was not a republican. He was loyal to our Federation and our Constitution, so, of course, he and his supporters had to go. Does this tell you anything about Scott Morrison, Mr Turnbull's right-hand man? It should!

The single-minded purpose of all republicans in all political parties is to move Australia from the protection of our Federation into a full-blown republic. But in the thirty years since the Republican Movement began in Australia, not one republican has ever told the Australian people what kind of republic they wanted us to become. I guess they thought we wouldn't like what they had in mind.

When COVID arrived, it was the opportunity they had been waiting for. It gave the republicans the impetus they needed to destroy our Federation and usher in their Republic. So finally, through the brutality Australians routinely experienced under the guise of 'keeping us safe", we were given a clear insight into the kind of repressive republicanism our leaders had in mind all along. Clearly, it is modelled on a Chinese-style dictatorship rather than on a French or American presidential-style democracy. No wonder republicans, over the last thirty years, have tried so hard to get us to cut ties with Europe and America and build closer ties with Asia!

DECADES OF GROUNDWORK

Republicanism is the fuel that has driven both sides of politics for the last thirty years. That's why the policies of the Liberal/National Labor/Green Parties are the same. They have been working together behind the facade of difference to move Australia from a thriving European-style democratic Federation to an austere Chinese-style Republic.

The Liberal/Nationals have not represented conservative views for a very long time. Neither do they stand anymore for business profitability and growth. Labor/Greens do not fight for the needs of workers, choosing instead to block new industry.

Both sides hide behind a facade of tradition while they work in unison to kill off the very Federation that allows them to exist. There is no such thing as a 'two-party system' in our Federation. That concept is a republican turn of phrase now used so often by a biased media that Australians have been brainwashed into believing there are only two parties worth considering at the polls - Labor or Liberal. That notion is an insult to our Constitution.

Look at the last thirty years of Liberal and Labor destruction. Under their tandem leadership, manufacturing has been shut down, and industry all but eradicated, education standards have dropped from one of the top in the world to almost the bottom and the health system is on the verge of collapse. No new dams have been built, our farms, water, energy, ports, houses and many businesses have been sold to overseas interests, and our conservative Christian values have been brutally thrown to the ground.

Is this what ordinary Australians want? We have said 'NO' loud and clear! A referendum in 1999 to establish a republic, led by Malcolm Turnbull, was soundly rejected. And yet, here we are...

SEVEN STEPS IN THE DSA SOCIAL EXPERIMENT

STEP ONE: Wait for a Global disaster.

The Global Financial Crisis of 2007-2009 was the crisis the Defence moguls were waiting for. They went into planning in 2007 and put the infrastructure in place in 2008. But, it wasn't until the beginning of the new financial year, July 2009, that it was implemented. In full swing, it became the financially lucrative, money-making golden opportunity they had hoped it would be. It didn't matter that they needed to break laws and override morality to bring their fiscal plan to fruition.

STEP TWO: Hide the truth behind a facade.

From the very beginning, walls of separation and physical divisions were built between DSA analysts and the Agency staff brought in to implement the illegal changes. It was imperative that analysts not find out what agency staff were employed to do. This was a very dangerous game! Separation, segregation and limited communication were vital for the deception to take root and the corruption to succeed.

STEP THREE: Focus attention on one law.

Working inside DSA, the overriding law, constantly on our minds, was the Secrecy Act. We were painfully aware that we could not speak about anything we saw or encountered while working in the intelligence arena. The trouble was that law was exaggerated, twisted out of context and used to blot out all the other laws that would have protected us. Under that one law, we were made to feel that all our other rights as Australians no longer existed. That was a lie! A ruse! Totally false!

SEVEN STEPS IN THE REPUBLICAN COUP D'ETAT

STEP ONE: Wait for a Global disaster.

The COVID pandemic was the *'pandemic we had to have'*, the opportunity to kill, steal and destroy our Federation, unity, national identity, freedom, livelihoods, health, economy and future, under the pretence of 'keeping us safe'. Was it a pandemic? No! COVID proved to be no more deadly than the flu, killing less than 1% of those affected, but it was a golden opportunity. It didn't matter that they needed to break laws and override morality in order to bring their republican plans to fruition.

STEP TWO: Hide the truth behind a facade.

Our Federation is a union of States. To destroy that union, borders had to be introduced. So, Australians were divided, not just from State to State but personally as well. COVID was the facade used to cover a capricious pathway to a dictatorial republic. Lockdowns, segregation, division and limited communication were vital for the destruction of the Federation and for the establishment of a republic to succeed.

STEP THREE: Focus attention on one law.

During the COVID deception, the overriding law used against us was 'Emergency Powers'. We were made to believe these powers made all the other laws written in our Constitution irrelevant. But, the truth is, those 'Emergency Powers' do not exist and cannot be enforced outside the framework of our Constitution. By exaggerating the supposed power of one law over all the others, we were made to feel that our full and free rights as Australians no longer existed. That was a lie! A ruse! Totally false!

STEP FOUR: Create confusion and insecurity.

DSA leaders deliberately created confusion, disorientation, and insecurity through constant rapid and unpredictable changes that brought instability and chaos to the established and legal vetting processes. The purpose of their confusion was to break down conformity to the old legal standards so they could establish their new, illegal standards as normal.

STEP FIVE: Destroy the concept of 'self'.

At DSA, we were warned our friends would pay the price for our decisions. And they did! This is typical communist reasoning. Communist means caring more about the community than yourself. *You* are no longer important.

STEP SIX: Torture, punish and penalise.

The leaders within DSA and their civilian henchmen were a particular breed. They were heartless and loved to torture. Like spoilt brats, they would provoke situations to cause reactions in others that they could then punish, also penalising anyone who tried to stand up against their savagery. For them, this was pure fun!

STEP SEVEN: Continually threaten job loss.

In DSA, sackings were never about individual work performance. They were always about something personal, like smiling too much or speaking to the wrong person. Though ordered by DSA, the sackings themselves were carried out by their civilian puppets. And the sackings were brutal. Like Russian Roulette, we never knew, from day to day, when it would be our turn to take the bullet.

STEP FOUR: Create confusion and insecurity.

Under the COVID banner, Federal and State leaders and bureaucrats have worked together to create confusion, disorientation, uncertainty and insecurity throughout Australia by introducing constant, rapid and unpredictable changes. They deliberately cultivated fear, instability, chaos and severe financial hardship and then informed us this was the 'new normal'.

STEP FIVE: Destroy the concept of 'self'.

To push untried drugs onto the unsuspecting public, our government used communist rhetoric, labelling people 'selfish' if they chose not to stumble blindly over a dangerous and experimental medical cliff like lemmings.

STEP SIX: Torture, punish and penalise.

Throughout the COVID deception, heartless State and Federal leaders have had lots of fun. Their nasty, abusive and power-mad use of punishment, sadly causing many deaths, has been bolstered by huge fines and police brutality against anyone objecting to their callous treatment of suffering Australians.

STEP SEVEN: Continually threaten job loss.

During COVID, qualified and experienced people have been sacked simply for refusing to take experimental drugs without question. The sackings were carried out by civilian puppets, leaving Australia with a severe shortage of skilled workers. Was this about drugs? No! It was about conformity to a new regime. Next time, the job losses will be for something else, like religion, ethnicity, or eating meat.

When DSA did this to me and others in 2009, they did it quickly. Slow doesn't work. Once they began their destruction, they had to move fast so that their victims would not have the time or the will to think about what they were being ordered to do.

The DSA moguls got away with everything they did because we 'good people' thought staying quiet and going along with 'those who know better' was the best way to serve Australia.

Likewise, the COVID moguls have been able to get away with everything they have done because the 'good people' of Australia have been made to believe that going along with this destructive madness is the best way to overcome a cold virus.

Is the virus the problem? No!

The virus is merely the excuse the moguls needed to 'cover their sneaky deed' and enforce their hidden agenda.

It wouldn't have mattered what kind of 'Global Crisis' came along; the crisis itself was irrelevant. Though COVID was the catalyst for the brutal authoritarian response, the crisis could just as well have been something else, like a significant terrorist threat, an imminent war, or a major stock market collapse. No matter the global crisis, the republican response in Australia would have been the same. Heavy-handed authoritarianism designed to become the 'new norm' forced on an unsuspecting public, 'for our own good'.

IT IS TOTALLY ILLEGAL

Everything described in each of the Seven Steps above is utterly illegal under our Constitution. Everything! Yet, both Liberal and Labor are working together to ensure this brutality continues.

When are Australians going to wake up?

The DSA pre-COVID social experiment, defended by the Labor Party, exposed two major loopholes. The Liberal Party closed those loopholes! Then, when the COVID opportunity came along, the Liberal Party unleashed the full destruction of the Federation on the Australian public, albeit with the keen cooperation of the Labor Party.

The 'good people' of Australia went quietly along with all the brutality. We didn't even object when the State Parliaments were shut down! Why not? Why haven't we cried out? How can we have a Federation when we have hard borders separating States? How is our Constitution served by closing our Parliaments? The National Cabinet was set up to override the Parliamentary system and allow for the unchallenged rule of an elite few, unfettered by the scrutiny of Parliament. Can people not see that a new totalitarian government is already in place?

This new totalitarian government's only real problem is that their authority to hold political office comes from the Constitution. Outside the bounds of the Constitution, they have no right to tell us to do anything! So, to take full control over us they *must* strip the Constitution of it's power, which they propose to do after the next election, under the guise of 'simplifying the referrendum process'.

When are Australians going to wake up?

It seems that a weird form of anarchy is at play here. The kind where the leaders are the ones who lift themselves above established law and break all the rules. The kind where the government organises the absence of government. The kind where those in authority choose non-recognition of previous authority. A true coup d'etat! Unstoppable? No!

THEY ARE *NOT* KEEPING US SAFE

In DSAland, when leaders smiled, it was not a good thing. A smile from a DSA team leader meant we were in big trouble. What trouble? We didn't usually know straight away. We had to wait for events to unfold before we understood how we'd been set up to be the subject of one of their cruel games. But, the smile was always a giveaway.

It's the same with the COVID crisis!

Today, when any bureaucrat, Premier or Minister tells you they are keeping you safe, that's when you need to be on your guard. That's when you need to run and hide your children. That's when you need to duck for cover and batten down the hatches because you know for sure big trouble is coming. When they say you are safe, you can be very sure you are not! That phrase is a dead giveaway. Every time it is used, we know they are about to do something cruel and nasty.

Look at their track record...

- Children in boarding schools not allowed to return home to parents during holidays.
- Wives unable to see husbands working in a different State.
- Businesses driven to bankruptcy.
- Farmers unable to feed or tend the animals on their land in an adjoining State.
- A pregnant woman arrested in her pyjamas for sending a non-government approved email.
- A disabled man brutally thrown to the ground by police for the crime of not wearing a mask.
- A twelve-year-old girl sprayed with pepper spray for not wearing a mask.

- An elderly man given a heart attack by police who forced him to the ground for not wearing a mask while walking in a park.
- Children kept away from dying parents.
- Parents kept away from sick children.
- Newly born babies ripped away from their unvaccinated mothers.
- Children's playgrounds locked with chains.
- A woman pregnant with twins turned away from a nearby Queensland hospital because she lived in a different State loses one of the twins as a direct consequence.
- A seventy-year-old woman brutally pepper-sprayed and thrown to the ground for the crime of holding up the Australian flag in public.
- Weddings cancelled, funerals banned, visits to the elderly and disabled outlawed.
- Suicides, particularly among men who have lost incomes and businesses, skyrocket.
- Mental Health issues and suicides in school children who are no longer allowed to attend school, skyrocket.
- Police in riot gear shoot rubber bullets into people's backs at peaceful freedom protests.
- Homeowners forced to live in cars and tents for months on end because they are not allowed back into their home State.
- People jailed without trial.

This callous, chilling and despicable behaviour can never be construed as 'keeping us safe'. This 'new normal' is what we can look forward to in any future Liberal or Labor totalitarian republic.

IS THIS WHAT AUSTRALIAN'S WANT?

Over the last thirty years, Liberal and Labor have been very good at keeping their secret plans and dirty deeds hidden from the Australian public. So much so that people today, even knowing all this horror has been enforced under a Liberal government, still believe Scott Morrison is an innocent bystander, blundering through the chaos and being pushed around by Labor Premiers. But is that true? That's not what the hidden record shows.

Since 2010, 167 billion dollars of Australian land, housing and business assets have been sold to China, yet lately, Singapore has outstripped China in the purchase of Australian assets. Do the maths, it's terrifying! It also begs the question, where does a tiny country of less than 6 million people find so much money? Who is behind Singapore's purchases of Australian assets? Is it China?

Take a look at what they own...

- *EnergyAustralia,* despite its name, is a wholly-owned subsidiary of the Hong Kong-based China Light and Power Co Ltd (CLP Group).
- *Alinta Energy* (signed off by Scott Morrison) is owned by Chow Tai Fook Enterprises.
- Tasmanian dairy processor *Bellamy's* is owned by China's Mengniu Dairy Company financially backed by the Chinese government.
- *Port of Darwin* (signed off by Scott Morrison) owned by Chinese company Landbridge.
- *Port of Newcastle* is 50% owned by China Merchants Port Holdings Co. Ltd.
- *Port of Melbourne* is owned by China Investment Corp. as part of a consortium.

- *Australian water.* Since 2017, 11% of Australia's water, the equivalent of six Sydney Harbour's worth has been syphoned off per annum by foreign interests, even in drought. They legally sell Australian water back to Australian farmers at prices so high it is putting our local farmers out of business. Who said this was okay?

- The largest exporter of *Australian wool* is now Chinese business tycoon Qingnan Wen who bought the large heritage listed *Mawallok Estate* in Victoria.

- Other *large agricultural properties* are currently being snapped up by the Chinese Company Harvest Agriculture.

- *Merredin Aerodrome* in WA (paid for by Australian Tax Dollars) was 100-year leased to the Chinese Government for $1 through their state-owned Chinese Southern Airlines.

- *Major Coal mine*s in Queensland, NSW and WA, including three in the Hunter Valley, have been aquired by the huge Yancoal Mining Co, owned by China's Yanzhou Coal Mining Co. Ltd.

- *Australian residential and commercial properties* to the value of $113.2 billion were purchased by buyers living in mainland China during 2018-19 (that amount is for just one year under this Liberal government). Do you wonder why Australians can't afford to buy homes? Stop wondering!

- *The largest dairy in Australia (in North West Tasmania)* was sold to the Chinese Moon Lake Investments in 2016 (approved by Scott Morrison). Two years later, the entire Dairy, globally regarded as the best farming land in the world, was broken up in to small lots and sold as 'Happy Farms'.

- *Forty-one Wineries* have been sold to Chinese companies, mostly in the Barossa Valley, Clare Valley, Langhorne Creek, Hunter Valley, Heathcote, Yarra Valley, Frankland and Margaret River areas.

The above list is not comprehensive. This wholesale sell-off of vital infrastructure and assets has been slowly increasing for decades. These few items show how Australia has been sold-out to China for hundreds of billions in the last twelve years alone. This is what the Liberal/National Labor/ Green republican coalition, behind closed doors, has been routinely doing to Australia since the Keating era. Has this sell-out/sell-off stopped? No!

It's not going to stop until *we* stop it!

It doesn't take a genius to see that China's wealth comes from western democracy. If they collapse democracy, they destroy the freedom that keeps them fiscally viable. Ultimately, their belt and road domination theory is doomed to failure. For this reason, Australians need to ask the right questions and demand clear answers. Like, why are Liberal and Labor so keen to sell Australia to the highest bidder rather than invest in developing our rich resources? Why has so much been sold to China? And why have they fallen for China's climate change/green energy belt and road lie? Australians want to know. We *need* to know!

THE BIGGEST LIE OF ALL

Scott Morrison's budget solution for his flamboyant spending spree during the so-called COVID crisis is to get Australians working so we can pay it off! Really? Why is the massive debt Scott Morrison has imposed on Australia the responsibility of the Australian people?

Why does Scott Morrison want to make our children slaves to poverty and live out their lives under the weight of a debt they can never repay? Should our children and children's children be burdened with this debt? Absolutely not! This is NOT their debt! To say it is, is a whopping great lie!

This is the Federal Government's debt!

The strong and powerful truth is the Federal Government has the MEANS to get itself out of this debt quickly, without using taxpayer money! So why do they want us to believe we, and our children, need to enslave ourselves to them for the rest of our lives? Simple! That's the communist way! They need the people to believe that the government OWNS them! Do they own us? No! No! No! The whole idea of enslaving our children to government control is a deception. It is the totalitarian dream. It is the fantasy of every dictator. Are Australians stupid enough to fall for this? Or will we call it out?

The solution for Federal debt is simple!

Australia is an exceedingly mineral-rich country. We have gold, copper, uranium, zinc, lead, diamonds, coal – you name it, we've got it! Just *one* government-owned and run mining project would pay off all our debts in a few years. This is not rocket science!

There is enough money in mining in this country to pay our debts, fund our pensions, build new infrastructure, equip our schools and hospitals, and provide suitable housing for pensioners, the aged and the poor. Yet, the Liberal/National Labor/ Green republican alliance refuses to put Australia and Australians first, preferring to burden our children with debt while continuing to bring in overseas companies to mine Australia, so the profits go overseas to them and not to us.

All of this nonsense needs to stop! And we are the ones who need to stop it! There is no point waiting for these die-hard republicans to suddenly change their ways. They won't change! They are living their dream. They have been waiting for the day when they could cut off freedom in this country and replace it with severe authoritarianism. That day is now. They're not going to let it go. We have to depose them!

These Liberal/National Labor/Green politicians have made themselves big and untouchable in our eyes. They have made themselves look like they are the dog, and we are the insignificant little tail. But it's the other way around. We are the dog, and they are the tail. We are 26 million, and they are less than 700. Who do they think will win this battle? A dog can survive very well without a tail, but a tail cannot survive apart from the dog. This selection of egotistic politicians believe they are more important than the Australians they are paid to serve, but they're not!

And we need to show them they're not!

WHAT CAN WE DO?

The Liberal/National Labor/Green republican coalition has become a cancer in our society. As a nation, we are at death's door because of them. The only thing that can save us now is surgery. The tail has developed a cancer, so we need to cut it off and rid ourselves of the cancer it carries before it does any more damage to our children and us. As a nation, we are not dead yet, but if we don't act now, the cancer will spread, and it will soon be too late.

One of the most arrogant delusions the republican coalition has promoted through the media over the last thirty years, while they have been destroying us, is the fantasy that no other party has the skills to lead this country.

What a load of rubbish! What a lie!

The most important thing about democratic leadership is that the politicians elected are willing to do the will of the people they are paid to serve. That is *not* the Liberal/National Labor/Green position!

In Australia, we have many skilled, talented and experienced people who could not only undo the damage Liberal and Labor have done over many decades but *want* to undo the damage.

- People who know the mining industry inside out and could turn the whole country around through wise mining activity.
- People who have a thorough knowledge of immigration policy and how it could be implemented for Australia's benefit.
- People who understand curriculum and how to protect our children from woke exploitation.
- People who would be willing to tell the truth about the so-called COVID pandemic.
- People who are skilled in international trade, commerce, taxation and Aboriginal affairs.
- People who know what needs to be done to build industry and exports and the infrastructure required to support our farmers.
- People who understand Defence and the needs of our military and our Nation.

They are out there, sitting in the minor parties, trying to prevent the damage being done by destructive policies, keeping us informed and stopping the rot, from the inside, whenever they can. They are the unsung heroes of our country and deserve our respect, rather than the sneering contempt they receive from smug republicans.

The minor parties are our hope of freedom. Working together as a united coalition, they have all the skills, talent and expertise we need to give us the future we thought we had lost forever. They can give us back the Australia we all know and love. A land of sunshine and happiness. A land of laughing children and relaxed, kind-hearted people. A land of sun-drenched beaches and easy-going smiles. A land where people are willing to give a helping hand expecting nothing in return. A land where everyone has a job, and the elderly are respected and protected. A land where everyone has a home and life is so good and so abundant, we have the time and the will to reach out to other nations and help them attain the same living standards we enjoy.

That was how Australia used to be before the nasties got hold of us and crushed the life out of us. That is how Australia can be again. Utopia! It's not a dream or fantasy. We've lived that way! The Australia described above is now our paradise lost. But, not for long! We can have our paradise again if we choose life over death when we vote.

It's time to trust the minor parties!

BEWARE OF VOTING FRAUD

Before you start thinking voting fraud would never happen in Australia or that our government Ministers, bureaucrats and their civilian henchmen would never try to defraud the voting system, remember what happened at DSA. That whole ugly scandal was about the corruption of official data and the lengths the government was prepared to go to cover their corruption.

Do not forget what they did!

And more importantly...

Do not let them do it again!

When paper applications were received at DSA, and the information written on them was entered differently into the database, that false information could later be fixed. It could be checked and corrected because there was a paper copy to start with.

But, when electronic applications were received via the internet, no one could check how the entries had been changed. They could see that someone had accessed the file but could not see what had been changed because there were no originals to check.

This is a dangerous scenario and a wake-up call for our voting system. The internet is not safe. We cannot afford to trust our vote to the internet or a voting machine because the people who operate them could be paid to ensure a republican win.

Don't think corruption doesn't exist in our government! It does! And we are the ones who have to guard against it! Those who can benefit from the fraud and corruption certainly won't try to eliminate it. On the contrary, they will be pushing hardest for internet voting and machine counting. Mark them! Such a push reveals hidden motives!

If we want an accurate count of our votes, we must do it the tried and true hands-on way. I've counted election votes. I know that when counted by hand, every vote is checked by two sets of eyes before being marked as accurate by a third person. This level of security doesn't happen with machines or the internet. With the internet, one hacker can change a lot of votes without anyone knowing what they've changed, and machines can be set to favour one candidate over another. Neither can be trusted!

Our vote is too important to leave to chance. Only hand-counting is secure. It may take a few hours longer to get a result, but it will be an accurate result.

If we want our vote to count and be accurate, we, the people, need to insist loud and clear that all votes be hand-counted. It's time to start writing to Senators, insisting that internet voting and machine counting be banned from every election. Those two 'time-savers' are open doors to fraud, and all doors to fraud need to be firmly shut at election time.

Members of Parliament who disagree with this
are already corrupt!

Take their names! And remember them!

There is so much corruption happening in the highest places of government at the moment that we cannot trust our current leaders to act with integrity. We must start being the dog. We must rise up and tell the tail what to do. And remember, if the tail doesn't listen, we have the power to cut it off!

ACCOUNTABILITY IS WAY OVERDUE

The DSA saga revealed the stark horror that those in high places will never be brought to account by other people in high places. That is just not acceptable! So, *we* need to make them accountable!

We need to make public what they do for all of Australia to see. We need an official voters website with a dedicated ABC TV channel. A place where people can go prior to an election to see at a glance what those who are seeking re-election have supported or done while in office. Like, for instance, pushing for internet voting and machine counting.

Since they won't regulate themselves
we need to regulate them!

Such a site needs to cover bureaucrats, like the Health Minister, a lawyer, not a doctor, handing out medical advice that must be obeyed. What are his political ambitions? We need to know!

Every decision Minister's and Senator's make for or against any bill or policy needs to be displayed for all Australians to easily see. That is real public interest TV! Every overseas deal they have agreed to needs to be broadly reported. Every sell-off of an Australian asset needs to be well publicised. The source of every political donation needs to be made public. Have they or their families received any kickbacks from the big pharmaceutical companies during COVID? What deals have been made? If they want to be leaders of this great nation, they need to be willing to be open books.

All of the above used to be the general role of the media. But now, most of the media is corrupt as well and cannot be trusted to ask any of the right questions, let alone follow up on the answers. Maybe we should also investigate the media 'stars' on this channel. Where does the money they make come from? What are their political affiliations?

These investigations should also include the civilian henchmen, the businesses, who have joined the government in this COVID corruption by sacking good employees for the so-called crime of not being willing to become drug addicts. The definition of a drug addict is a person who takes dangerous, illegal drugs regularly. Since the COVID deception began, being a drug addict has become a mandatory part of the job criteria. If you are not a registered drug user, you will *not* get a job in Australia.

This is madness! How did it come to this?

We need to bring what is in the dark out into the light. If we don't stop the corruption in high places, it will continue to worsen, and our children and children's children will be taken down a long dark path of destruction that will become almost impossible to escape. Is this what Australians want?

For those wondering about my previous statement - yes, these COVID drugs are illegal! They have not been approved for general distribution and will not be approved until 2023 after the initial trials are completed. We are, in fact, guinea pigs in a drug trial! If these drugs kill or permanently damage too many people during this trial period, they will not be approved when the trial concludes. In the meantime, they remain illegal except for 'emergency use' in extreme cases where life is likely to be lost unless the drug is administered. Is life likely to be lost through Omicron? No! Omicron is not life-threatening!

Let me paint a simple picture...

When sellers of disinfectants tell you their product kills 99.9% of germs, they mean it kills ALL germs, but they are not allowed to say it kills 100% of germs because the regulators won't allow them to say so for insurance purposes. So, what do you think it means when experts tell us Omicron is 99.9% safe for those who get it? It means the same thing. Omicron is not a killer! Therefore, there is no need for 'emergency use' of trial drugs! So, why is our government still pushing them? The stark reality is drug pushing is the only way Liberal and Labor republican despots can keep in place their 'emergency powers', which they need to cover all their other sneaky, illegal deeds.

When are Australians going to wake up?

DESPOTS ALWAYS OVERPLAY THEIR HAND

The pre-COVID social experiment conducted in DSA between 2009 and 2012 revealed the shocking reality that, with strong coercion, 70% of Australians would be willing to submit to a totalitarian regime. And worse, some of those would willingly become vicious enforcers of extreme authoritarianism.

Therefore, when the COVID opportunity arrived, the leaders of the republican coup d'etat assumed that, with strong coercion, 70% of Australians would give over their freedom without a word of dissent. And they were right! Until they did what despots always do - they went too far!

In the history of warfare, when leaders push too hard and go beyond the limit of what people will bear, it's at that point that their victims lose their fear. When the people lose their fear, they stop being pushed and start fighting back. That is the defining moment! That's when despots lose their power. Pushing people too hard is a mistake that dictators always make - and our despotic Liberal and Labor leaders have just made that mistake.

If they had stayed within the boundaries of their previous experiment, they would've kept their 70%, and a new order would've been born. Instead, in their pride and arrogance, they pushed ordinary Australians beyond what we could accept. That was a fatal error! When they did that, it was game over! So, what stupid thing did they do?

They came after our children!

It was one thing to cancel our children's education and another to lock up their playgrounds so they couldn't play. But when they ordered us to hand our children over to be used as guinea pigs in therapeutic drug trials, using experimental drugs with unknown side effects, drugs that had the potential to kill some and permanently injure others, on the pretence of protecting them from catching a cold - well, that was going too far!

Our children are not owned by a communist dictatorship! The Australian government has no right to punish our children and us for not complying with their illegal drug regime. Yes! Illegal!

Despite Scott Morrison's "No jab No pay" child vaccination rules, we still have a Constitution! And under our Constitution, all Australians are protected from drug mandates and enforced medical procedures. That is the law! No one in the Australian government has the right to override this Constitutional law! In order to take office, every politician in this country had to swear that they would uphold our Constitution! Not one of them has any right to now go against the Constitution and force Australians to submit to vaccination or any other kind of medical procedure!

> *Government must not authorise (condone or coerce) any form of civil conscription in regards to medical procedures.* (Constitution of Australia, Section 51 23a)

> *Consent must be given voluntarily and in the absence of undue pressure, coercion or manipulation.* (The Australian Government, Health Department, Immunisation Handbook)

> *Consent may be withdrawn by the person concerned at any time and for any reason without disadvantage or prejudice.* (UNESCO Universal Declaration on Bioethics and Human Rights - International Law)

Limited 'emergency powers' do not give politicians the right to override Australian and International law or to encourage businesses to breach the intent of the Constitution and enforce drug mandates on the Australian population on their behalf. Companies that have implemented illegal drug mandates have shown themselves to be the enemies of Australia and need to be deregistered. The heads of Government Departments that have breached the law in this way need to do jail time.

Can we fight back and win? Absolutely!

Liberal and Labor politicians and their government bureaucrats lied to the Australian people. They made all sorts of false claims about the danger of a disease that has all but petered out. They lied about the safety and efficacy of an experimental therapy that was supposed to stop it but didn't. They buried the truth about the dangerous side effects of the drug therapies by threatening medical professionals who wanted to speak out. They callously ignored all the carnage their brutal dictates unleashed on so many ordinary Australians, smiling as they faced the cameras! After all of that, they can't now smugly say, "oops - my bad," and get away with it! They must be held to account and brought to justice!

Talk about going too far...

It's like the story of an annoying fly that came to a small village. The officials got out the armoured tanks and heavy artillery and let loose until not one building was left standing. When the dust cleared there in the midst of the rubble was the fly, still buzzing around. All the village officials needed to do from the start was issue everyone with fly spray, and the problem would have been solved. But the truth was, they didn't care about the fly. It was the village they didn't like. This was their excuse to tear it down and build back better.

How do we bring supposedly untouchable leaders to account? That was the question a handful of ordinary Aussies asked during the trial run of this scenario ten years ago. Thankfully, the government was not the only one who learned lessons from the horrors of the pre-COVID social experiment at DSA. A few ordinary people found a way to take them on and win! One simple but extremely powerful weapon gave us victory then, and it will give us victory now. That weapon has nothing to do with the closed loopholes!

BYPASSING THE LOOPHOLES

After our win against the might of Australia's Defence Intelligence, the government quickly closed the two loopholes we had used to bring attention to the problem. That was a bit of a waste of taxpayer time and money because, in any global crisis, those loopholes become irrelevant. They are bypassed automatically. Back during the DSA saga, whistleblowing was a tool we used to bring attention to the problem. But in the current crisis, the whole world is aware of the problem, so whistleblowing is not needed. Likewise, back then, we used the media to bring the brutality and breaches of law to the attention of the Senate, and as we had hoped, when our stories hit the Senate, things changed. This time, media coverage is not needed because the Senate is already aware of the brutality and breaches of law.

But, being aware is just the beginning...

The Senate is aware but can't act without evidence. Ten years ago, when we set out to bring hidden government corruption into the light, we used a weapon more powerful than whistleblowing and the media combined. A weapon the government couldn't touch or fight then and cannot touch or fight now. The weapon we used is the kind of evidence no government in the world can ever legislate against or control, and no courtroom can deny. What did we use? Our personal stories! Our experiences! Our eye-witness testimonies! Undeniable evidence!

Today, personal stories, testimonies and undeniable eye-witness accounts of the way ordinary Australians have suffered under multiple cruel and heartless government edicts have the power to stop the horror and bring this nightmare to an end. Personal testimonies are the supporting evidence the Senators need to hold the government to account.

A KLIEG LIGHT OF COMPASSION

Finally, through the foggy darkness of buried truths, hidden agendas, orchestrated chaos, crass brutality, coerced confusion, organised insecurity, stolen freedoms, manipulated segregation and the destruction of everything Australian, there has come a bright shining light calling for kindness and truth.

That light is coming from the Senate!

The Senate, fully aware of the suffering in our nation, is now calling for a Royal Commission into the bizarre nature of the Liberal and Labor COVID response. They are demanding transparency from Members of Parliament, Ministers and government officials regarding the health advice they claimed they were following as they implemented their extreme pandemic measures.

They are also calling on the Australian people to send them their personal testimonies of the pain and suffering they have experienced at the hands of their anything-but-safe government. Filled with compassion for the suffering of fellow Australians, these Senators have opened a wide door. They want undeniable evidence! They know that your stories have the power to bring this whole terrible episode in Australia's history to a close.

So, this is where this book ends - with a klieg light of compassion being shone onto the pain and suffering felt by ordinary Australians because of the despotic ambitions of a few ruthless politicians.

I have no doubt there will be a Royal Commission and that it will uncover a mountain of truth so devastating that laws will be passed to ensure this kind of despotism never happens again. To get this result, all the Senator's need is the undeniable evidence of your personal story.

So many terrible things have happened to good people during this attempted coup d'etat that they need to be recorded. Future Australians need to know what a corrupt government looks like and how to see beyond the smiling public face of individual politicians to the pain their actions cause.

When I look back in history, I can recall many smiling family photos and home movies taken of Hitler and his friends in his private mountain abode. And I also remember seeing a video of him standing in front of a large crowd of flag-waving Germans in 1933 pretending to be a godly man. Yet, we all know now that while he was pretending to be a normal family man and openly using prayer to gain the Christian vote, he was secretly planning to kill all Jews and Christians once he took full power. Only the Pope's direct intervention stopped him from killing Christians the same way he killed Jews.

> *We don't ask the Almighty, "Lord, make us free!" We want to be active, to work together, so that when the hour comes that we appear before the Lord we can say to him: "Lord, you see that we have changed. The German people are no longer a people of dishonor and shame, of self-destructiveness and cowardice. No, Lord, the German people are once more strong in spirit, strong in determination, strong in the willingness to bear every sacrifice. Lord, now bless our battle and our freedom, and therefore our German people and Fatherland."* (Adolf Hitler, May 1, 1933)

This is a powerful lesson from history. We must look past what politicians claim to be and judge them for what they do.

ORDINARY PEOPLE CAN MAKE A DIFFERENCE

I am the same as you, an ordinary person, and the destruction of my country breaks my heart. That's why I've written this book. None of this is new to me. I've seen it all before. I've lived through it, and I've overcome it!

The strategy I used to overcome the trial run has the power to overcome this coup d'etat! Our personal eye-witness experiences are so absolute they cannot be disputed in any court of law, in any Royal Commission, or in any government hearing. The combined power of our various testimonies cannot fail to overcome all this horror and stop the rot. I know this for a fact, and now you know it too.

None of us has to accept the dystopian 'new normal' that a few hearless and despotic politicians have planned for us. We can choose life and smiles, hope and freedom! That's what I choose, and I'm an ordinary Aussie. I love what our country used to be, and I miss it. I want my country back!

The more eye-witness testimonies there are, the more powerful each of them become. No testimony is too small or insignificant. Every story is important! All we have to do, as individuals, is write our personal stories on paper and send them to the Senate. That's not a hard thing to do, but it could save a lot of future hardship. In Australia, this is where to send your story:

Senators for a Royal Commission
GPO Box 228
Brisbane QLD 4001

When all this is over, I will do a revised edition of this book with a new section showing how we have overcome again and the glory of our victory. Until then, God bless Australia!

God has chosen
the foolish things of the world
to confound the wise;
and the weak things of the world
to shame the strong.

(Bible: 1Cor.1:27)

Monica Bennett-Ryan

Thank you for taking the time to read my personal story. I'm an ordinary Aussie, a mother and grandmother. There is nothing special about me, and yet I was able to make a difference. If a grandma like me can make a difference, so can you!

Ordinary people CAN make a difference!

My battle with DSA took three very long years and when it was over, I needed time to recover. That's why I feel for so many of my fellow Aussies today. Going through the horror is only half the story. Giving yourself time to recover and get back to normal is the other half. But that's pretty hard to do when you've lost your health or home or income or a cherished family member. The monsters who have done this to us have a lot to answer for!

As one who has been through the horror and understands the pain, I would like to add one last word. Be kind to yourself and be kind to others. All the battle-scarred people in this country need to bathe in some loving-kindness for a while; until we can recover and get back to the real normal.

Until that day comes, God bless you!

CPSIA information can be obtained
at www.ICGtesting.com
Printed in the USA
LVHW020254090322
712998LV00003B/25

9 780645 351354